Supervision and Dramatherapy

of related interest

Essays in Dramatherapy
The Double Life
Robert Landy
ISBN 1 85302 322 1

Imagination, Identification and Catharsis in Theatre and Therapy
Mary Duggan and Roger Grainger
ISBN 1 85302 431 7

Dramatherapy
Clinical Studies
Steve Mitchell
ISBN 1 85302 304 3

Dramatherapy for People with Learning Disabilities
A World of Difference
Anna Chesner
ISBN 1 85302 208 X

Dramatherapy with Families, Groups and Individuals
Waiting in the Wings
Sue Jennings
ISBN 1 85302 144 X pb
ISBN 1 85302 014 1 hb

Drama and Healing
The Roots of Drama Therapy
Roger Grainger
ISBN 1 85302 337 X

Staff Supervision in a Turbulent Environment
Managing Process and Task in Front-Line Services
Lynette Hughes and Paul Pengelly
ISBN 1 85302 327 2

Good Practice in Supervision
Statutory and Voluntary Organisations
Edited by Jacki Pritchard
ISBN 1 85302 279 9

Supervision and Dramatherapy

Edited by Elektra Tselikas-Portmann

Foreword by Paolo Knill

Jessica Kingsley Publishers
London and Philadelphia

The lines from the poem reprinted on p.200 is from *Horses Make a Landscape Look More Beautiful* by Alice Walker, published in Great Britain in 1985 by the Women's Press Ltd, 34 Great Sutton Street, London EC1V 0LQ. It is reproduced by kind permission of David Higham Associates.

The material reproduced on pp.104–106, 108, 110 is taken from *The Little Prince* © Gallimard 1944. The first edition was published in 1945 by William Heinemann Ltd. The extract is reproduced by kind permission of Egmount Children's Books Ltd, London, and Harcourt Brace Inc, New York.

First published in the United Kingdom in 1999 by
Jessica Kingsley Publishers Ltd
116 Pentonville Road, London
N1 9JB, England
and
325 Chestnut Street,
Philadelphia, PA 19106, USA.

www.jkp.com

© Copyright 1999 Jessica Kingsley Publishers

Library of Congress Cataloging in Publication Data
A CIP catalog record for this book is available from the Library of Congress

British Library Cataloguing in Publication Data
A CIP catalogue record for this book is available from the British Library

ISBN 1 85302 738 3

Printed and Bound in Great Britain by
Athenaeum Press, Gateshead, Tyne and Wear

Contents

FOREWORD BY PAOLO KNILL   7

PREFACE AND ACKNOWLEDGEMENTS   9

Introduction   13
Elektra Tselikas-Portmann

I. Supervision and dramatherapy

1 Dramatherapy supervision: Historical issues   39
and supervisory settings
Anna Chesner

2 Theatre-based supervision: 62
A supervisory model for multidisciplinary supervisees
Sue Jennings

3 Supervision in playtherapy   80
and dramatherapy with children
Ann Cattanach

II. The supervisory relationship and dramatherapy

4 Supervisory triangles and the helicopter ability   95
Katerina Couroucli-Robertson

5 Role model of dramatherapy supervision   114
Robert J. Landy

III. Supervision with dramatherapy in different fields

6 Supervision of crisis intervention teams: 136
The myth of the saviour
Mooli Lahad

7 Supervision and coaching of teams in business   155
Reinhard Tötschinger

8 Supervision and consultancy of art-based research   168
Roger Grainger

IV. Supervisor training with dramatherapy

9 Training the supervisor-dramatherapist I: 185
A psychodynamic approach
Marina Jenkyns

10 Training the supervisor-dramatherapist II: 202
The theatre-based approach
Elektra Tselikas-Portmann, Sue Jennings,
Katerina Couroucli-Robertson and Demys Kyriacou

Appendix 1 Dramatherapists' views of supervision   220
Madeline Andersen-Warren and Lorraine Fox

Appendix 2 Dramatherapy supervision training courses   226

Appendix 3 The Supervision Subcommittee of the   228
British Association of Dramatherapists

THE CONTRIBUTORS   229

SUBJECT INDEX   232

AUTHOR INDEX   239

Foreword

Elektra Tselikas-Portmann has skilfully edited a book that acts like a kaleidescope, projecting the compelling thoughts of the finest authors in this field onto the screen of our imaginations. With each turn of the page we are able to get a picture of the domain of supervision from a distinctly different perspective. Many of these perspectives engage with topics for the first time and are essential to the field. Cultural differences are clarified, in particular as they are displayed in the history of British–American and German traditions. The issues of professional approaches through the applications of supervision are portrayed.

Even though there are distinct differences in the orientation of the drama presented and its application, there is a strong unity in this work, which embraces the supervisory functions of 'irritation' or 'perturbation' as an essential part of human existence, to gain alternative narration. This unity is achieved by sticking to the art of theatre at its best. There is a thread of 'art-based' or 'theatre-based' research that guides us through many applications and a variety of tools within the method of dramatherapy. We learn, for instance, that supervisees can respond to familiar popular tales or newly encountered stories from literature on creative journeys, in a collaborative enterprise between supervisor and supervisees; or we discover focal points in the role model of supervision that allow us to look into the different scenarios and relationships that evolve within the supervisory process; or we are shown ways of supervising professionals who are involved in interventions immediately following a disaster with victims of emotional trauma. In the sequence of these chapters the outcome will point toward a concept of aesthetic distancing that can be particularly fruitful. The de-centring into theatre, out of the problem-saturated discourse that really starts a supervisory process, can lead into a 'state in-between' that allows us to look at a professional situation through identification and distancing at the same time. We will discover that the gift eliciting in supervision is indigenous to the arts and is genuinely presented by theatre. Besides the need for supervision training in general, there is therefore a necessity for dramatherapy supervision training in particular.

A text of the achievement presented here can only be created by writers who have a deep understanding and firm faith in their supervisory work through dramatherapy, and a masterful eloquence in the language of phenomenological psychology.

Paolo J. Knill
Professor Emeritus, Lesley College, Massachussetts
Provost, European Graduate School, Switzerland
April 1999

Preface and Acknowledgements

This book focuses on the application of dramatherapy principles and concepts to supervision, providing examples of dramatherapy supervision practice.

In dramatherapy and related arts therapies, where artistic processes are at the centre of professional activity, supervision cannot only rely on verbal analysis. Supervision can also operate through artistic imagination and creation, i.e. in and through the 'in-between' or liminal space inherent in the dramatic activity. In the case of supervision with dramatherapy, the concept of aesthetic distancing can be particularly fruitful. It describes this 'in-between' state, allowing one to look at a professional situation through identification and distancing at the same time.

The book points to the need for dramatherapy supervision for dramatherapists. Dramatherapy supervision helps these professionals stay in contact with that particular attitude characteristic to the practising of dramatherapy: keeping aesthetic distance, trusting the process, and bearing the obliqueness inherent in metaphorical expressions instead of interpreting dramatic/artistic creations.

The book also shows how supervision with dramatherapy can be helpful to other professionals, how fuelling the imagination can be part of the supervision process in order to widen perception and enlarge the ability to gain overview.

Putting this book together in collaboration with some of the pioneers in dramatherapy has been particularly inspiring. I would like to warmly thank all the contributors to this book for what they allowed me to learn through this collaboration and for their trust in my comments and feedback.

Many people have guided me on my way up here, dramatherapists and non-dramatherapists alike. Although I do not belong to the first generation of dramatherapists, I think that I shared the same fate as many of them by being a dramatherapy practitioner in an area where dramatherapy was unknown. Part of this fate was the lack of 'ancestors' and specialist support close by.

As the first results of Andersen-Warren's and Fox's survey on dramatherapy supervision show (see Appendix 1), the majority of British dramatherapists who responded to the questionnaire regard having a dramatherapist as a supervisor as being very important. Indeed, this is a particularly relevant finding. Initiating discussion about the need for dramatherapy supervision qualification and training is one of the reasons for producing this book.

In my own career, training and practice, finding an appropriate supervisor has always been an adventure. Even in very early times when I first started training in Britain, while I was living in Switzerland and planning to do my first placement in Germany, one of the first challenges I was confronted with was trying to find a supervisor (dramatherapy was, it could be said, non-existent in these last two countries at that time). Sue Jennings, my trainer, said; 'Any approach will do provided the supervisor accepts art and artistic expression for what it is and does not dismiss it under the term of "sublimation".' With this advice I went off to search. Although I made some wonderful discoveries, supervision with dramatherapy remained a basic need for me. Yet, I tried to live with what life gave me and I finally found my way through the jungle of supervisors and approaches.

While dramatherapists (supervisors, trainers and therapists) enabled me to understand dramatherapy through identification, professionals from other approaches helped me to understand dramatherapy through differentiation. It is through these movements and the balance between identification and differentiation, inclusion and exclusion, that my identity as a dramatherapist and as a dramatherapist supervisor was built. Here is a good place to give these professionals my acknowledgement.

First I would like to mention the people 'at home' – my supervisors and teachers from the field of dramatherapy and theatre who guided me and shared their experience and wisdom with me. With them I learned through identification, which enabled me to develop a grounded and positive self-image as a dramatherapist and find that particular attitude that is at the basis of the dramatherapy activity.

Sue Jennings has been an endless source of wisdom, encouragement, inspiration and comfort for over ten years. Like a 'down-to-earth Martha Freud, a no-nonsense Jewish grandma who "never dreams – well, hardly ever", and yet has all the love and intuition that come naturally to women' (Elizabeth Rees reviewing Sue's and Joan Walker's performance 'Mrs Freud and Mrs Jung' in *Context 30*, Spring 1997) she has often shown me the way back to everyday reality and modelled how I can live this reality with imagination and creativity. My special thanks also go to her for encouraging me to edit this book.

Through the teaching of his role model, Robert Landy has helped me enter and inhabit the realm of dramatic reality, touch other levels of consciousness and understand the importance of proper and explicit closure.

With Grotowskian theatre director, Richard Nieoczym, I discovered how to contact the wisdom and fire of the body.

And it was actor Daniel Prieto who led me to the power connected with the voice.

Next I would like to acknowledge what I owe to those who, as supervisors and therapists, allowed me to understand what dramatherapy is through differentiation. My thanks go to the 'sympathizers' from other schools who as supervisors or therapists have guided me and given me support: Martha Koukkou-Lehmann (psychoanalyst), Martin Odermatt (Jungian analyst), Jörg Burmeister (psychodramatist), Renate Frühmann (integrative gestalt-therapist), Ute Volmerg and Klaus Antons-Volmerg (both trainers and supervisors in group dynamics). They all offered me acceptance, sometimes even admiration, encouragement and support for what I was doing or trying to do. They all advised me using their ways of thinking and working, speaking their different languages although they were in several points so similar. They helped me to discover 'universal truths' about supervision and therapy across borders. The exchange was particularly enriching. It was also often challenging. It motivated me to think and to select, to accept and to reject, much more than if I had stayed in a uniform discourse.

Dramatherapy is expansive, we say. It is also integrative. Dramatherapy and dramatherapy supervision helped me integrate the many, often divergent or contradictory, life and professional experiences. It allowed me to respect the need to live not just a double (Landy) but a multiple life. To live it by finding the balance.

This is what this book is about. How to facilitate finding balances in professional practice, and by that, how to initiate, preserve and move on the processes of change.

There are also some other people I would particularly like to thank here: Ian Robertson and Sarah Mercer for their assistance as native speakers with some parts of the text; Jessica Kingsley and Helen Parry for their patience while witnessing the book dynamically changing in its making until it found its final form. Paul, my guide, my mentor, my counsellor, my supervisor in life, who always finds a wonderful way to reword my accounts so as to make me better understand the essence of my own sayings.

My mother gave me a wonderful present last Christmas. For the first time she honestly showed me her vulnerability. Thereby she appeared and acted as authentically strong as never before. Through this image I discovered what goes to make the strength of a good therapist and a good supervisor. Words are not enough to express my gratitude to her for this present. I would like to dedicate this book to my mother.

Elektra Tselikas-Portmann
Graz, Austria, January 1999

Introduction

Elektra Tselikas-Portmann

My life has been a long series of journeys through countries, languages, cultures and professions. On those journeys I came across an almost endless variety of discourses and I developed the capacity to live 'in-between' – in-between countries, in-between languages, in-between cultures. My existence developed in some kind of liminal space where usual self-evidence is non-existent, where in spite of personal identification distance remains an imposed or often chosen necessity, where finding balances becomes a conscious endeavour. All this sounds challenging. It is full of chance – in both senses. It allows you to develop the 'eye of the stranger' that watches from a distance because it often understands but does not share the same self-evidence of the narratives of the groups she is participating in. (I use the female form throughout this Introduction to mean both sexes.)

I realize that here I have just described some main characteristics of the supervisor. The supervisor senses, understands, yet stands at the edge, looks with the 'eye of the stranger', does not subscribe to the self-evidences of the supervised system and can thus become a 'perturbator', an 'intruder'. I also realize that I have described many of the factors that constitute dramatherapy: liminal spaces, distance, balance, in-between. I might now maintain that dramatherapy is the approach *par excellence* for the practice of supervision. However I will refrain from a missionary zeal and will instead try to guide you, the readers, through the landscapes that I discovered while preparing this book.

My first voyage led me into the land of supervision. What at first sight seemed clear, revealed itself through the existing literature as an almost endless amount of endeavours for conceptualizing the act of supervision. Different cultural traditions (the English–American and the German); different professional approaches (supervision in business, supervision in the helping professions, clinical supervision), and finally different clinical approaches. Through all this variety one thing remains constant and clear: supervision is about reflecting on one's professional practice. The 'what-to-do's' and the 'how-to-do's' vary, obviously, according to the cultural tradition and the approach that is being adopted.

My next voyage took me into the continent of arts therapies and notably to the land of dramatherapy. While there is a considerable amount of literature about supervision based on theories of psychotherapy, communication, constructivist and systemic approaches, I did not find any discussions on supervision in the arts therapies. This book appears to be a first in this field.

On the basis of my album of souvenirs and the diaries that I kept during these voyages I have prepared a sightseeing tour for you. I have tried to collect the materials and to choose the places as objectively as possible, yet it cannot be avoided that the presentation will bear my personal mark and the focus will be through my own (maybe in the broadest sense multicultural) glasses. Someone else would maybe approach this subject in a different manner. My comments will sometimes look like fiction and sometimes they will look real. Just bear in mind: what looks like fiction is real and what looks real is fiction....

I will start with sightseeing in the land of supervision. I will present to you the different traditions in the English and the German speaking areas. (When writing about the 'English speaking area or world' I mainly refer to the USA and Britain. When writing about the 'German speaking area or world' I mean Germany, Switzerland and Austria.) I will state the principal aim of supervision as it seems to crystallize through both traditions. I will subsequently discuss the different theoretical assumptions that result from the different approaches to supervision. The supervision process is influenced by the values that underlie these approaches. These values guide the supervisor's actions and interventions and also the supervisee's understandings. Here, I will also make some reference to 'creative' methods being used in supervision. Next, I will go into the land of dramatherapy. I will present similarities and differences between dramatherapy and the approaches discussed before. I will, then, attempt to build a bridge between supervision and dramatherapy. I will illustrate the tasks and functions of supervision as they can be understood within a dramatherapeutic framework. I will refer to the specific qualities required for dramatherapy supervisors, I will point to the dramatherapy models and, finally, I will discuss specifics of the supervisory relationship that forms within dramatherapy supervision. Before presenting the chapters of this book I would like to draw your attention to the importance of a clear contract before starting dramatherapy supervision.

I will now invite you to ride with me on a hop-on hop-off bus. At each stop I will briefly state what the attractions there are. You can decide at which stop you would like to stay, and at which you would prefer to continue.

On supervision

Entering the land of supervision I will first take you to an 'ethnographic museum' that contains some historical artefacts and shows how the term supervision evolved in the two different cultural areas, the Anglo-American and the German. The exposition here is interesting for those who have been concerned with questions such as, for example, 'Should the supervisor be simultaneously a superior and what can this dual role mean? Or should she rather be a "neutral" person from outside the organization?' Such questions can be important for employed professionals (e.g. dramatherapists) who ask for supervision at their place of work or freelance supervisors being asked by organizations for their services. The events I intend to show here give some hints on different possible developments as well as on risks and chances connected with the dual role of the internal supervisor or the 'intruder' role of the external supervisor. Such questions might deserve some thought when engaging for supervision or when designing and planning policy strategies demanding supervision for dramatherapists. A glance into other cultural areas might offer some ideas about alternative developments.

Those not interested in this 'ethnographic museum' can continue their tour at the next stop, 'Supervision: one term, one aim' which is a must for the serious-minded traveller.

Supervision: one term, several traditions

The term 'supervision' has had different meanings according to the context in which it has been used. Originally the term developed in the context of social work; in the English-speaking world it was and is mainly connected with what is called 'administrative supervision'. Apart from its educative function it involved a certain amount of control. Yet, although control and administration are part of the supervisor's tasks, they are not predominant characteristics of her role. The supervisor is usually an experienced professional, on a hierarchically higher level than the persons being supervised, who also has an educative and counselling function. Indeed the

terms counselling, consultation and supervision are often used inter-
changeably, counselling also being part of the task of a supervisor (Holloway
1995, p.13).

According to Kadushin (1985) (cited in Belardi 1994, pp.43–44) there
are three types of supervision that emerge when reviewing the discussion
surrounding supervision in the USA: administrative supervision (attaining
the goals of the organization); educational supervision (informing and
guiding); and supportive supervision (preventing burnout). In fact, the
supervisor 'integrates and co-ordinates' the work of the supervisees. This
development in the English-speaking countries stems from the fact that
originally people working in the helping professions were employed by
charity organizations and received much of their training on the job (Belardi
1994, p.34). It is in the 1990s that the term has begun to shift in meaning.
According to Stoltenberg and Delworth (1987), American literature
differentiates between 'administrative' and 'clinical' supervision. Its
connection to the administrative aspect remains, however, in most of the
English-speaking publications. The supervisor usually has the dual role of
both management and support which obviously causes certain conflicts (see,
for example, Hawkins and Shohet 1996, p.23; and in the case of trainee
supervision Holloway 1995, pp.3, 63 and 69). This situation might also be
one reason why agencies often do not fund supervision for their members, as
it is supposed that this role is carried out by the superiors. (Most of the
supervision literature has been produced in the USA and concerns mainly
administrative supervision. Yet, according to Belardi (1994), the
developments in Britain have been quite parallel to those in the USA.)

The development in the German-speaking world has been different.
Here, the managers were originally not experienced professionals but
'administrators', strangers to the profession, usually lawyers. Accordingly, the
aspect of 'control' was predominant and the educative as well as supportive
aspects were lacking. The first generation of consultants or supervisors that
became active in the German-speaking world were educated in the USA. Yet
introducing supervision as a form of consultation that involved the dual
function of control and help was not an easy task. The systems that were to be
supervised reacted with resistance and mistrust. The existing dominant
hierarchical structures as well as the experience of national socialism did not
allow the role of the supervisor as simultaneous controller, educator and
helper to be established. In contrast to this, demands for 'neutral' supervision,
reduction of hierarchies, more teamwork and co-operation were articulated

within the helping professions. Control and help appeared as two incompatible concepts (Belardi 1994, pp.65–67). One of the roles of supervision was to challenge the structures of the organization. According to this, supervision evolved in Germany into an emancipatory instrument of professional development. Supervision should aim at independence for the worker from external control (Kersting 1992, p.23). The role of the external supervisor was born. As a result of this, a great amount of literature was produced, particularly in the 1990s.

An animated debate evolved on the professional profile of the supervisor, the tasks of supervision and the training of the supervisors. In short, the profession of supervisor began to develop and to shift ever more into the role of organizational developer or organizational consultant. An organizational developer or consultant is a specialist, a counsellor who facilitates change in the organization. Indeed, the supervisor may supervise individuals, or teams, yet an important part of the focus here will be on structural issues concerning the context and the systems in which the professionals operate.

An external supervisor will perhaps have a better overall view as she will naturally have more distance from the practices of the organization. On the other hand one danger connected with the supervisor's role in this instance is that she can more easily be seen as an intruder who disturbs or even disrupts ongoing practices. Connected with this is the possibility of an increased danger of using her as a scapegoat.

Supervision: one term, one aim

This stop here is actually a must. It tells you what supervision is about. You should not miss it, otherwise you will have missed out a substantial bit of information.

A review of the literature shows different forms of supervision: trainee supervision (which is part of the professional socialization) work supervision (which can be useful for every professional, whether in a helping profession or not); and clinical supervision (which concentrates on the clinical therapeutic work).

Independently of the form of supervision and the tradition it comes from, the aim of supervision is defined in the existing literature as improving professional competence, i.e. the practice of supervisees or trainees on a pragmatic and ethical level (practice is 'successful' in a pragmatic sense and 'correct' in an ethical sense; Schreyögg 1994, p.19). Supervision offers a framework where professional experiences can be survived, reflected upon and learnt from (Hawkins and Shohet 1996, p.3). The themes of supervision then result from the constituents of professional practice, that is the professional interactions between supervisees and clients. I will be using the term 'client' mainly in the clinical sense, although it can also be understood in its commercial sense for example. All but one of the contributions to this book come from the clinical domain. The one that doesn't (Chapter 7) comes from the domain of business. I believe that the principles of supervision and particularly dramatherapy supervision as I present them in this Introduction apply both to the clinical and the non-clinical domains. Additionally, the aim of this book is to give a first impulse for a discussion about supervision and dramatherapy. Accordingly, I would rather focus on expansion than on reduction.

It is particularly important to be clear about the significance of the professional interactions between supervisees and clients, as the temptation to blur the boundaries between supervision and therapy is often present. This is particularly so in the case of clinical supervision or when supervisors outside the clinical field have a therapeutic background. Accordingly, personal issues of the supervisee that need to be worked through are to be referred further to therapy. Yet, despite the clarity of what is said here, it is equally important to bear in mind that supervision is, nevertheless and after all, a process of balancing between several poles: between self-experience and instruction; between descriptions of the psychodynamic and the sociodynamic; between structuring and following the process; between self-analysis and other-analysis (Rappe-Giesecke 1994, p.11).

Some of the main themes addressed in supervision would be (Schreyögg 1994, pp.15–16):

- the understandings and action-oriented patterns the supervisee uses based on her professional knowledge, i.e. the 'planned', knowledge-based understandings and actions
- the 'not planned' understandings and actions that result from the supervisee's own history and her interaction with the client (transferential and countertransferential patterns as well as subconscious or semiconscious role definitions within the professional relationship)
- the institutional context with its formal and informal structures. These formal and informal organizational structures influence the interactions in the field of practice. Furthermore, workers in organizational/institutional contexts basically live in an ambivalence

between security and constraint, which might also influence their professional understanding and action patterns

- the way the supervisee(s) mirrors the content and dynamic of their work with the client(s) in their presentation to the supervisor-dramatherapist.

All these characteristics as they manifest themselves in the person of the supervisee are potential themes for supervision. The supervisor can help the supervisee to see things on the levels mentioned above in other perspectives. She can also help the supervisee(s) to expand their horizons.

Supervision: one term, several approaches

At this stop we will visit a market with industrial and handmade products from different provinces of the land of supervision. You will find a brief description of how the main schools of psychotherapy conceive supervision. These schools have also influenced dramatherapy and if you stop here you will have the background that will later on help you to better understand the specificities in the land of dramatherapy and dramatherapy supervision. Apart from this, you might want to take some souvenirs with you from this colourful market.

In the following I refer to clinical supervision mainly, although several of the approaches I present are also applied in supervision more generally, to help professionals who work in non-clinical settings reflect on their practice.

In general terms, the approach that is the basis of the supervision model used, as well as its underlying values, will influence the definition of roles, relationships, and interventions applied. Let me briefly present these theoretical discourses in a first step.

Supervision from the point of view of *psychoanalysis* focuses on the personal specificities of the supervisee, the 'not planned' understandings and actions that result from the supervisee's own history and her interaction with the client. Emotions that emerge as transference and countertransference in her relationship with the client are discussed (Schreyögg 1992, p.14).

In the light of *behavioural therapy,* supervision focuses on skill training. The focus is on the action-oriented patterns used by the supervisee based on her professional knowledge. Her ability to recognize existing problems and to choose the appropriate methods for the socialization of the client is promoted (Schreyögg 1992, p.14).

In a Rogerian *client-centred* approach it is the supervisee's personality that is at the centre of supervision. However, the focus is more on the promotion of the personal development of the supervisee than on uncovering her deficits (Schreyögg 1992, p.15).

From an *integrative gestalt-oriented* point of view Schreyögg proposes an integration of different approaches, notably gestalt and psychodrama, in order to overcome what she defines as shortcomings of gestalt theory when applied to supervision. As examples of such shortcomings she sees the orientation of gestalt theory on psychoanalysis for the explanation of interaction as well as its impossibility to seize systemic phenomena. These shortcomings of the gestalt approach can be met, according to her, by psychodrama which is more interactionist and systems-oriented (Schreyögg 1992, p.314) (on the practice of psychodrama supervision see Williams 1995 and Buer 1996).

Holloway proposes a *systems approach* to supervision according to which the goal of supervision would be the enhancement of the supervisee's empowerment resulting from feeling capable of making a difference in one's world and the world of others. According to this approach the relationship is the core factor and contains the process of the supervision interaction. Around it the client, the supervisee, the supervisor, the institution, the tasks and the functions of supervision unfold as contextual factors (Holloway 1995, pp.7–8). According to Holloway, the process of supervision consists of tasks that define *what* the teaching/learning is about, and of functions that define *how* these tasks will be accomplished in supervision (Holloway 1995, p.37). I will come back to this point when we come to the stop 'On supervision and dramatherapy'.

Finally, Kersting presents us with a *constructivist approach,* maintaining that reality is a linguistic construction. In this context, reality is constructed through the stories that group members share that enable them to reduce complexity and arrive at a consensus. Supervision is the space in which diagnosis (or enlightenment) (Kersting 1992, p.16) takes place, in which the different views are presented and in which explanations occur. The supervisor functions as an 'irritator' or 'perturbator' (Maturana and Varela 1984) who 'perturbs' the system through alternative narrations. These narrations interrupt repetitive stories and facilitate the construction of new ones. The supervisor also functions as a 'broker of views' (Kersting 1992, p.20) who helps raise and collect 'diagnoses' (understandings of narratives). Interestingly enough, though, by constructing diagnoses the supervisory system constructs the reality that it believes it observes (Kersting 1992, p.70)! The new stories that members create again help reduce complexity and through these new constructions arrive at a consensus that enables the survival of the group. Within this approach, one important goal of supervision is to help supervisees construct as many different narratives as possible rather than to stick to the same repetitive narration.

All the above approaches are strongly verbal and rely on words, verbalization and reflection for the gaining of insight.

Increasingly many approaches now use *'creative' and action methods* in supervision, particularly drawing/painting, stories, role plays, puppets and musical instruments. Schreyögg defines these as 'media' and sees their function as transmitters of rational and non-rational information on the one hand and as 'means through which human beings express themselves' on the other (Schreyögg 1992, pp.385–386). These 'media' help to present and formulate the problem, promote change of the not-planned understandings and action patterns and also facilitate expression (Schreyögg 1992, p.404). This would imply, in fact, that the artistic creations (as 'carriers of information' that form the basis of communication and understanding; Schreyögg 1992, p.386) gain their full power only after they have been verbalized and interpreted.

On dramatherapy

Now we have reached the land of dramatherapy. I hope you are not too tired. If so, take a rest. At this and the next stop there are some exciting attractions waiting for you like taking off with an air-balloon and seeing the world from above or watching a firework. You should risk stopping here – these experiences are thrilling and beyond what you normally experience in your everyday life. You may, however, be assured that we will take you back safely.

Dramatherapy shares several characteristics with the above approaches: transference and countertransference that build the focus of the psychoanalytic approach are dramatic phenomena (see Landy 1986, p.19). Dramatherapy draws from cognitive approaches when working with task-centred role-play (see Emunah 1994, p.31). The relationship to psychodrama is well known. Theatre is the space *par excellence* where entangled systemic relationships can be seen and shown on stage (see Davis 1995). Finally the dramatherapeutic model on story making can be linked to the constructivist approach (see Gersie 1997). The methodology of dramatherapy consists of creative and action methods and, indeed, many of these methods are also common to the gestalt approach.

What is it then that differentiates dramatherapy from other approaches, what forms its identity? One important difference characteristic of dramatherapy is the assumption about the *dramatic nature of the human being and the human mind* (Jennings 1998). Transference and countertransference phenomena are seen in the context of psychoanalysis as 'problems' that are to be restricted and dealt with. In dramatherapy, these phenomena are seen as essentially dramatic and as inherent to every human interaction. Consequently, transference and countertransference will shift constantly between the supervision partners as well as the roles of supervisor, supervisee and guide (see Chapter 5 in this volume). It is through the promotion of aesthetic distancing that the individual boundaries can be preserved and the therapeutic or supervisory setting respected.

The *concept of distancing* (Jennings 1998, pp.115–117; Landy 1986, pp.98–100; 1996) is thus a further central concept that is specific to dramatherapy and contributes to its identity. In task-oriented role-play, it is not only the skills that are being learned but also the finding of the right balance between identification and distance while carrying out the task. The concept of distance and the explicit reference to the here and now differentiates dramatherapy from psychodrama.

Dramatic reality (Jennings 1998, pp.117–121) is another concept characteristic of dramatherapy. It differentiates dramatherapy from the gestalt-oriented approach as well as from the systemic approach. Dramatherapy places emphasis on working with fictional contexts and uses the power of metaphors. It does not simply present 'constellations' but represents them aesthetically through body images, projective play and theatrical/dramatic role play.

The concepts of *role* and *role-play* (Landy 1986, p.97; 1993, p.30) are, of course, very important in dramatherapy. In contrast to psychodrama the theatrical role is not perceived as 'conserve' but as archetypal gestalt. Role-playing is seen as a form of dramatic impersonation. Through role-playing the person (self) identifies with the persona (the mask, the social archetype, the role that hides the person by revealing it). In role-play the person projects qualities of herself onto the persona. In that sense role-play takes place on the basis of a relationship between person and persona and between identification and projection. Chapter 5 is a vivid illustration of how the different roles (according to the role model) interact in supervision and therapy and how these interactions are made visible in the process of dramatherapy supervision.

Hence dramatherapy works not only with verbal means but builds on the principles of *embodiment, projection and role* (Cattanach 1994; Jennings 1994; Jennings 1998, p.121–122). The processes of insight, change and growth begin in and with the body. Dramatherapy offers a wide range of possibilities for the construction of realities, using also the body as non-verbal means. In that sense it is different from a strict constructivist approach that sees reality formed out of linguistic constructions. I do not ignore the fact that 'words are not mirrorlike reflections of reality' (Gergen 1991, p.119) and hence they are also representations and bear, as a result, artistic potential. What I am particularly referring to here is the integrated and expansive experience that theatre/drama – or to put it more directly in contemporary and integrative terms: performance (see Huxley and Witts 1996) – can convey through all the senses. (On fundamental processes within dramatherapy see also Jones 1996.)

In this sense, the perturbation of the system through irritating interventions is possible within the scope of dramatherapy even if it is not restricted to verbal interaction; still, more important is the fact that the practice of drama and theatre is, *per se*, expanding or 'perturbing' (to say it in constructivist terms). To quote Artaud (1996, p.26):

> … we believe there are living powers in what is called poetry, and that the picture of a crime presented in the right stage conditions is something infinitely more dangerous to the mind than if the same crime were committed in life. We want to make theatre a believable reality inflicting this kind of tangible laceration, contained in all true feeling, on the heart and senses.

Thus, still using constructivist terminology, when acting or practising drama, the danger of repetitive narratives will be minimized. Apart from that, the artistic activity will be inspiring and expand provided that supervisor and supervisee have the courage to trust the process of creation although they might not know where it will lead them (McNiff 1998). This is an important difference to the approaches mentioned above and to all those which use 'creative' methodologies: art in dramatherapy is not the medium but the end. Art, in the case of dramatherapy meaning drama and theatre, is the very process of supervision; the artistic creation is at the centre of the process and not its interpretation. Therefore, enhancing and maintaining the artistic capacity of the supervisee, and subsequently the client, is one of the main goals in dramatherapy supervision.

While discussing with a friend about art, communication and the relationship in supervision an animated debate developed. My friend maintained that communication and the relationship are at the basis of supervision. I countered that it is the art form that is at the basis of dramatherapy supervision. What do you think, reader?

Let us consult Pina Bausch. Pina Bausch is an internationally known German choreographer and director of Wuppertal Dance Theatre (Germany). 'Bausch's work is remarkable in both the scale and detail of her theatricality ... Her dance theatre emphasizes how people behave, presenting them in real time, as real people, yet writ large' (Huxley and Witts 1996, p.60). Her favourite themes are the relationships between men and women. An interview by Jochen Schmidt (Bausch 1996, pp.58–59) went as follows:

> *You mentioned the word process. Process means development. You yourself have developed considerably ... Do you have any idea where the process is leading or where you yourself are going? Could you imagine retiring from dance completely and becoming a theater director, for example?*

> That's possible. I don't know. I'm always trying. I keep desperately trying to dance. I'm always hoping I'm going to find new ways of relating to movement. I can't go on working in the previous way. It would be like repeating something, something strange.

> *Might it also be that movement simply no longer suffices for what you want to say — that you also require words?*

> Words? I can't say exactly ... It is simply a question of when is it dance, when is it not. Where does it start? When do we call it dance? It does in fact have something to do with consciousness, with bodily consciousness, and the way we form things. But then it needn't have this kind of aesthetic form. It can have a quite different form and still be dance. Basically one wants to say something which cannot be said, so what one has done is to make a poem where one can feel what is meant. And so words, I find, are a means – a means to an end. But words are not the true aim.

> *What would you describe the true aim as being? Communication, or is it art?*

> I don't know. I don't know.

The message in Pina Bausch's answers leads to a reversal of what supervision (and also therapy) is supposed to be in conventional terms: an activity based on words. As we saw earlier – when talking about 'creative' and action methods in conventional supervision – these methods are 'media', means, whereas it is the words that lead us to reflection (and insight). In the quote above (and I see here an analogy to the dramatic process in dramatherapy) it is the words that are seen as a means – a means to an end. It is through the body that discoveries can be made, and projected, and expressed. Words are not the true aim. In the above quote, the true aim is the exploration of new ways of relating to movement, of finding bodily consciousness and of finding new ways to form things, all of which is analogous to the EPR (embodiment, projection, role). In the sense of such artistic activity, art *is* communication. Art and artistic activity respectively open up other perspectives that can lead professionals to alternative solutions other than those known to them through their routines. This means for dramatherapy supervision that the communication that takes place in dramatherapy supervision through the dramatic activity will have a quality quite different from communication in conventional supervision. This difference will also influence the kind of relationship that evolves between supervisor and supervisee, supervisee and client.

This is a crucial difference between dramatherapy and the above-mentioned approaches. This difference is important and needs to be considered when formulating supervision concepts and models for dramatherapy (see also Lahad 1997, p.31).

On supervision and dramatherapy

We are reaching one of our last stops. We can now attempt to combine our impressions so far. The chapters of this book will give you detailed examples of how this all works in practice.

In the previous section I have presented the core concepts of dramatherapy that differentiate it from other approaches. I have also mentioned that the approach being used and its underlying values will influence the 'what-to-do's' and 'how-to-do's' of supervision. In fact, there are certain 'what-to-do's' (tasks) and 'how-to-do's' (functions) that have been worked out through research on supervision and could be said to be valuable for supervision in general. Drawing on Holloway (1995, p.39) I would like to define the tasks of supervision as promoting the reflection on professional practice, the building up of professional skills, developing or preserving the ability to conceptualize the situation (case), reflecting on the professional role, preserving emotional awareness and enabling self-evaluation (thus promoting autonomy). The functions could be defined as follows: advising; eventually instructing; modelling; consulting; supporting and sharing; monitoring. The combination of tasks and functions defines the process of supervision (Holloway 1995, p.37). These tasks and functions will also be valid for dramatherapy supervision; however, we will try to keep in mind that the process of 'reflection' will take place here – as described above – through the senses. In dramatherapy supervision, these tasks and functions can be carried out by drawing on the dramatherapy models as they are mentioned in the next paragraph. The chapters of this book will demonstrate the use of such models within the supervisory process.

Particular qualities that supervisor dramatherapists are required to have and that are connected to the very nature of dramatherapy are the capability of risk-taking (connected to the ritual-risk paradigm of theatre), the artistic/expressive capacity, the capacity to play, the sense for bodily and non-verbal communication, the sensory awareness and finally the imagination and the sense for the metaphysical, also inherent in theatrical activity. These are also obviously qualities that dramatherapist practitioners need to have and that are useful to other professionals as they expand their resources for dealing with demanding and challenging professional situations. Accordingly, dramatherapy supervisors will use and promote these qualities through the process of supervision. To do this the supervisor dramatherapist will use interventions that can be, for example, prescriptive, informative, confrontative, cathartic, catalytic or supportive (Rowan, as quoted in Burnard 1989). She will draw on her fund of metaphors and images from myths, plays and fairy tales. Furthermore she will base these interventions on the different dramatherapy models, for example, developmental/aesthetic (Jennings 1998), paratheatre (Mitchell 1992), role (Landy 1993), story-telling (Gersie and King 1990) and story-making (Lahad 1992). The chapters in this book illustrate, with various examples based on these models, relationships and roles as they form within the dramatherapy supervision process. They also present several dramatherapy supervision processes as they unfold in different settings (individual, group and team) as well as in interdisciplinary supervision (e.g. a dramatherapist supervising a music therapist in Chapter 10).

Before giving brief summaries of these chapters I would like to refer to a specific feature of dramatherapy supervision that differentiates it from supervision that is based primarily on verbal communication. This feature is also characteristic of other arts therapies and concerns the relationship in dramatherapy supervision. I will here introduce the terms 'non-artistic' and 'artistic' supervision to refer to mainly verbal supervision that uses art as a means versus supervision that builds on the artistic process.

In non-artistic supervision the relationship unfolds mainly between supervisor and supervisee in that the supervisee relates the case and the supervisor facilitates the realization of tasks and functions keeping the 'helicopter ability' (focusing on the client, and keeping the overview over the supervisee's process, the supervisor's own process, the here and now process of the relationship with the supervisee(s), and finally the client and the work within the wider systemic context in which it takes place) (Hawkins and Shohet 1996, p.37). Here, the process of supervision is realized mainly through verbal communication and interpretation. As I have mentioned, artistic creations – if they occur – are mainly media, means to facilitate expression of pre-rational material that underlies the not-planned actions of the supervisee and their interpretation.

In dramatherapy supervision – and I suppose in other artistic supervision, too – the relationship develops between supervisor, supervisee and the method, i.e. the art form. The three form a triangle that is the basis for other triangles to unfold during the process. The process of supervision takes place here mainly through 'poiesis' (Levine 1997) made possible through the parties' involved letting go within the artistic process. The helicopter ability as described above, coupled with the capacity for aesthetic distancing, enables the supervisor dramatherapist to help the Dionysian power express itself and transform it by Apollonian clarity. 'The result would be living form. The "chaos" of the Dionysian, joined with the "cosmos" (order) of the Apollonian, would give birth to the "dancing star" of an artistic culture' (Levine 1997, p.14), a culture that we – dramatherapists and arts therapists alike – believe to be healing and preventive of dysfunction and illness. Hence, through facilitating the artistic creation of the supervisee, the supervisor affirms the supervisee's creativity, thus role-modelling to her how to affirm the creativity of her client and help him find the courage to affirm it for himself, too (see also Levine 1997, p.89). (On supervisory triangles and the helicopter ability see also Chapter 4 in this volume.)

In a culture that bases professional activity on rational thinking, that believes in and propagates the power of reflection for the gaining of insight and growth, the question arises: in which way does such a process help the professional cope with the demands of her professional situations?

The artistic creation (whether the creation of or work with a story, or a painting, or the play with mini sculpts, or a performance with the body, or a role-play on the basis of imagined or borrowed roles from theatre and fiction) allows a contact with the 'depths', a 'sounding' (Richard Nieoczym: personal communication) that expands perception, puts us in contact with the imagination and allows us to feed the soul, see with many eyes, speak many languages, particularly those which are beyond linguistic constructions. This expansion – which needs no interpretation – allows us to see what we do with our clients, to imagine alternatives to our interventions and actions, and to create solutions that meet the demands of our professional situations. The artistic activity also distances us from situations we perceive as challenging, thus enabling us to look at them with a helicopter view and preventing us from getting stuck in them. In that sense, dramatherapy supervision is not only 'perturbing' our stuck narratives. It does not just allow us to construct new narratives, narratives that again help us reduce complexity. (I am referring here to the constructivist approach as I presented it above and as has been applied to supervision (Kersting 1992). As I said before, the aim of supervision is to 'perturb' the system by countering the existing narratives. Through this perturbation, new narratives are created which, however, again have the function of reducing complexity. Within this approach, a way of helping the system (whether this is an individual, a team, a group or an organization) to cope with the complexity is to encourage it to create as many narratives as possible.) It promotes our very capacity to bear complexity, to live and play with imbalances that in the flow of our imaginative and real actions transform into balances and again into imbalances, following an endless stream of transformations. Complexity within this play therefore becomes not only bearable but even enjoyable. Supervision with dramatherapy promotes the capacity to cope with complex professional situations. It enables supervisor and supervisees to deal with the processes of balancing between several poles that are the very aim of supervision (as quoted above from Rappe-Giesecke 1994, p.11): between self-experience and instruction; between descriptions of the psychodynamic and the sociodynamic; between structuring and following the process; between self-analysis and other-analysis.

On the dramatherapy supervision contract

We are reaching the end of our sightseeing tour now. Before we part, I need to draw your attention to the subject of contract. You certainly know how important it is to make proper arrangements before embarking on a journey. Let me remind you of some preparations that you should make and some points that are not to be forgotten when you plan a supervision process.

Gathering information about the system to be supervised (what they do) and clarifying the needs and motivations of the supervisee(s) to be (what they want) as well as negotiating a clear contract before entering whichever supervisory relationship, is essential. It is important also for the supervisees when they negotiate with a new supervisor to be clear about her way of working and the approach she will apply. The following matters should be agreed upon and mentioned in the contract:

- the contracting parties
- the length and frequency of sessions
- the number of sessions
- the meeting place
- the persons participating (this is particularly important for teams (whether, for example, the team leader will participate in supervision or not) and for groups in institutions (where different hierarchical levels might want to attend the supervision sessions)
- confidentiality
- particularly in the case of non-clinical supervision, the support of the top management for the supervision process (process of reflection on the working practice)
- the price and other conditions related to payment in case of cancelling of sessions.

Particularly in the case of dramatherapy supervision it is important that the contracting institution, team, group or individual knows what dramatherapy supervision is and what the terms and implications are. I have already mentioned the expanding potential of theatre and drama. Drama and dramatherapy can very quickly have strong impacts of change on individuals, teams, groups and institutions. The support of the upper management – particularly in institutional settings – is necessary in order to minimize set-backs and scapegoating practices against the supervisor. Chapters 3 and 7 refer to the significance of the surrounding systems and to the importance of the management's understanding, agreement and support.

Conclusion

The specific resources of the supervisor-dramatherapist are her ability to structure time, space, role and process with artistic, specifically dramatic, means, as well as the possibility of using aesthetic distance to gain insight with respect to professional practice. These are some of the characteristics that differentiate dramatherapy from other approaches that are based on interpretations and use drama and play as a means to an end rather than an end in itself. These aspects and resources are illustrated throughout this book. It is demonstrated how, through the artistic orientation and the work with dramatic distance, the client and the organization can be included, how the supervision process can be moved on, how blocks can be overcome, how support for the discovery and nourishment of the internal supervisor can be given. Through an expanded perception the supervisee can find new ways in her practice and become a role model for the client.

On the chapters of this book

Chapters 1, 2 and 3 introduce dramatherapy supervision generally: historical issues, a theatre-based supervision model for multidisciplinary supervisees and the importance of supervision for the playtherapist and the dramatherapist working with children.

In Chapter 1, Anna Chesner discusses in the first part the historical issues of dramatherapy supervision in Britain. In the discussion she includes comparisons with other countries and other approaches. In the second part she presents the specifics of supervision with individuals/trainees, groups, teams and peers. She highlights particular characteristics that should be noted when working within each setting; she also gives an overall view of the several interventions that can be applied in the different settings and richly illustrates these different processes with corresponding examples of practice.

In Chapter 2, Sue Jennings presents a theatre-based model of dramatherapy supervision and its application in practice. She shows how the Mandala, the EPR and the text-based story, as well as socially constructive narratives, are essential ingredients in dramatherapy supervision practice. This type of supervision puts tremendous demands on the dramatherapist in terms of their broad base of knowledge of therapeutic practice, as well as a working knowledge of a wide variety of stories and plays. Supervisees can respond to known and popular stories, even from books such as the Old Testament, as well as stories that are new to them. This means that the dramatherapist supervisor has to be willing to take risks with their own intuition and hunches. They also have to be able to admit it when they get it wrong. However, as Sue Jennings maintains, and as this and the other chapters in this book show, supervising in this mode is a very rich and rewarding experience, and takes us on creative journeys in a collaborative enterprise between supervisor and supervisee.

In Chapter 3, Ann Cattanach explains the importance of supervision for the playtherapist or the dramatherapist working with children. Current ideas about childhood are explored and how these can impact on the therapist who has to cope with pressures from the external world. The ethics and objectives of the agencies that support work with children and the imperative to 'make it better' for the child are examined. The tendency for agencies to use children in therapy as objects to get information from about their families or what has happened to them, rather than change the adults who are more frightening to confront, are issues that are also tackled. In supervision, these social issues are untangled as are the personal feelings of therapists about their own childhoods.

Chapters 4 and 5 focus on the supervisory relationship as it unfolds within supervision with dramatherapy. In Chapter 4, Katerina Couroucli-Robertson deals with different supervisory triangles that form during dramatherapy supervision, for example, the triangle between client/therapist/supervisor and the mirroring of the client/supervisee relationship with that of the supervisor/supervisee relationship, both contained in the art form. The idea here is that during supervision the therapy session is reproduced very closely in its original form and at the same time it takes on a life of its own. This parallel process is a universal phenomenon. The failure to observe its presence in supervision may be an indication of a natural resistance on the part of the supervisor and/or the supervisee against facing the full impact of those forces which they are asking the client to face in him or herself.

In Chapter 5, Robert J. Landy presents the application of the role model of dramatherapy in supervision. In a series of four dialogues that correspond to four focal points of the role model of supervision he allows us to look into the different scenarios and relationships that evolve within the supervisory process: the relationship of role–counterrole–guide within the therapist; the relationship of role–counterrole–guide within the client; the relationship between client and therapist; and the relationship of role–counterrole–guide in the relationship among client, therapist and supervisor.

Chapters 6, 7 and 8 deal with supervision in different fields. In Chapter 6, Mooli Lahad takes us into the field of crisis intervention. He describes the parallel processes between the experience of a victim and that of a helper; the problem of not being able to perform the protective rituals, the trance-like influence of the situation, and some reflections on the myth of creation and chaos, the experience of encounter with darkness over abyss. Using stories and myths he shows ways of supervising and helping professionals who are involved in intervention immediately after and following a disaster with victims of emotional trauma.

In Chapter 7, Reinhard Tötschinger offers insight into the world of business. He explains why supervision with theatre/drama and dramatherapy is important in business. He shows us how it can be applied as well as the effects it has on the people and systems supervised. He presents personal and organizational stages and how these stages are kept alive. He shows how theatre methods can be used for diagnosis and as irritating interventions within organizational systems. With examples he shows us how dramatherapy can be used to deal with unconscious or subconscious *mise-en-scènes* in institutions and business organizations, and how these can be challenged, expanded or changed.

In Chapter 8, Roger Grainger introduces the field of art-based research. He discusses the principal aims of consultation and research supervision respectively. He refers to the particular attitude of mind required by the supervisor of art-based research, namely one that shares the same basic perspective as an art critic – 'albeit an art critic who is also an artist'. Grainger points to the supervision of dramatherapy research being a very different activity from that of supervising dramatherapy itself. Some dimensions of the relationship between therapist and supervisor are changed in an important way, as the primary focus is shifted away from the therapist's relationship *with* clients to that of her involvement in research activities *concerning* clients.

Chapters 9 and 10 are concerned with issues of training of supervisor dramatherapists. In Chapter 9, Marina Jenkyns considers aspects of supervision training, referring mainly to her own training course which is run in London. The aims, rationale, content and teaching/learning methods in relation to the eventual roles and tasks of a supervisor dramatherapist are considered. A psychodynamic perspective in relation to dramatherapy supervision is adopted and attention is paid to issues of projection, transference and countertransference. The issue of the trainer's task in helping trainees to take their own authority in the supervisory role is emphasized.

In Chapter 10, Elektra Tselikas-Portmann, Sue Jennings, Katerina Couroucli-Robertson and Demys Kyriacou discuss the need for supervision training in general and the necessity for dramatherapy supervision training in particular. They present some principles that underly the structure of curricula and apply them to the concept of a theatre-based supervision training course. The arguments presented are illustrated with examples from theatre-based supervision training sessions that demonstrate the learning process of an individual trainee and a training group as well as the placement of theatre-based dramatherapy supervision in an interdisciplinary setting.

Finally, the Appendices contain the results of research on dramatherapy supervision and the addresses of institutions or people offering drama-therapy supervision training courses, as well as a presentation of the Supervision Subcommittee of the British Association of Dramatherapists. Madeline Andersen-Warren and Lorraine Fox have carried out the first research on dramatherapy supervision. The questionnaires asked for length of time since qualification, information about client groups, major theoretical influences on practice, form and frequency of supervision, as well as the perceived importance of having a dramatherapist as a supervisor and whether the supervisor's clinical practice should be the same as the supervisee's. They were sent out to all dramatherapists on the BADTh register who are resident in Britain. The first results contain relevant information concerning, among others, the imbalance between named theories of psychology versus those of drama/theatre, the importance the respondents attach to supervision and the possibilities they have to receive it. Interestingly enough, most drama-therapists do not receive clinical supervision in their place of work. Perhaps this is due to the assumption that supervision is provided by the dramatherapists' superiors. This tendency is obviously a result of the situation regarding supervision in the English-speaking countries as I have described it above (under 'Supervision: one term, several traditions').

Another interesting result of this research is the importance drama-therapists attach to being supervised by a dramatherapist supervisor. On the basis of what I have described as the characteristics of dramatherapy, this is not astonishing. Indeed, supervisors qualified in other approaches will find it hard to understand and practise the principles that underlie the process of dramatherapy supervision. By contrast, it will be possible for supervisor-dramatherapists to understand professionals from other fields and help them expand their own understandings.

Acknowledgement

I warmly thank Robert Landy and Paul Portmann for their feedback and comments on this Introduction. Of course, I bear the sole responsibility for the thoughts expressed here.

References

Artaud, A. (1996) 'Theatre and cruelty.' In M. Huxley and N. Witts (eds) *The Twentieth Century Performance Reader.* London: Routledge.

Bausch, P. (1996) 'Not how people move but what moves them.' In M. Huxley and N. Witts (eds) *The Twentieth Century Performance Reader.* London: Routledge.

Belardi, N. (1994) *Supervision. Von der Praxisberatung zur Organisationsentwicklung.* (*Supervision. From Counselling to Organizational Development.*) (2nd edn.) Paderborn: Junfermann.

Buer, F. (1996) 'Methoden in der Supervision – psychodramatisch angereichert. (Methods in supervision – Enriched with psychodrama)' *Organisationsberatung – Supervision – Clinical Management 1/1996,* 21–44.

Burnard, P. (1989) *Counselling Skills for Practitioners.* London: Chapman Hall.

Cattanach, A. (1994) 'The developmental model of dramatherapy.' In S. Jennings, A. Cattanach, S. Mitchell, A. Chesner and B. Meldrum (eds) *The Handbook of Dramatherapy.* London: Routledge.

Davis, D.R. (1995) *Scenes of Madness. A Psychiatrist at the Theatre.* London: Routledge.

Emunah, R. (1994) *Acting for Real. Drama Therapy Process, Technique, and Performance.* New York: Brunner/Mazel.

Gergen, K.J. (1991) *The Saturated Self.* New York: Basic Books.

Gersie, A. (1997) *Reflections on Therapeutic Storymaking. The Use of Stories in Groups.* London: Jessica Kingsley Pubslishers.

Gersie, A. and King, N. (1990) *Storymaking in Education and Therapy.* London: Jessica Kingsley Publishers.

Hawkins, P. and Shohet, R. (1996) *Supervision in the Helping Professions.* Buckingham and Philadelphia: Open University Press.

Holloway, E. (1995) *Clinical Supervision. A Systems Approach.* London: Sage.

Huxley, M. and Witts, N. (eds) (1996) *The Twentieth Century Performance Reader.* London: Routledge.

Jennings, S. (1994) 'The theatre of healing: Metaphor and metaphysics in the healing process.' In S. Jennings, A. Cattanach, S. Mitchell, A. Chesner and B. Meldrum (eds) *The Handbook of Dramatherapy.* London: Routledge.

Jennings, S.E. (1998) *Introduction to Dramatherapy. Theatre and Healing. Ariadne's Ball of Thread.* London: Jessica Kingsley Publishers.

Jones, P. (1996) *Drama as Therapy – Theatre as Living.* London: Routledge.

Kadushin, A. (1985) *Supervision in Social Work.* New York.

Kersting, H.J. (1992) *Kommunikationssystem Supervision. Unterwegs zu einer konstruktivistischen Beratung (Communication System Supervision. On the Way to Constructivist Counselling).* Aachen: Institut für Beratung und Supervision.

Lahad, M. (1992) 'Story-making in assessment method for coping with stress: Six-piece story-making and BASIC Ph.' In S. Jennings (ed) *Dramatherapy. Theory and Practice 2.* London: Routledge.

Lahad, M. (1997) 'The story as a guide to metaphoric processes.' In S. Jennings (ed) *Dramatherapy. Theory and Practice 3.* London: Routledge.

Landy, R.J. (1986) (2nd enlarged edition 1994) *Drama Therapy. Concepts and Practices.* Springfield, IL: Charles Thomas Publishers.

Landy, R.J. (1993) *Persona and Performance. The Meaning of Role in Drama, Therapy, and Everyday Life.* London: Jessica Kingsley Publishers.

Landy, R.J. (1996) 'The use of distancing in dramatherapy.' In R.J. Landy (ed) *Essays in Drama Therapy. The Double Life.* London: Jessica Kingsley Publishers.

Levine, S.K. (1997) *Poiesis. The Language of Psychology and the Speech of the Soul.* London: Jessica Kingsley Publishers.

Maturana, H.R. and Varela, F. (1984) *El Arbol del Conocimiento (The Tree of Cognition).* Santiago/Chile.

McNiff, S. (1998) *Trust the Process. An Artist's Guide to Letting Go.* Boston and London: Shambhala.

Mitchell, S. (1992) 'Therapeutic theatre: A para-theatrical model of dramatherapy.' In S. Jennings (ed) *Dramatherapy. Theory and Practice 2.* London: Routledge.

Rappe-Giesecke, C. (1994) 2nd revised and enlarged edition *Supervision. Gruppen- und Team Supervision in Theorie und Praxis (Supervision. Group and Team Supervision in Theory and Practice).* Berlin: Springer.

Schreyögg, A. (1992) *Supervision. Ein integratives Modell. Lehrbuch zu Theorie und Praxis (Supervision. An Integrative Model. Handbook for Theory and Practice).* Paderborn: Junfermann.

Schreyögg, A. (1994) *Supervision. Didaktik and Evaluation (Supervision. Didactics and Evaluation).* Paderborn: Junfermann.

Stoltenberg, C.D. and Delworth, U. (1987) *Supervising Counsellors and Therapists.* San Francisco.

Williams A. (1995) *Visual and Active Supervision.* New York: Norton.

PART 1

Supervision and Dramatherapy

CHAPTER I

Dramatherapy Supervision
Historical Issues and Supervisory Settings

Anna Chesner

This chapter is divided into two sections. It begins with a historical overview of dramatherapy supervision in Britain including some comparisons with other countries where dramatherapy is practised as a profession. There follows a consideration of the settings in which supervision can take place, with particular reference to dramatherapy. Here I give examples of dramatherapy-influenced supervision in a variety of settings. These include supervision of dramatherapists and non-dramatherapists; trainees and experienced practitioners.

It is important that a consideration of dramatherapy-influenced supervision situates itself not only in the smaller perspective of the specialized profession of dramatherapy but also in the wider perspective of the world of counselling and psychotherapy; a world where multi-disciplinary teamwork and constructive dialogue between professions are vital.

A historical perspective

In summer 1977 the first newsletter for the British Association for Dramatherapists (BADTh) appeared. This was twenty-one years ago at the time of writing. Of course 'the intentional use of the healing aspects of drama in the therapeutic process' (BADTh Code of Practice definition of dramatherapy) has a much older history, reaching back more than two millennia in Europe alone. It is the profession of dramatherapy that has recently come of age, and its maturational history has been one of ever-increasing professionalization.

The history of supervision within the British association can be placed into the context of this professionalization. It has occurred alongside developments such as the placing of dramatherapy as a 'profession supplementary to medicine' and the formal recognition of the need for personal therapy for trainees. As well as receiving supervision during their training British dramatherapists commit to and must substantiate forty mandatory supervision sessions in the first three years of their postqualifying practice. While it is encouraged that dramatherapists and trainees receive their supervision from a dramatherapist, the system which has been in place since 1992 makes it currently not an absolute requirement in Britain. There are considerable variations between different countries. In Israel a system operates which is rather more rigorous than in Britain: it follows the rules of the Israeli Psychology Association and leads to registration with the umbrella Association of Arts Therapies. Graduates of a dramatherapy training must complete over 2000 hours of supervised postqualifying dramatherapy practice. Forty out of 200 hours of postqualifying supervision must be with a dramatherapist. The rest can be with a qualified supervisor who may be an arts therapist, a psychologist, a social worker or a psychiatrist. In Greece there is a stipulation of 96 hours of supervision during training as a dramatherapist or playtherapist and a subsequent requirement of two hours supervision per month for as long as they are practising in the field. The preference is that this takes place with a trained dramatherapy or playtherapy supervisor, but otherwise with a qualified supervisor from another discipline with a knowledge of the field. In the USA (information based on the NYU course) there is a requirement for supervision during training at the rate of a minimum 40 hours per year for a 780-hour clinical internship. Supervision is provided by the faculty as well as on placement. Qualifications for supervisors are not completely formalized due to limited availability of experienced dramatherapist supervisors. This is a factor which appears to be common to all relevant countries and relates to the relative youth of the profession worldwide.

It is, however, clear that supervision is a core element in the process of becoming a professional dramatherapist. The British Association for Dramatherapists' Code of Practice enshrines it as 'an essential component of good practice' and one which must be clearly differentiated from training or therapy.

The profession in Britain has reached a point now where there is not only a list of practitioners and trainees but a register of dramatherapy supervisors. These have been trained in a BADTh accredited course and themselves make a commitment to be supervised on their supervision as a further level of professional quality assurance. The register exists as a resource, but there is currently no requirement that a trainee receives supervision from someone on the supervisors' register. There is an expectation that trainee supervision be with a registered dramatherapist with at least three years of post-qualifying experience where possible. It is understood that there are local differences in availability of such supervisors and alternatively trained supervisors are also being used. The need for dramatherapy supervision from within a dramatherapy framework has led to the emergence over the last decade of several supervision training courses run by dramatherapists. Such courses have begun to contribute to the availability of appropriate specialist supervision for dramatherapists. They have also brought a creative and action-based dimension into the supervision of practitioners from other backgrounds and furthered the awareness and recognition of dramatherapy within the wider professional world.

A brief glance through the looking glass of history shows that the acceptance of supervision as a core part of the British dramatherapist's commitment to good practice has not been without resistance and controversy. During the mid-1980s a series of educational workshops introducing the concept and exploring the need for supervision to the membership were set up. Initially these were poorly attended, suggesting perhaps some reluctance to engage with the concept. By 1986, however, Dramatherapy North West reported on a study day led by Dorothy Langley in which models and techniques were clarified and practitioners' own hopes and needs from supervision as related to practice were listed. The participants had the following hopes for supervision:

> being acknowledged and understood, validated and reassured, being able to share and learn, get things in perspective, recognize the source of difficulties, share our anxieties without fear of censure, be challenged and questioned by the Supervisor, ventilate our feelings, get help and training, clarify less well understood areas and publicly state our intentions and have them checked out. (Dramatherapy North West 1986, p.1)

There is also an acknowledgement

that supervision [is] not personal therapy, but could elucidate the sources of difficulties which could then be taken to personal therapy. (Dramatherapy North West 1986, p.1)

The list demonstrates the multiple functions of supervision and a growing enthusiasm for what it can offer. The report was front page news in the *Newsletter*, indicating the prominent place the subject had for the professional association at the time.

Three years later questions arose amongst the membership around the issue of the association's role in monitoring supervision. The executive had recommended a three-tier system of membership whereby anyone wishing to be registered as a 'full practising member' would have to provide annual written evidence of their supervision, presumably for the rest of their professional life. This was regarded by some members as elitist, restrictive and inflexible, sentiments expressed in a letter published in the *Newsletter* (Casson *et al.* 1989).

The debate seems to me to have been an appropriate one for a profession in its adolescence. There was a desire to maintain and be seen to maintain high professional standards. At the same time there was a determination amongst trained dramatherapists to assert their adult status in the face of a quality control mechanism which was perceived as parental and infantilizing. A balance was being negotiated between trusting the practitioner and monitoring good practice. The outcome in terms of the current status quo is that trainee and newly trained dramatherapists provide written evidence of their supervision. It is assumed that this experience is internalized and lays the foundation of good practice. The dramatherapist is then in a position to make an informed and free choice to continue in supervision subsequently, a choice which is clearly backed up by the code of practice as quoted above.

If we look at the broader view we can see that dramatherapy as a profession in Britain has positioned itself somewhere between the traditions of counselling and psychoanalysis as regards supervision requirements. The British Association of Counsellors (BAC) quantifies the amount of supervision recommended in relation to the amount of clinical contact time. This applies to trained as well as trainee counsellors, and must be substantiated when accreditation is renewed every five years. In some analytic traditions by contrast, after an initial period of post-qualifying supervision, those wishing to become training analysts have to demonstrate a period of time without supervision! This may reflect differences in the approaches to and lengths of training, but also perhaps alternative views of the function(s) of supervision.

In a Department of Health-run Clinical Supervision Conference in 1995 the issue of supervision was debated from a number of perspectives. The concluding statements began: 'This conference believes that clinical supervision should be developed, supported and evaluated throughout the health services' (Bishop and Butterworth 1995, p.39). While the emphasis of the conference was on the clinical supervision of nurses this was explicitly broadened to 'all health care professionals' (p.38). The conference recognized clinical supervision as being of value on a number of counts, which I consider useful in considering the function of supervision for dramatherapists working within a health care or other agency. In addition to its 'intrinsic value' (p.42) it is 'normative' in the sense that it addresses organizational and quality control aspects of practice; it is 'restorative' (p.4) in that it provides supportive help to professionals 'working constantly with stress and distress'; it is 'protective' in that it is a proactive device to help with difficulties, which is preferable to reactive solutions to damage already done (p.43); and it is 'formative', in terms of educating and developing new skills (Bishop and Butterworth 1995, p.4). The document also suggests that the value of supervision could be audited through existing mechanisms such as rates of sickness and absence, staff satisfaction scales, numbers of patient complaints and retention and recruitment of staff. Those dramatherapists who have to struggle to achieve time and funding for supervision within the workplace may resonate with these suggestions and find the document useful in making their case. In Israel there is an expectation of continuing post-qualifying supervision at the rate of one hour per ten practice hours whilst in Britain and other countries the rate of supervision is a matter for negotiation.

Settings for supervision

Should the dramatherapist be supervised by a dramatherapist? Should supervisors be trained in supervision or is it enough to be an experienced and insightful practitioner? These questions are of current interest to dramatherapists and the debate will inform our future view of good practice and the continuing development of the profession. In terms of the first question I believe it is helpful to make a distinction between supervision for the trainee and supervision for the qualified and experienced practitioner. In the case of a trainee or newly qualified therapist there is much to be said for supervision taking place predominantly in the method being learned. This facilitates the process of internalizing the method, mastering its language and strengthening a professional identity. When supervising trainees more time is devoted to the questions of what happened in the session and what interventions were used. This is particularly the case in an action-based method like dramatherapy, where there is a virtually limitless range of structures and interventions to choose from and to be arranged together into a coherent and whole session. The dramatherapist is artist as well as therapist and the supervision needs to take both these elements into account.

The trainee or neophyte dramatherapist may reap significant benefits from being supervised by an experienced dramatherapist, who thinks dramatherapeutically and knows the methods and processes which distinguish dramatherapy from 'talking cure' therapies and from other arts therapies. The non-dramatherapist is less qualified to engage critically with the implications of a particular choice of dramatherapy structure in practice. They may view the 'therapy' of dramatherapy as something which happens outside or after rather than within and through the 'drama'. The outcome for the trainee in the process of developing their own internal supervisor can be a lack of confidence in their own therapeutic rationale, a lack of rigour in questioning their own choice of dramatherapy structure or approach within a particular therapeutic context, and even a personal sense of alienation from the very language they are learning.

In the particular case of dramatherapy supervision there is an added complexity when we look at transference and countertransference issues. These processes, even in verbal counselling and psychotherapy, are in themselves dramatic processes, whereby one party (and it can be either the client or therapist) 'casts' the other in a particular 'role'. When the transference is directed at the therapist he or she may take on that role in a reciprocal manner, or deliberately take on an alternative role to challenge the transference. How much more complex this becomes in dramatherapy when the intentional playing of imaginary or remembered roles is the very language of the therapy. So, in addition to paying attention to transference phenomena as they emerge on the boundaries of the dramatic work and in the process as a whole we must also look at the potential levels of meaning within the dramatic work itself. For dramatherapy supervision we need to pay particular attention to:

a) the symbolic content of the client's dramatic material and its significance to the client

b) the relationship of the dramatic material to the group process including the group–therapist dynamic

c) the significance of this material as reflected in the supervision process.

Vignette: dramatic imagery and the group process

An example of b) above:

> Trainee Pam working with a group of eating disordered women registered mixed feelings when her group began a session by presenting her with a gift. She brings these feelings to supervision and various approaches to untangling them are explored in the supervision session. It is only towards the end of the session that she comes to a clearer view about what may have happened. The supervision focus at this point is on the heart of the dramatic work of the group. She describes how the group work together in finding a solution to one group member's imaginary story. The imagery involves distracting a sharp-toothed tiger from the vulnerable heroine by the other animals dressing up as beautiful butterflies and doing a seductive dance, while the heroine escapes. By staying with this imagery and playing with the idea of the therapist as tiger Pam recognizes that she had to some extent been seduced by the gift and diverted from looking at the rageful feelings that had been present in the group in their previous session. The group had succeeded in deflecting attention from their own and the therapist's 'teeth'.

For the trained and more experienced dramatherapist the situation may be quite different. When a body of core skills and modes of thinking are in place there is much to be gained from viewing the therapeutic situation through the eyes of another system. The process is analogous to travelling in a foreign country, using a foreign language to communicate and receive new ideas, then returning home with the benefit of a fresh perspective to cast new light on the familiar.

As for the question as to the necessity for training in supervision my view is that clinical wisdom is usually gained through experience and informal learning in the field. A formal training in supervision assumes that this wisdom is largely in place. The supervision training adds the further advantages of giving a theoretical framework to the supervision process, and opening up the possibility of new perspectives and approaches.

Supervision settings currently fall into four categories: one-to-one; group; team; and peer. With the development of new technology we may be moving towards a time when supervision happens through telephone or on-line conferencing, which will bring its own advantages and disadvantages. My discussion of each setting assumes live and face-to-face contact.

One-to-one

This form of supervision often takes place weekly, fortnightly or monthly for a therapeutic hour. The advantages are that the supervisee has the full attention of the supervisor, and it is possible to devote more time to looking at the material in detail. A closer relationship may be built than in group supervision, and some supervisees may find it easier to disclose mistakes and insecurities in a one-to-one situation.

On the downside the supervisor–supervisee relationship is more prominent in this setting. If there are difficulties in the relationship there are no other participants to provide an alternative perspective. The supervisor may be perceived as more authoritarian in this model or may collude with the blind spots of the supervisee. Even where the relationship is satisfactory it may be considered a limitation that the dialogue is restricted to two people, although in defence of this form it must be remembered that each individual may bring with them the perspective of other parts of the therapy system.

I favour one-to-one supervision for dramatherapy trainees especially at the beginning of their practice. This is for a number of reasons. First, trainees at this time of transition tend to be insecure, full of questions and in need of time. Having to share and negotiate for time in a group supervision situation can add to feelings of insecurity in an unhelpful way. Second, early placement experiences offer the trainee multiple challenges, all of which can usefully be explored. These challenges include dealing with a placement agency; preparing for and conducting assessments; planning, conducting and recording the clinical work; engaging with individual and group therapeutic processes; dealing with the emerging dynamics of the agency; establishing a professional dramatherapy identity. Exploration of each of these perspectives takes time, which makes the one-to-one framework the setting of choice. Most dramatherapy placements, especially those early on in the training, tend to be group therapy experiences. It might seem incongruent to engage in one-to-one supervision when the therapy being practised is a group one. However the considerations already mentioned often outweigh the benefits of other frameworks.

One-to-one supervision may also be the setting of choice for experienced therapists at times of particular challenge such as a new project or a difficult dynamic. Furthermore it can be a welcome change for those who work predominantly in groups to be in a one-to-one setting for supervision.

There are a number of dramatherapeutic techniques suited to the one-to-one supervision context. Some of the possible techniques are as follows:

1. *Representing the workspace*

    The supervisee walks and talks the supervisor through the space 'as if' it were contained within the supervision room. This allows the supervisee to contact feelings and reflections around the physical environment and the dynamics of the agency in a spontaneous way and the supervisor to get a sense of the work context and some of the issues which may be associated with it.

2. *Mini role reversal*

    The supervisee *shows* the supervisor a posture, gesture, movement, facial expression or vocal expression. This allows a momentary identification and 'feeling into' the client (or colleague) whilst falling into the overall structure of a conversation or dialogue with the supervisor rather than a dramatic representation.

3. *Macro role reversal*

    The supervisee inhabits the role of the client (or colleague) for longer in order to describe the person in the first rather than the third person, and in order to allow the supervisor to conduct an 'interview in role'. The device of an empty chair or the assumption and relinquishing of a cloth or prop associated with the person may be used to create a distinction between being 'in role' and 'deroling'. The device is particularly useful where the supervisee feels mystified by an aspect of the client or of the therapy relationship, or when there is a countertransferential issue blocking the process. To some extent all counsellors and therapists engage in an empathic role reversal during the therapeutic encounter. The dramatherapeutic device makes this process explicit within the supervision session and allows an imaginative extension of the partial identification with the client.

4.   *Addressing the client in the 'as if'*

The supervisee is invited to imagine the client present in the room, on an empty chair or in the part of the room where they imagine them. They are invited to address them more openly than they would do if they were actually present. This device allows the supervisee to contact the feelings and unspoken thoughts in relation to the client and to make this countertransferential material both explicit to themselves and open for discussion with the supervisor.

5.   *Spectogram and symbolization*

The spectogram or button sculpt is a representation in miniature of the therapeutic system as perceived and constructed by the supervisee in the here and now of the supervision session. Small objects such as buttons, stones, marbles, or miniature animals and people are chosen to represent people, inner objects, client or therapist imagery, issues relevant to the therapy relationship (see Williams 1995 for his use of magnetic figures on a board). Spatial relationships between the parts are used to express the dynamics in non-verbal terms. The supervisee can explore possible directions, impulses and outcomes by making changes in the represented picture. They may also role reverse with different parts of the picture, giving voice to these as the dynamics are fleshed out. One of the advantages of the method is the perspective and scale. By working in miniature the supervisee has an overview and can take in the wider picture.

Symbolization works on similar principles to the spectogram but is not confined to small objects. Chairs, cushions, cloths and any other objects may be used to represent a larger three-dimensional image, through which the supervisee may choose to move. They may enter the represented world in role reversal with any of its parts to explore it from within.

EXAMPLES WITH A DRAMATHERAPY TRAINEE

The following examples describe two moments where the supervision moves into action, but for contrasting reasons.

Gaining distance and the value of the overview

Dan is about to conduct a one-to-one placement with a learning disabled adolescent. He has already run an assessment session and spoken to the staff at the referring agency. He is about to start a short series of sessions and comes to supervision feeling 'daunted by the impossibility' of the task. This is despite the fact that he has already completed two group placements successfully. This client seems to have so many problems, the agency has so many expectations and time is so limited.

The supervisor offers the trainee the opportunity to make a spectogram of the client and the potential foci of the work. Projective materials available in the room are: cloths of various colours, size and texture; a tub of small objects and musical instruments; a collection of model animals.

Dan welcomes the opportunity to take action, to handle the objects and sort out the overwhelming and jumbled feeling into discrete but connected components. Working on the floor he lays down one cloth as background and uses mainly clusters of smaller cloths to differentiate the main issues: a recent bereavement; a query around sexual abuse; the client's adolescent concerns; and a query around the client's psychiatric state in terms of their habit of talking out loud.

Each of these areas is visited and discussed, teasing out above all Dan's sense of the client, but also his concerns relating to agency expectations and to what extent Dan can take these on. The intervention succeeds in engaging Dan's creative and reflective energy. The scale of the spectogram is such as to enable an overview ('super-vision') of the situation. Dan acknowledges its complexity and sorts through what he will give overt focus to and what he will be peripherally watchful for in the sessions.

In retrospect the supervisee evaluates this intervention as follows: 'It helped me sift through my own projections. It was useful to have a perspective on the client before starting the therapy.'

Reducing distance and the value of empathy

Dan's placement is now well under way. The client has responded better than expected to the dramatherapy form. The relationship with Dan appears to be close and meaningful. At the same time the client is taking initiative and leadership in the sessions, and addressing some important issues. The placement is becoming a 'success story' and supervision sessions reflect the growing level of comfort and confidence.

Shortly after the half-way point of the placement Dan arrives unusually agitated. The supervisor registers some surprise at this, having been lulled to some extent into the expectation of a continuing 'success story'. This jolt parallels the situation Dan is bringing to supervision.

He had gone into the therapy session with expectations of continuing to work with the client where they had left off previously. The client, however, arrived at the session unable to concentrate or to engage with Dan other than from a stereotyped 'stupid' and 'childish' role. Dan's countertransference feelings are strong. He feels angry with his client for letting him down and angry with himself for getting it wrong.

Again a spectogram is used to explore the situation. This time the focus is on the therapeutic process and relationship, the therapist's counter-transference in terms of both client and supervisor. The shift in focus since the earlier supervision session above is commensurate with the changing depth of work. As the therapeutic process is under way the less conscious factors have come into play and need to be addressed in the supervision at this pivotal point. While the earlier spectogram facilitates an overview and distancing function the later one incorporates moments of role reversal in order for Dan to get closer to the client's perspective. Dan begins by concretizing his own feelings and attitudes. He represents his anger at himself with an enveloping red cloth. He uses a clown's red nose to represent his question to the client: 'Are you making a mockery of this?' He chooses a witch puppet for the self-attacking view: 'I demand the impossible of my client, I am a bad and destructive therapist.' A tortoise represents another aspect of this, the self-view: 'I am ineffectual and slow. I won't have time to achieve all I should.' A wide-mouthed hippopotamus dominates the picture as the therapist's anger at the client: 'I want to scream at you.' A small, flat plastic tree is placed at the edge of the spectogram representing Dan's own expectations of what he should be as the ideal good therapist and his assumption about the supervisor's expectations of him. The supervisor relativizes this with the observation that the tree looks two-dimensional, and the supervisee introduces a long-necked giraffe into the picture as an acknowledgement 'I know I aim too high.'

So far the spectogram is all about the therapist's self-perception. He then brings the client into the picture. A baby ostrich represents the client's attitude 'I need to hide' while a neatly folded black cloth represents the client's pain: 'It's there, but it's folded away.' Dan makes a role reversal with the client and is asked to comment on the therapist. Of all the symbols of the therapist the client focuses on the gaping hippopotamus. From the client's perspective this represents Dan's demand for the client to feed him, to 'come up with the goods'. Dan continues in role reversal speaking as his client: 'All I want right now is to play, to have fun, be a kid.' This is a revelation for the supervisee who comes out of role and spends the rest of the session re-evaluating his approach to the client and making a decision to be more client-led in future sessions.

In retrospect Dan values this session as a turning point: 'By getting under the client's skin I learned about what I was doing in the relationship. It was the beginning of a deepening of our contact, a clearer approach to the therapy sessions and a more authentic quality of empathy on my part.'

Group

The frequency of group supervision may vary from weekly to monthly or even longer intervals. Ideally the duration of a session is longer than in one-to-one supervision in order to hear the views of different group members and perhaps to focus on more than one case in each session. As with group therapy there are a number of models in group supervision. The group may be open, closed or slow-open (i.e. with a gradually rolling membership). Participants tend to work in different settings (as distinct from team supervision). They may also work with different therapies. The group offers the advantage of eliciting varying perspectives and the chance to learn through difference and multiple dialogue.

The issue of how to use time in the group needs to be clarified. Time may be divided equally amongst all participants in each session in a small group. More usually a session will be devoted to one or two presentations, allowing more time for reflection and perhaps including time for 'any other business', where issues pertinent to the moment or demanding urgent attention can be brought up.

Since there may be an extended period of time before each supervisee's 'turn' comes the group setting presupposes a significant ability for the individual to contain anxiety and to self-manage. As in group therapy there is an assumption that there is a benefit to applying ourselves to the dilemmas and dynamics of each others' work. Not all group supervisors have the skill or inclination to use the group to its full advantage and financial considerations may be behind the choice of a group setting. At worst, there is the danger that what takes place is one-to-one supervision in the context of the group as silent witness. At best the setting offers a highly creative and participative process. Different perspectives and identifications expressed by supervision group members may be viewed as mirroring the perspectives of the different parts of the therapeutic system, whether it be a group or individual therapy situation which is being explored. The group setting often reveals the 'truth' as complex and multifaceted. The supervisor using dramatherapy techniques in a group setting has a wider repertoire of tools to choose from, such as:

1. *Supervisee-led group sculpt*

    Here the supervisee 'sculpts' group members in terms of posture, gesture, relative position and distance to represent a particular theme. Typical themes might include an individual client's family or social atom (significant people in their life); the supervisee's perception of the dynamic within a therapy group; a metaphorical image which the supervisee associates with the client(s) or which the client(s) have worked with.

    The supervisee 'doubles' each part or role within the sculpt, i.e. they make contact and speak for that part, expressing succinctly and in the "I" form what they are doing/feeling/saying in that position. The group member holding the role can then take up the role and develop it further *in situ* or as part of a reflective process after the action. This allows new perspectives to be expressed through their identification with the role.

2. *Group-led group sculpt*

    The supervisee-led group sculpt begins as the subjective expression of one person who is presenting their case for exploration. In the group-led sculpt group members choose the role they wish to explore and position themselves in relation to each other accordingly and in response to how they understand the initial presentation. The presenting supervisee has the opportunity to question the choices made and 'correct' them or conduct interviews in role for further exploration.

    In both forms of group sculpt the presenting supervisee gets to view the system from outside, the 'mirror position'.

3. *Role reversal and role feedback*

    Role reversal can be used in conjunction with the group sculpt or with a simpler staging such as empty chair(s). The presenting supervisee chooses one or more group members to hold roles from the therapy system. As well as viewing the pattern from outside, they adopt one or more of the roles themselves and experience them also from within. This enables a dialogue to emerge through which questions and feelings can be addressed. Such a dialogue will be informed not only by the supervisee's perception of the roles, but also by that of the group member(s) holding the roles. Indeed, the different perspectives can be so useful that the supervisor may invite those group members who have no role allocated to them to enter the stage area and contribute 'doubling' statements as described above.

After an exploration in action of this kind it is helpful to allow some time for reflection, both on the experience of playing the roles and on resonances from other group members' own personal and work experience.

4. *Symbolization with people*

    The supervisee uses other group members to set up a representation of a moment from the therapy. In addition to the external aspects of the situation (e.g. how the client enters the room), aspects of the inner world are also 'concretized' (e.g. the subtextual messages between therapist and client). A composite picture emerges where covert transferential and countertransferential forces are made visible and audible. Exploration continues through doubling, role reversal and role feedback.

    The method is useful in bringing to light personal issues for the therapist as they impact on the therapy relationship. Further working through might then be appropriate within a therapy as opposed to supervision setting.

5. *Playback theatre*

    In this procedure the playback theatre form is used. The supervisor takes on the function of playback theatre 'conductor', the supervisee becomes the 'teller' and members of the group are either players or audience. (For details of the form see Salas 1993 and for a more detailed description of the use within supervision see Chesner 1997.) The supervisee describes the situation of concern to them and the players improvise a scene or number of scenes from the account, in expressionistic style aiming to capture the essence of the 'story'. Initially both supervisee and supervisor watch the scene unfold. Subsequently the supervisee may wish to suggest a change in a 'transformation scene' or address a part of the scene from the outside. The form is suited to a group with highly developed expressive skills as well as the ability to listen for the heart of the story told. The group has a high degree of autonomy in the presentation and the chance to give feedback in a creative way.

EXAMPLE FROM GROUP SUPERVISION OF COUNSELLORS

The group meets weekly in the context of an advanced training course. Sessions last for ninety minutes, during which time there are one or more case presentations for the purpose of shared learning.

Bob brings his clinical work with a couple to the group. The traditional mode of presentation involves reading a brief case history and description of key moments in the work so far to the group, followed by questions and reflections from the group and a final résumé from the presenting supervisee.

On this occasion the supervisor places three empty chairs as a focal point in the room and names them as the man, the woman and the counsellor. The presentation is delivered in the usual way, but the presence of the three chairs provides a continuing reminder to the group of the three-way dynamic under consideration. Bob describes the relationship difficulties of the couple, which are intensified after the death of the man's mother. As he speaks he acknowledges feelings of irritation with the woman and confusion as to what is going on in the counselling sessions.

The supervisor invites him to sit in the woman's chair and try to adopt her body posture as he enters her role for a while. He agrees to do this but experiences some difficulty in getting a sense of her. The supervisor interviews him in role both about her relationship with her husband and about how she experiences her counsellor in the sessions. She expresses anger and disappointment towards her husband and a sense that Bob is more in tune with him than her. Other group members continue the interview. When Bob finds it difficult to answer in role those group members who feel they may have a sense of the role offer a number of 'doubling' statements which he accepts or rejects in role according to how well they capture the feeling he was struggling to identify. The process is repeated with the other two roles. It is immediately clear that Bob has a strong identification with and sympathy for the man, settles easily into his physical posture and can talk with more fluency in that role. When he enters his own role he begins to integrate the new information he has accessed from the roles of his clients. He is able to reflect on his own difficulty in encouraging the expression of anger in the counselling sessions whilst recognizing how strong the need was for this from the position of the woman.

The structure is valued by Bob as giving him insight into the couple and himself and helping him through a feeling of blockedness. The group values it as allowing them to be powerfully involved in the dynamics and to explore their identifications with different parts of the therapy system.

Team

Team supervision is a form of group supervision where all group members are involved in working together, whether in a specialist or multidisciplinary team. A team may be as small as two and theoretically there is no upper limit.

In addition to exploring clinical work as described above, team supervision has the function of maintaining a healthy working relationship within the team. It is a forum for team building, airing grievances, clarifying expectations and roles and exploring change. The dynamic within the team in the supervision tends to mirror what happens between the team and the clients and part of the work is to keep an eye on and learn from this parallel process.

The dramatherapist as supervisee is more likely to be in a multi-disciplinary than specialist team, since the profession is a relatively small one. The setting offers the opportunity for educating colleagues about the work as well as learning about other approaches. The setting is unlikely to offer specialist guidance in the method, although the experienced practitioner may gain as much from viewing their work from other perspectives.

Dramatherapeutic interventions are well suited to the team setting, particularly in terms of cutting through the everyday styles of comm-unication. Non-verbal approaches (when appropriately used) can help give each team member a voice and the spirit of play can allow new perspectives to emerge. The kind of techniques used are those already described. What differs is the focus and the intention, which need to be negotiated and clarified as part of the process.

EXAMPLES OF DRAMATHERAPY TECHNIQUES IN TEAM SUPERVISION FOR NON-DRAMATHERAPISTS

In the following account the supervisees are a team of four art therapists working in a specialist mental health setting. The supervision takes place every three weeks for a year. The contract is for consultancy supervision, whereby the therapists take co-responsibility for setting the agenda. There is an experimental element to the supervision in that the team is curious about exploring a new form, having been supervised for a long time by an art therapist.

The work explores three main foci:

- the work of selected clients;
- the place of the team within the organization setting;
- the internal dynamics of the team itself.

The focus changes over time: the shift from client work to the relationship with the agency happens after some months, and only towards the end of the year does the focus settle on the dynamics of the team itself. This transition reflects a growing level of trust within the team, towards the supervisor, and towards the method.

Focus on the client

A number of approaches to working with the client's material are explored. In the first and least successful one a series of paintings or other art work of one client is displayed. The team reflects verbally on them and the supervisor suggests exploring one element in some depth through dramatic representation. The approach requires more time than is available in a one-and-a-half-hour session.

A second approach involves the therapist bringing a client's art work, but not showing it until towards the end of the session. This ensures that the team works with the therapist's subjective experience of the client and therapeutic relationship. After a brief movement-based warm-up for the whole group the presenting therapist poses a question or states a concern they wish to explore. They use the team to sculpt key symbols from the client's work. These may be symbols and stylistic features from one piece, or a synthesis from several pieces of art. Staging and the use of three-dimensional space, psycho-dramatic doubling and role reversal are used to 'let the symbols speak' and to facilitate the therapist to explore different perspectives. Team members are put in role as, for example, 'the spiky black arrows' or 'the room at the top of the house'. Team members use their empathic resonance with such roles to offer insights to the therapist and to explore potential relationships between diverse symbols. Comments made *in situ* or during deroling help flesh out the picture of the client and to stimulate further discussion based on the professional and personal experience of the team.

A third approach involves using the team to set up a short scene showing the interaction between therapist and client. A moment from the beginning of a session or what is felt to be a typical moment within a session is put under the microscope on stage. Team members are available to be used in a number of ways. As the therapist's double they enable the therapist to view the scene from the mirror or audience position and to hear colleagues giving empathic voice to the therapist's thoughts and feelings. Colleagues give both professional feedback and feedback from played roles.

Focus on the setting

Context is vital to the understanding of the client's world. It is also highly significant in terms of the work of the therapeutic team. How referrals are made, how space and time are allocated to the work, the degree of autonomy and integration of the team into the service as a whole, the status given to the therapy by colleagues and the agency; these issues address the broader picture and have a political dimension some therapists may rather not look at. Dramatherapy structures lend themselves well to such an exploration. While working with the client–therapist system as described above, figures from the wider agency context begin to emerge. Despite an initial reluctance on the part of the team to use the supervision to explore this level they eventually make the decision to look at the context of their team within the agency.

The structure used is a collaborative whole group sculpt depicting the hierarchy of the agency by the use of chairs, cloths and props. It spreads through most of the work space. One end of the room represents 'the top' and the other end 'the bottom'. The art therapy team is placed towards the bottom, a notch lower than other therapists in the agency. Team members are invited to role reverse with any of the positions in the hierarchy and to make a statement from role about the agency as a whole, their own place in it and how they view or interact with the art therapy team. They are also encouraged to make a statement from their own position.

What emerges initially is a strong sense of mutual self-valuing as a team; an island of solidarity in a sea which is at times benevolent, at others indifferent or denigrating. It is significant that some difference emerges at this point between the team leader's and the rest of the team's use of the structure. The team leader has some interest in exploring the higher and middle levels of the hierarchy, whilst the interest of the other team members remains more local. The overt focus of the exercise is hierarchy and role in the external world of the agency, but in the process the inner hierarchy of the team is inevitably highlighted alongside the implicit questions, 'Where are we and where should we be in the organization and whose responsibility is it to get us there?'

The team is all-female and has presented itself as minimizing any internal differences in status. The exercise confronts them with the reality of difference and provides a bridge into focusing on the team dynamics.

Focus on the team dynamics through the use of metaphor

The team describes itself as non-hierarchical and co-operative, a perception which minimizes difference, alliances and conflict. In order to facilitate a look at its internal dynamics the supervisor suggests the dramatherapeutic approach of exploration through metaphor in action. The metaphor of the team as family is offered. It is oblique but provocative enough to arouse interest in the team. The metaphor is an implicit acknowledgement that feelings and issues in the team are powerful and have deep roots informed by family and other group experiences of team members.

The work takes place over two sessions, in which each team member is invited to sculpt their view of the team as family, using the team members to hold family roles and a chair to represent the place of the sculptor. The structure allows different subjective perspectives to be concretized, experienced and acknowledged by the team as a whole. It also allows valuable third party observations about relationships in the team to be made indirectly through the metaphor.

Two key themes emerge. These are around age and seniority in the team; and the issue of territory and 'give and take' in the workplace.

The youngest and most junior team member makes the first sculpt. Her exploration reveals a direct parallel between her relationship with the team leader and that with her mother. She experiences both as relationships of affection combined with a compulsion to protect from potentially dangerous other family members. Having looked at the sculpt from the outside she expresses the wish to loosen the bonds that ally her with the team leader and to experience the freedom to disagree.

The oldest and most experienced member of the team is not the team leader. In her own sculpt she portrays herself as an equal sister with her colleagues, reflecting her desire to be accepted as an equal. The discrepancy between her own view and that of her colleagues is revealed in their sculpts, where she is represented as an experienced sage figure (grandmother, aunt, big sister) implicitly questioning the authority of the team leader and wishing to be recognized for her seniority. A further perception of her is as martyr. She has a longstanding conflict with one of the younger team members, which centres on the question, 'Who clears up shared workspaces?' She has readily given up her own desk and practice space for use by her junior colleague when there is a shortage of space. This has involved clearing the space of personal and clients' work, a courtesy which is not returned by her junior colleague on the completion of her work. In terms of the family metaphor there is an echo of the stereotypical housewife/mother complaint: 'It's always me who does the washing up.' Her self-sacrifice brings out the stroppy adolescent in her younger colleague, who has let the pattern continue for as long as she can get away with it.

The pattern of communication between these two team members has been characteristically indirect. One result of the metaphorical approach within the supervision is that it brings to light the transferential nature of their relationship. At a very practical level appropriate to the supervision context it highlights the necessity for direct communication and a renegotiation of ground rules. This happens overtly within the deroling and reflection phase of the supervision session and is seen as a positive outcome. The ideal of a co-operative team is revealed as something which requires conscious work and some risk-taking.

It would be unrealistic to expect immediate resolution at every level when working with team dynamics. Teams, like families, have a tendency to find a delicate balance of roles which enables a certain level of functioning but at the cost of potentially creative change and growth. Here the junior members of the team confront their elders with the lack of clarity in the family hierarchy. Their perception is that the team leader's authority is challenged by her more experienced colleague. This is a painful observation and is denied by the latter, but opens the way in the team leader's sculpt to an exploration of her difficulty in being 'in charge' of an 'older sister'. Her sculpt and the ensuing discussion reveal her vulnerability and fear of loneliness within the role of leader and the reasons behind her tendency to avoid the authority and political features of her role in favour of being a regular team member. Her style has repercussions both within the team and for the team within the agency as a whole. Within the team it brings out protective tendencies in her colleagues, and the locating of any conflicts in the team amongst the other team members rather than with her. In terms of the agency as a whole it means that the team has to take shared responsibility for promoting its work and status within the agency – or challenge her to rethink her approach to representing them.

In this example it is clear that the metaphor of the family is effective in focusing the attention of the team on its dynamics and in providing a language for addressing them. It is a powerful medium and there is a corresponding responsibility on the part of the supervisor to be sensitive to the appropriate level of risk for individuals and the team as a whole. It would be counterproductive to push the team further into disclosure and challenge than they feel able to process. It would also be unhelpful to offer the language and form of the metaphor and then block the process it sets in action. There are a number of ways the supervisor can help the team find an acceptable balance:

- *The negotiation of a contract accepted by all.* In this case the contract involves the structure (a sculpt from each person); the metaphor (team as family); the time frame (two sessions).

- *Holding the boundaries of the subjective space.* In this case that each sculptor has the right to sculpt their own perception including doubling statements to be voiced by the team members.

- *Holding the boundaries of the feedback space.* In this case that statements of discomfort with allocated roles, agreement or disagreement with the subjective perception of the sculptor are dealt with in a feedback circle and not *in situ* in the sculpt. In other words there is a distinction between the space for the sculptor's subjective perception and the space for commentary on it.

- *Providing space for a closure.* Work of this nature disrupts the status quo. Team members by definition continue to meet and function in the work context. The supervisor makes an explicit acknowledgement of this fact and provides time at the end of the session for the team to use as a bridge into that reality.

Peer

In peer supervision two or more therapists come together to supervise each other. The function of expert or consultant is shared amongst peer group members. Meetings may be informal and free-flowing or may follow a schedule whereby it is agreed who presents a case when and for how long.

One of the attractions of peer group supervision is that it is free. Another is that expertise is explicitly 'owned' by all members. At best this setting can provide an effective forum for learning, support and challenge and the development of a good collegial network. On the negative side there is a danger that the group dynamic may be unchallenged; in particular that power issues and competitive dynamics remain covert.

In terms of dramatherapeutic techniques any of the approaches already described could be integrated into a peer supervision setting, provided one or more group members take on the function of facilitator for the appropriate period of time.

Conclusion

I have attempted to give a sense of the background to supervision in dramatherapy and the broader application of the dramatherapeutic tradition within supervision. I have given examples of one-to-one and team supervision; in the context of training and for experienced professionals; for those who define themselves as dramatherapists and for those from other traditions. The focus on supervision requirements and provision has contributed significantly to the development of dramatherapy as a profession over the past decade and continues to do so. One of the strengths of dramatherapy is its breadth of application. It is practised with an impressively diverse range of client groups because it is flexible, accessible and inclusive. These strengths extend also to the field of supervision, where dramatherapeutic structures and concepts can make a contribution to other disciplines and multidisciplinary environments.

References

Bishop, V. and Butterworth, T. (eds) (1995) *Proceedings of the Clinical Supervision Conference.* London: Department of Health.

Casson, J., Feasey, D., Mitchell, S. and Smith, H. (1989) 'Letter.' *British Association for Dramatherapists Newsletter,* April, pp.21–22.

Chesner, A. (1997) *Dramatherapy, Psychodrama and Playback Theatre: Three Dramatic Modalities in Group Work.* In O. Kruse (ed) *Kreativät als Ressource für Veränderung und Wachstum.* Tübingen; DGVT Verlag.

Dramatherapy North West (1986) 'Study Day and Business Meeting.' *British Association for Dramatherapists Newsletter,* October, p.1.

Salas, J. (1993) *Improvising Real Life.* Dubuque, IA: Kendall/Hunt.

Williams A. (1995) *Visual and Active Supervision.* New York: Norton.

CHAPTER 2

Theatre-Based Supervision
A Supervisory Model
for Multidisciplinary Supervisees

Sue Jennings

I have had a most rare vision. I have had a dream – past the wit of man to say what the dream was.

A Midsummer Night's Dream, IV ii

Introduction

Theatre-based dramatherapy is a working model of theory and practice which can be applied with all client groups. Its basis lies in theatre art rather than psychotherapy and perhaps its nearest therapeutic neighbour would be systemic practice. In theatre-based dramatherapy stories and themes and structures from plays and myths are used as a framework for drama-therapeutic exploration. Participants also create their own stories and improvise plays, but the essence of the structure is the same:

exposition $\longrightarrow$ exploration $\longrightarrow$ resolution

This means that the structure of any session goes from expressing the issue to exploring it and then finding a resolution. Dramatherapy is the term used for the application of theatre art in special situations with the intention that it will be therapeutic, healing or beneficial for the participants (Jennings 1998a, p.33).

Dramatherapy is primarily an artistic therapy which gives opportunities for expanding our perception and understanding of the world through witnessing the drama in the world of the theatre. Rather than work with the client's own immediate material, the theatre-based therapist will use dramatic distancing of a play text which contains a universal story rather than an individual personal story. Of course everybody has their own personal relationship with the universal story, but the individual is able to experience being related to and being part of a wider whole rather than only focusing on the self and the individual story. The process of development through the bigger story means that everyone is acknowledged both as an individual and in relation to others and the outside world.

A theatre-based model of dramatherapy has the potential not only for dramatherapy supervision but also for supervision of people from many orientations. For example I have applied it in the supervision of counsellors, psychotherapists, professional teams, youth workers, social workers and other arts therapists. Many of these practitioners have worked in a wide variety of theory and practice, which includes Jungian and Freudian, cognitive, existensional, person-centred, systemic, group analytic and task-centred.

The supervision process that I will describe in this chapter includes:

- consultation supervision for a single session
- crisis supervision for the medical team
- group supervision for ongoing practice
- individual supervision for ongoing practice.

This practice will be linked to specific stories and plays that seemed appropriate to contain and structure the process at the time.

Dramatherapy principles in supervision

The Mandala

The Mandala concept illustrates how we all have a dramatic structure of the mind and have internalized a range of roles and practices as we approach adult life. As I see it, we have four major areas of being a person.

- our skills
- our guiding principle
- our creative artist
- our vulnerability.

Figure 2.1

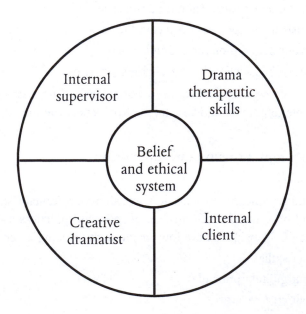

Figure 2.2

These internal states are mediated through our belief system, which may be an organized religion or a philosophical or ethical set of standards. Figure 2.1 is a simplistic illustration of how the Mandala is for most people.

When I have asked people to fill in the Mandala with words, or colours or patterns, they often find the creative artist the most difficult to fill in, the vulnerability the most painful, the skills become very selective and the guide is often very supportive or soothing. This Mandala exercise can be done as a starting point with anybody in any group including children (see Jennings 1999). In Figure 2.2 we see the Mandala applied to the practising dramatherapist.

After a dramatherapist has trained, we anticipate that they will have internalized a strong supervisor, a variety of dramatherapeutic skills, that they will have acknowledged their own vulnerability as an internal client and that their internal creative dramatist will be enhanced. All these states are underpinned by a personal belief system on the one hand and a professional ethical system on the other.

This is the Mandala that supervisees will bring to supervision to illustrate their own process of dramatherapy practice. The supervisor is able to facilitate the supervisee looking at:

- the connection between the internal client and the client
- the choices of dramatherapeutic skills
- the function of the internal supervisor
- the stimulus and structure from the creative dramatist.

Sometimes the supervisor will find that the supervisee is over-identifying with the client, a practice which gets in the way of empathic intervention. Perhaps the supervisee and client have similar life histories or have both been subject to a similar traumatic event. The supervisor needs to be able to assist the supervisee to differentiate between their understanding *of* the client and their identification *with* the client. Through the Mandala the supervisor can see the type of therapeutic skill that is being applied and can help the supervisee understand their rationale for choosing certain dramatherapy techniques, rather than applying a recipe.

The internal supervisor for some supervisees can be a harsh critic or judge who disables the supervisee, rather than having benign qualities and enhancing practice. The creative dramatist can sometimes appear quite separate from the other internal states, rather than being seen as a source of stimulus and nourishment. I often find with supervisees that the 'rescue' in a

Figure 2.3

difficult situation, or the unblocking of practice that feels stuck, will come from the artist rather than the guide. It is useful for the supervisor to relate the supervisee's Mandala to the Mandala of the client. Whether or not the dramatherapist has actually used the Mandala with their client, the supervisee can create the Mandala 'as if' they are the client. What we often find is that the vulnerability has taken over the whole picture and that the client is perceived as a walking bag of problems.

Figure 2.3 illustrates a supervisee's perception of a client, which is not necessarily how the client actually perceives themselves. The therapist does not always perceive that the client has their own skills, their own guide, their own creativity, together with a belief system.

Some clients of course may believe this about themselves. In particular, those people who have suffered major trauma, and resulting post-traumatic stress disorder, will often find that they feel de-skilled, hopeless, non-creative and have total loss of faith. However I want to emphasize that many therapists reinforce this total aspect of the client and think it is their job to work only with problems. Whereas, if we can keep the Mandala model in mind, we can see how our therapeutic intervention can keep all aspects at least addressed and in time strengthened and functioning. All therapists can use the Mandala with supervisees and clients and perhaps one of its most important functions is to strengthen and enhance the artistic and creative side of everybody.

The EPR (embodiment, projection, role)

The developmental paradigm of embodiment, projection and role (see Jennings 1990; 1992; 1993; 1994a, 1994b; 1997; 1998a) provides a developmental structure for all therapists and supervisees to explore and communicate their experience. The EPR follows the development of children from birth to six years and can be used as an organizational principle to structure therapeutic sessions. For example, embodiment work can include sensory work, movement, warm-ups, sounds, dance and all bodily means of expression. Projection can include sand play, painting, drawing, clay work, writing, object sculpts and body sculpts. Role can include improvisation, script work, role play and enactment.

The importance of understanding EPR development is to guard against the hapless young therapist thinking that dramatherapy is only about dramatization and therefore becoming very frustrated if clients feel unable to engage in role play. Since very few people can do 'instant drama', the dramatherapist becomes despondent and decides to go into an allied therapy practice rather than look at the dimensions of the dramatherapy itself. If the dramatherapist had started with projective work such as a life map or Mandala, or embodiment work, such as breathing, exercises, relaxation or physical warm-up, the end result might have been very different.

The EPR paradigm enables the supervisor both to monitor the logistics of the supervisee's practice and to give form to the supervision itself. For example, the supervisee may bring issues to supervision which they can physicalize through movement or posture or gesture; or they may present material in projective form, such as object or body sculpts. This may then facilitate a deeper exploration of the issues when they are dramatized. A group representation of a supervisee's session by the group as a whole can be an in-depth exploration which will lead to the growth of all participants.

By using EPR in the supervisory session with either individuals or groups, the supervisee is communicating directly about the dynamics of their practice, rather than telling the supervisor about their practice. A sample EPR recording chart is included at the end of this chapter as Figure 2.4.

Supervision through text

The quotation at the beginning of this chapter from *A Midsummer Night's Dream* leads me into the example of the application of this text in supervision. The actual structure of the play is most appropriate for supervisory process in relation to what we said earlier on about:

exposition $\longrightarrow$ exploration $\longrightarrow$ resolution

The play starts with an exposition of the conflict between the families in relation to Egeus and his daughter Hermia, Hermia's preference for Demetrius over Lysander, the rivalry between Lysander and Demetrius, the intervention of authority through Duke Theseus as well as the uneasy relationship between Theseus and Hippolyta and the strained friendship between Hermia and her friend Helena (Act I, Scene I). We then see the workmen coming together with a plan for the production of a play and the dynamics of leadership expressed through Bottom and Quince (Act I, Scene II). Puck and one of the fairies set the scene for the conflict between the Fairy King Oberon and the Fairy Queen Titania (Act II, Scene I). This is quickly followed by Oberon and Titania, then Demetrius and Helena, enacting their conflicts (Act II, Scene II). These various conflicts are explored in the forest with resulting chaos, cruelty and power struggles (Act II, Scene III; Act III, Scenes I and II). The story moves towards some kind of compromise and resolution in Act IV, Scenes I and II, and in Act V we see the final transformation through the wedding rituals of the court, the play of the workmen and Puck's final speech. There is a resolution for the chaos and permission from Puck to treat it all as a dream if any of the story has offended:

If we shadows have offended,
Think but this – and all is mended –
That you have but slumber'd here
While these visions did appear.
And this weak and idle theme,
No more yielding but a dream,
Gentles, do not reprehend;
If you pardon, we will mend.
And, as I am an honest Puck,
If we have unearned luck
Now to 'scape the serpent's tongue,
We will make amends ere long;
Else, the Puck a liar call:
So, good night unto you all.
Give me your hands, if we be friends,
And Robin shall restore amends.

A Midsummer Night's Dream, V ii

The motifs throughout the play are family conflict, jealousy, imposition of authority, age versus youth, class distinction, gratuitous cruelty, the importance of the spirit world and its impact on ordinary human beings. We could ask our supervisees to reflect on Titania's speech quoted below. It describes how jealousy and dissension can disrupt the order of day-to-day life and the certainty of a belief system. Similarly any disruption in the centre of the Mandala, which is a stabilizing influence for ourselves as well as our clients, can cause uncertainty and anxiety. Titania emphasizes the importance of the security of the seasons and the predictability of occupations and the weather. When these are disrupted even artistic activity and games come to an end:

These are the forgeries of jealousy:
And never, since the middle summer's spring,
Met we on hill, in dale, forest, or mead,
By paved fountain, or by rushy brook,
Or on the beached margent of the sea,
To dance our ringlets to the whistling wind,
But with thy brawls thou has disturb'd our sport.
Therefore the winds, piping to us in vain,
As in revenge, have suck'd up from the sea

Contagious fogs; which, falling in the land,
Have every pelting river made so proud
That they have overborne their continents;
The ox hath therefore stretch'd his yoke in vain,
The ploughman lost his seat; and the green corn
Hath rotted ere his youth attain'd a beard:
The fold stands empty in the drowned field,
And crows are fatted with the murrain flock;
The nine men's morris is fill'd up with mud;
And the quaint mazes in the wanton green,
For lack of tread, are undistinguishable:
The human mortals want their winter here;
No night is now with hymn or carol blest:
Therefore the moon, the governess of floods,
Pale in her anger, washes all the air,
That rheumatic diseases do abound:
And thorough this distemperature we see
The seasons alter: hoary-headed frosts
Fall in the fresh lap of the crimson rose;
And on old Hyem's chin and icy crown
An odorous chaplet of sweet summer buds
Is, as in mockery, set: the spring, the summer,
The chiding autumn, angry winter, change
Their wonted liveries; and the maz'd world,
By their increase, now knows not which is which:
And this same progeny of evils comes
From our debate, from our dissension:
We are their parents and original.

A Midsummer Night's Dream, II i

You might like to do a Mandala based on Titania's speech and look at the relationship between the different segments.

As supervisors we can invite our supervisees to consider which of the characters they see themselves as, as a dramatherapist, and which of the characters might be useful to them in assisting them with their work. As a supervisor myself I have found the ordinariness of Bottom extremely useful to stop me getting too lofty in my ideas and the poetry of Titania has pushed the borders of my understanding in relation to both supervisees and clients. It is of particular significance, in relation to the supervision of people involved in family work or adoption and fostering, to reflect on the conflict between Oberon and Titania in relation to the little Indian boy.

Examples of supervision practice

Consultation supervision for a single session

I was asked to provide a day of supervision for a clinic for people with mental health problems, who were about to be moved out of their building into another building some twenty miles away. It meant a move from a rural setting, surrounded by trees, into a suburban setting within a larger hospital institution. The staff were engaged in ongoing transition work with the clients, some of whom would be unable to move to the new place, but would be absorbed into other institutions, and a small number who would move into the new clinic and where there would be new clients joining shortly after the move. The staff team, apart from two, would all go to the new place and they requested a supervision day to help them deal with their own transition, since all of their energies were going into their client work. The staff team of twenty included psychiatrists, psychologists, social workers, nurses, occupational therapists, as well as an art therapist and a dramatherapist.

The story we worked with was Hansel and Gretel and we took the theme of children being abandoned by parents in a dangerous forest and being lured by a house covered in sweets, only to find that a monstrous witch wanted to subjugate and devour the children that went inside, ultimately to be rescued by the forethought of one child and the guidance of a little blue bird.

The story seemed to encompass the feeling of being abandoned by authority to a dangerous place, which might be dressed up in all sorts of attractive incentives such as colour schemes and new furniture, only to find that there was a devouring danger that would threaten them. One of the constant themes seemed to be about being taken over and being bribed, so we created the forest and built the house, an amazing structure created out of garbage. We were able to dramatize the search for the solution which, although it had many question marks, nevertheless had both an internal guide of every individual, and a guide of the philosophy and good ethos of the clinic, to support them on their way through. The day was able to contain the many and varied feelings and to bring them as energy into the story. There were some people who just wanted to get the whole thing over with and didn't see the new venue as an issue. There were others who felt the anxiety of not knowing what to expect and there were some who felt that the whole of their past was being destroyed. The bird motif enabled the rediscovery of individual and group resources that could mobilize this transition in a less fearful way. When we all stood outside the witch's house in the forest that they had made, we realized that it actually looked like a ship, with a mast and sails. We were able to load up all our symbolic treasures onto the ship and sail away into the unknown.

Crisis supervision for the medical team

I was called in to a team of doctors, embryologists and nurses, who felt they had a crisis of confidence in relation to their fertility work. The stress levels appeared to be very high, as people snapped at each other and gave orders rather than developing a discourse. Success rates in the clinic were at an all-time low and funding had been cut back for the service. It was a big step for them to ask for outside supervision and I was unclear at the outset just how many people thought it was a useful idea. My hunch was right as bleepers started going off and some of the male staff kept rushing in and out of the room to speak on their phone. We then agreed to have calls diverted, unless literally there was a life or death situation, when the medical secretary would actually come and fetch somebody.

Looking round the group, this phrase came into my head, 'Doctors don't like dancing.' I'm not sure where that came from, but it certainly influenced my decision to use projective work as a starting point. I placed a large piece of paper in the middle of the group, with a supply of felt pens and crayons and finger paint and I invited them to create the picture of the clinic right now, using images and symbols rather than literal representations.

Initially everyone worked in their own space and there was a picture of the medical symbol of the Caduceus; there was a section of exploding fireworks, and a coffin, dollar bill signs, tears, a brick wall and a woman pushing a pram. Everybody was working very industriously in their own patch and not relating to anybody else. We sat back and looked at the picture and I asked people to make any comments they wanted to and somebody remarked that the fireworks could also be exploding sperm, and the woman with the pram was the whole raison d'être of the clinic, but then someone else remarked that the coffin was the strongest image and that the clinic was a failure. One of the women suggested that the tears were not only her own, but those of the patients who had been unable to conceive.

I said that there were many symbols of life and death in the picture, but nothing that connected them all together and I asked whether it was possible to create a fertile landscape. Slowly they began to draw again, and trees appeared, and water, and caves, and rocky outcrops, which both contained and expanded the picture into a flowing, living entity. The landscape images crossed over all the territorial borders, as people worked together on different sections, and the feeling of despair in the group shifted into a gradual, positive, energy. I then read them the story of Makendaya (Jennings 1998b).

[The journey of Makendaya]

Many, many, many years ago it seemed as if the world had come to an end. There were no living creatures to be seen and the face of the earth was covered by an enormous cold and icy swamp. In the distance there appeared one man on the horizon who seemed to have escaped and his name was Makendaya. He was old and exhausted. His clothes hung in shreds and he continued walking over the barren landscape. He walked and walked and found no cave or trees to give him shelter. Everything seemed to have come to an end. All he could feel was a deep sadness and desperation. On some new impulse he turned round and saw that a tree, a fig tree, was growing out of the swamp and underneath the fig tree stood a small smiling child. Makendaya paused, wondering at the beauty of the child.

The child looked at him and said, 'Makendaya, you need to rest your weary body. Come inside my body.' The child opened his mouth wide, and suddenly an enormous gust of wind lifted up Makendaya and carried him into the mouth of the child and he seemed to be falling, falling and falling, into the belly of the child. Very, very surprised, Makendaya looked around him and saw living things again. There were cattle, and birds, and he saw people in a city. Women were coming to the well to fetch water in large pitchers. There were green, fertile fields, clumps of trees and a stream leading to a river. He started walking through this beautiful landscape and he could see the whole of the Universe, the sky and the ocean leading to infinity. He continued walking without ever reaching the end of this landscape. He was walking for more than 100 years. Suddenly, again he felt the strong wind and the wind took him upwards, through the body of the child, and he came through the child's mouth. He saw again the fig tree with the child now sitting beneath it.

Makendaya was quite silent, wondrous at all that had happened to him, and the child looked at him, smiling, and said; 'Makendaya, I hope you now feel rested.'

Adapted from the Mahabharata
Copyright Sue Emmy Jennings, 1998

The final part of the session was a reflection on ideas of collaboration rather than competition, renewal of energy instead of staff burnout, and the thought that people working in fertility are working on the edge of death and creation as part of their daily life. The barren landscape became a more fertile landscape, and there was a general feeling of release. I nevertheless wondered whether it was possible to bring about change when, the moment the session closed, several members raced to fetch their bleepers!

Some months later I heard from the team that they felt a corner had been turned and that it was now a more co-operative endeavour. Apparently there was now an increase in conception rates. Perhaps there is a relationship between the creativity and fertility of the staff and the fertility of the patients they treat.

Group supervision for ongoing practice

A group of supervisees who were all involved in dramatherapy meet with me on a regular basis for supervision of their practice. The basic structure that I use is that everybody presents a short update of their work and that anybody with urgent issues has a slightly longer time, and then we reflect on the process as a whole as well as the individuals within it. I often find that there is a similar theme running throughout the group. On this occasion a member of the group, who was working with clients with terminal illness, was struggling with her own personal feelings about her clients who were about to die. The theme of loss and grief was palpable in the group, and I asked the individual dramatherapist to create a sculpt of the last piece of work she had done with one of her clients. The client had got to a point of calmness about her own death and shared with the dramatherapist her sadness at what she would leave behind, but nevertheless would not wish to prolong her life any further after the pain of her debilitating disease. The sculpt included two people representing the people who would be left alive, i.e. the person's family. One person represented the client, another person represented the thoughts going on in the client's head, and another person took on the role of the dramatherapist with another person voicing what was going on in the dramatherapist's head.

The motif that came out of this sculpt, when it began to find a voice, was a theme of seeds and the dying client was able to talk about her own death in relation to the regeneration, or indeed generation, that she was leaving behind. The family members were able to express their feelings of loss, but also relief, and were able to acknowledge that they could go on and live their lives, even though they would experience grief and sadness. The supervisee playing the role of the dramatherapist talked about being the gardener and how she was able to create a garden in which some things grew, and some things died, in her dramatherapy work.

The dramatherapist who presented the material was visibly moved, and realized that her own distress was not only to do with this client in particular, but also the losses that she had personally experienced in her own life. We reflected together on the story of *The Secret Garden* (Burnett 1949) where a beautiful garden, which had been created for someone who suddenly died, is then discovered as a source of healing the two damaged children. This session enabled all the supervisees to face up to issues of death and loss, both in their clients and in their lives, and also to deal more fully with the theme of bereavement when clients are ready to stop therapy.

Individual supervision for ongoing practice

I was supervising an individual dramatherapist who was working with individual children who had been taken into care. She was using EPR to structure her work and also containing the situations through a ritual of the client's own devising, and allowing the children to create their own spontaneous stories. One girl in particular stands out in this supervisory process as a clear example of how narrative is socially constructed and can facilitate the supervisory process. Indeed, the therapeutic narrative in turn becomes the supervisory narrative.

The main motif for this girl was the Spice Girls, and my supervisee, although of riper years, entered wholeheartedly into her given role of Old Spice, preparing to go to parties with Baby Spice. They had to make up and dance and respond to invitations and adventures. The Spice Girls became both the containing ritual, as well as the exploration of role relationships. Within that frame, various stories of loss and discovery, anger, grief and reparation were told through different cartoon characters. The supervisee brought a very complex set of issues to supervision, which included both her own role as practitioner and researcher, the content and structure of a brief intervention, as well as issues around innovatory practice of using arts therapies in transitional situations.

By allowing her young client to socially construct the interventions in relation to the Spice Girls and the cartoon stories, and by dealing with feelings of impotence, when her client became all powerful and dictatorial, she was also able to construct the model of supervision that was going to be most helpful to her. It was very important that the contemporary icon of the young, i.e., the Spice Girls, could be allowed to have meaning in relation to the construction of this young girl's experience. I think perhaps this example demonstrates that the symbolic material of myth, or story, or play, does not necessarily have to be great literature or classical in its origins. Both as therapists and supervisors, we need to be able to enter the current mythology that is relevant to our client.

Conclusion

This chapter is concerned with the application of a theatre-based model of dramatherapy in supervision practice. I have shown how the Mandala, the EPR and the text-based story, as well as socially constructive narratives, are essential ingredients of our practice.

Of course supervisees need to be encouraged to factually record their practice and a sample recording sheet is illustrated at the end of this chapter (Figure 2.5). However, the factual report will not bring alive the actual dynamic that can be reached through the supervisory narrative.

This type of supervision puts tremendous demands on the dramatherapist in terms of their broad base of knowledge of therapeutic practice, as well as a working knowledge of a wide variety of stories and plays. Supervisees can respond to known and popular stories, even from books such as the Old Testament, as well as stories that are new to them, such as the Makendaya story. It means that the dramatherapist supervisor has to be willing to take risks with their own intuition and hunches. They also have to be able to admit when they get it wrong. However, supervising in this mode is a very rich and rewarding experience, and takes us on creative journeys in a collaborative enterprise between supervisor and supervisee.

EMBODIMENT-PROJECTION-ROLE OBSERVATION				
Name _____ Dramatherapist/Playtherapist: _____				
DOB_____ Session Aged _____ Date	1	2	3	Recommendations
EMBODIMENT:				
1. Touch, Eye-contact				
2. Spatial Awareness				
3. Working With/Against				
4. Whole Body				
5. Body Parts				
6. Body Self/Image				
7. Mimicry/Innovation				
8. Other				
PROJECTION				
1. Sand/Sand and Water				
2. Clay/Plasticine				
3. Pencil/Crayons				
4. Paint (finger/brush)				
5. Single Image/Whole Picture				
6. Single/Large Toys				
7. Environmental*				
8. Other				
ROLE				
1. Body Movement/Gesture				
2. Sound/Speech				
3. Mimicry/Innovation				
4. Brief/Sustained				
5. Relationship with another role				
6. Role Development				
7. Development Scene/Situation				
8. Other				
GENERAL OBSERVATIONS				
* houses/jungles ,etc., with boxes and material.				

Figure 2.4

BRIEF RECORDING OF PLAYTHERAPY/DRAMATHERAPY SESSION	
Client's Name _____	Dramatherapist/Playtherapist: _____
Session Number _____	Date _____
Therapist's reflections before session:	
Possible media and themes:	
Mood/atmosphere at beginning:	client
	therapist
Description of actual media and methods used:	
E	
P	
R	
Description of content expressed through above:	
Graph of levels of engagement throughout the session:	
Mood/atmosphere at closure:	client
	therapist
Thoughts on the session:	the client
	the drama and play
	the self
Any action which needs to be taken?	
Thoughts for the next session:	

Figure 2.5

References

Burnett, F.H. (1949) *The Secret Garden*. Kingswood, Surrey: Windmill Press.

Jennings, S. (1990) *Dramatherapy with Families, Groups and Individuals*. London: Jessica Kingsley Publishers.

Jennings, S. (1992) *Dramatherapy Theory and Practice 2*. London: Routledge.

Jennings, S. (1993) *Play Therapy with Children: A Practitioner's Guide* Oxford: Blackwell Scientific.

Jennings, S. (1994a) 'Unravelling dramatherapy: Ariadne's ball of thread.' *Family Context 1*, 21, 39–42.

Jennings, S. (1994b) 'The theatre of healing: Metaphor and metaphysics in the healing process.' In S. Jennings, A. Cattanach, S. Mitchell, A. Chesner and R Meldrum (eds) *The Handbook of Dramatherapy*. London: Routledge.

Jennings, S. (ed) (1997) *Dramatherapy Theory and Practice 3*. London: Routledge.

Jennings, S. (1998a) *Introduction to Dramatherapy*. London: Jessica Kingsley Publishers.

Jennings, S. (1998b) *The Journey of Makendaya*. Adapted from the *Mahabharta*.

Jennings, S. (1999) *Introduction to Playtherapy Playing and Health*. London: Jessica Kingsley Publishers.

Shakespeare, W. (1967) *A Midsummer Night's Dream*. Harmondsworth: Penguin.

CHAPTER 3

Supervision in Playtherapy and Dramatherapy with Children

Ann Cattanach

Here we go round the Mulberry Bush,
The Mulberry Bush, the Mulberry Bush.
Here we go round the Mulberry Bush
On a cold and frosty morning.

This is the way we clap our hands,
Clap our hands, clap our hands …

This is the way we wash our clothes,
Wash our clothes, wash our clothes …

This is the way we clean our rooms,
Clean our rooms, clean our rooms …
On a cold and frosty morning.

Introduction

This chapter examines the importance of supervision for the playtherapist and dramatherapist working with children. Like the children dancing round the Mulberry Bush learning to 'clap our hands, wash our clothes, clean our rooms' we begin to think again about play and work mixed up together.

Creative-expressive play is the medium used by the playtherapist and dramatherapist to help the child explore their world when they come to therapy. This process uses sensory play, projective play with toys and media and dramatic role play to enable the child to express creatively the issues they want to bring to play with the adult therapist.

Dramatherapists focus on dramatic role play and work with groups of children as well as individuals. The playtherapist operates mainly with individual children and does not focus on dramatic role play but explores the stories and narratives the child brings to the therapeutic space. These are sometimes expressed through dramatic play but often are narrated through projective play with toys and media or through sensory play with 'messy' materials with perhaps no verbal content at all. This may also be the experience of the dramatherapist who might be working with children who are unable to use dramatic roles as part of their repertoire of play.

Both playtherapy and dramatherapy are action therapies and use symbolic processes to help children make sense of their experiences. Dramatherapy and playtherapy are not the same as child psychotherapy. The healing in arts therapies is through the creative processes employed by the child. Psychoanalytic interpretation of children's material is not an integral part of the playtherapy and dramatherapy. It is important for the therapist working with children to recognize what is unique about playtherapy and dramatherapy and explore that uniqueness rather than try to take on some of the concepts of another form of therapeutic work.

There are a variety of models of working in dramatherapy and playtherapy from humanistic child-centred methods underpinned by psychodynamic theories to post-modern narrative approaches developed through theories of social construction. Whatever the approach, all models emphasize the role of action.

Supervision is a mandatory part of the professional life of playtherapists and dramatherapists. Children are especially vulnerable to the abuse of power in a therapeutic relationship and supervision can explore this dynamic to keep children as safe as possible in therapy. As well as practice issues the therapist has a space to heal the hurt experienced by listening to some of their clients' stories. It is always difficult to acknowledge what cruelty adults can inflict on children and stories of hurt are often very hard to bear.

As the therapist dances round the mulberry bush in supervision she begins to untangle some of the issues about 'playing with children':

- *What is childhood?* Ideas about childhood need to be examined, including those of the supervisor and supervisee. These ideas are the starting point for the therapist and impact on the relationship with the child and influence her practice. The therapist's idea about childhood can become an issue about power in the relationship.

- *Agencies which work with children.* The ethics and objectives of the agencies that support work with children must be considered. There is often a pressure to ' make it better' for the child. There is also a tendency for agencies to use children in therapy to get information from them about their families or what has happened to them rather than challenge the adults who are more frightening to confront.

- *Play is for the powerless.* Play itself is marginalized and those who play with children lose their status because play is not 'work' and therefore not serious. Playing aspects of a tragic life can also bring conflict to the therapist if their belief system does not include the idea that play can help make sense of difficult experiences. There can be a conflict between the idea that play is 'fun' and the use of play to express hurt.

- *The therapist's childhood.* And finally the untangling of the therapist's own childhood and separating this out from the client's life is painful.

Theories and models of childhood

Developmental models

The model of childhood that has become dominant in Western cultures connects biological development with social development and in this model all children's activities become significant markers of developmental progress. An example of such a model might be Piaget's account of predetermined stages of development, which lead to the achievement of logical competence. Jenks (1996) states that the difficulty with this model is the assumption that the desired process for the child is the development of cognition. This development is then defined as a natural process towards the structure of adult rationality. In this model the value of play as, for example, a preparation for participation later on in adult society is dismissed as peripheral and diverts the child from his true destiny and logical purpose within the scheme of rationality.

In his book *The Philosophy of Childhood*, Matthews (1996) warns us against letting developmental models of childhood caricature children and limit the possibilities we are willing to recognize in our dealings with them as fellow human beings.

Dominant discourses about childhood

FROM THE ROMANTIC CHILD TO THE PUBLIC CHILD

Hendrick (1990) delineates a variety of constructions of children through an exploration of dominant discourses about children in particular contexts from 1800 to the present. The constructions which emerge are, in chronological order: the Romantic Child; the Evangelical Child; the Factory Child; the Delinquent Child; the Schooled Child; the Psycho-medical Child; and the Welfare Child. Then two further reconstructions: from 1914 to the late 1950s the Psychological Child and the Public (child in a care system) Child.

CHILDHOOD INNOCENCE AND CHILDHOOD WICKEDNESS

Many referrals for playtherapy come with narratives about 'loss of innocence' through abuse or narratives about evil behaviour. Jennie the Angel and Cathy the Cat Killer come to mind as tags with which to burden the child. Children who have experienced difficulties are often categorized as children who have experienced a loss of innocence or children who are bad and this seems to be congruent with the view of children as either 'angels' to be protected or 'devils' to be contained and controlled.

There is also a somewhat sentimental discourse about adults getting in touch with 'the child within' as though that creature was the source of innocence and creativity. This concept of being a child is a social construction and I should imagine that many children who have experienced brutal beginnings to their lives are perfectly content to leave their past behind and their 'child without'.

POWER DISCOURSES

Many of these theories are about the power relationship between children and the adults who must protect the 'innocence' of children but also 'tame' their uncontrollable natures.

The issue of power is one of the major concerns explored in supervision. How can the therapist keep children safe in the therapeutic space but establish a relationship based on shared responsibility so that each individual has something to offer the other?

If children's material is respected as their part of the therapeutic relationship then the therapists' responsibility is to explore their material and keep the child safe at the same time. It is in the exploration of the children's material and the structure of the relationship that the differences in theoretical models of therapy emerge. But whatever the model presented to the child there is a need to constantly examine the power base of the relationship.

There has been much criticism of models of therapy with the power and knowledge held by the therapist, and the dangers of the abuse of power are perhaps greatest in working with children. However, the other side of the coin is the struggle to be accepting of the child's material without becoming a victim of the client's desire to abuse.

These issues of an abusive relationship are a source of much of the content in supervision and it can be helpful to replay some of these encounters to examine the nature of the relationship and then perhaps reframe interventions.

Living the child's burden does not help, and supervision can be the place to dump or discard that burden. It is often a shock for the new therapist to discover the ease with which the roles of perpetrator and victim can be learnt. And the therapist can become tainted with information about cruelty, which is very hard to keep in perspective. Some of the work in supervision is to find a balance.

Sometimes in supervision we play out the power roles of child and adult. In one group supervision we enacted a mother and child scene. The setting was in the morning getting ready for work and school. The instruction to the mother was that she was in a hurry because she was late for work. The instruction to the child was that she was trying to tell her mother that her teacher had touched her in a way she didn't like and today he was going to see her on her own in the break time at school.

The scene was enacted and it proved impossible for the child character to tell her mother about her fears so a variety of avoidance strategies were employed like becoming ill or delaying her mother who then got irritated.

In discussion after the enactment we all felt the overwhelming guilt of the mother, the helplessness of the child and the difficulties of communication in the stress of the moment.

Prout and James (1990) suggest a new paradigm for the sociology of childhood and this can be used as a baseline when thinking about our relationship with children:

1. Childhood is understood as a social construction. As such it provides an interpretative frame for contextualizing the early years of human life. Childhood, as distinct from biological immaturity, is neither a

natural or universal feature of human groups but appears as a specific structural and cultural component of many societies.

2.   Childhood is a variable of social analysis. It can never be entirely divorced from other variables such as class, gender or ethnicity. Comparative and cross-cultural analysis reveals a variety of childhoods rather than a single and universal phenomenon.

3.   Children's social relationships and cultures are worthy of study in their own right, independent of the perspective and concerns of adults.

4.   Children are, and must be seen as, active in the construction and determination of their own social lives, the lives of those around them and of the societies in which they live. Children are not just the passive subjects of social structures and processes.

There should be a constant dialogue in supervision about our discourses on children and childhood so we can critically evaluate how these constructions might impinge on our interventions with children.

The therapist and the institution

Where and how the playtherapist and dramatherapist do their work is a constant theme in supervision. If the therapist is employed by an agency there are often issues about roles within the workplace. If a therapist is self-employed it can be important to explore the agenda of the employer to keep clear boundaries about the task in hand.

Conflict of roles for the therapist

Many therapists are employed in a variety of roles in their work, in particular in social services or education. This can impact on referrals for therapy and a key task of supervision is to clarify roles and tasks for the therapist. If a therapist also works as a social worker, for example, it is important that referrals for therapy come from other social workers and these children are not the therapist's clients in her role of social worker.

Teachers who are also therapists equally need to keep the two roles separate for the children. If these roles are not carefully separated then the child will feel confused about the differences between the task of the social worker or teacher and the task of the therapist. Confidentiality can be compromised and the child loses trust in the relationship.

This confusion of roles is always a problem within the therapeutic relationship and many therapists have to struggle with the difference in the tasks they undertake in their working lives.

Referrals for therapy

There are many issues about the referral process which are brought to supervision. The child does not in the majority of circumstances personally ask for therapy – the referral comes from adults who have some control over the life of the child. It is important to consider carefully how helpful an intervention can be, who will support the intervention with the child and whether the child really wants to participate.

There is often a subtle – or not so subtle – subtext from the referrer about getting information from the child about their family, or persuading the child to tell about abuse, or expecting the child to learn to keep themselves safe from abuse even though nobody is working with the abusive adults. These are issues of child protection and referrers should be firmly told that therapy is not possible in these circumstances before the child protection issues have been clarified.

A refusal to work with a child because of the lack of safety or support from the child's carers can often lead to unpleasant encounters with the referrer who might be experiencing extreme stress about the safety of the child. It is difficult in these circumstances for the therapist to resist the temptation to be a 'rescuer'.

Ways of communicating with other professionals in these kinds of circumstances is an ever-present theme in supervision.

Code of ethics for work with children

Both playtherapists and dramatherapists have a Code of Ethics, which supports their practice and maintains standards for therapists. A re-reading of these codes can be a great comfort for therapists bruised by encounters with professionals who do not quite understand the nature of the therapeutic encounter. If the Code is shown to referrers it can be helpful when conditions for the work are less than adequate.

Confidentiality

Confidentiality is covered in the Code of Ethics for therapists, but with children there are circumstances when the therapist has a responsibility to protect a child who might disclose abuse. In the Code of Ethics for playtherapists there are two references to confidentiality:

B1.1 Issues of responsibility
Whereas the therapist–child relationship is the primary ethical concern, the playtherapist has a responsibility to conform to the local authority child protection procedures.

B3.1 Confidentiality
Playtherapists should take all reasonable steps to communicate to both child and carer the extent of confidentiality they are offering to their clients (see B1.1). This normally should be clarified before commencing therapy.

One of the topics brought to supervision is how to tell a child about issues of confidentiality. This can be doubly difficult if a child has been abused and the perpetrator has used the idea of 'secrets' as a way of keeping the child from telling. The difference between 'confidentiality' and 'secrets' is complex and each therapist will explore criteria for themselves within the boundaries of ethical practice.

The degree of confidentiality is also variable. A therapist might for example have to write a court report about the impact of abuse on a child. In these circumstances it is important to ask permission from the child and read the report regardless of the age of the child.

These ethical issues are complex and need to be thought through and connected to those ideas we have about children and their right to autonomy.

The Code of Ethics for playtherapists states:

1.2.3 Client autonomy
Playtherapists should recognize at all times within the therapy that the child/young person is an individual in his/her own right and has the capacity to facilitate their own healing through the therapeutic process.

Play is for the powerless

The social construction of childhood as a process for cognitive development to become a rational human adult is a powerful discourse. In this view of the child and the care of children, the place of play is little valued. For the dramatherapist and playtherapist the value of play and drama as the central healing forces in therapy is their discourse about their work, but it is often difficult to convince other professionals.

However, the work of sociologists like Jenks, Corsaro, and James and Prout have brought new ideas and ways to think about childhood. Evaldsson and Corsaro (1998) describe how aspects of game playing are appropriated by children in their negotiations of social identity. In their description of the jump rope game Cradle of Love the authors describe the 'as if' nature of the play which is a key concept in both dramatherapy and playtherapy.

Anthropologists are now producing studies on play and *Child's Play* by Goldman (1998) offers an anthropological account of make-believe behaviour as a way to examine the imaginal life of Huli (Papua New Guinea) children.

If play as a healing force is to be valued then it is up to playtherapists and dramatherapists to do their own research into what they do and what outcomes might be expected from an intervention.

Supervision should be the place and space for the therapist to explore aspects of their work, which might be audited for effectiveness. From small audits the therapist can then explore what aspects of their practice could be researched. The professional development of the therapist is critical for the evaluation of therapeutic interventions and should be supported in supervision.

The therapist's childhood

Children's narratives about their lives in therapy can be harrowing and shocking. It is important that the therapist through their own personal therapy has explored aspects of their own childhood so that the two narratives, that of therapist and client, are separate stories. It is not helpful for the child if the therapist drowns in the details of a shocking story and is not able to hear what the child is saying about the experience. Sometimes the stories are purloined by the professionals and taken away from the children because this feeds the need of the professional to tell the child's horror story. In these circumstances the ghoulish elements take over and the therapist ceases to listen to the child.

These shocking narratives which emerge in therapy need to be deconstructed in supervision so that the therapist can think constructively about the child's story and not just repeat the horror as a kind of indulgence. Sadly, many abused children only gain attention through retelling their story until they believe that is the only interesting aspect of their identity.

Conclusion

When the therapist works with children, the burden of responsibility is great. The child's ecosystem of carers and the wider world of school, work pressures of the adult carers and political decisions about child support all impinge on the decision to offer therapy to a child.

The danger of becoming a 'rescuer' is great and the precariousness of some children's support systems can make the offer of therapy seem hazardous.

It is therefore crucial to offer very clear boundaries in all the work we do. The safety of any intervention will be supported by the quality of supervision offered to the therapist and that safe space is a mirror of the therapeutic space offered to the child. The therapist tries to support the resilience of the child through difficult times.

The Russian story of *Snow White in the Forest* describes a resilient child who makes a 'good enough' choice. There is no prince on a white charger here! This is a true heroine who knows the really dangerous creatures and can evaluate who could help her. Let us hope we can support children to develop such judgement.

[Snow White in the Forest]

Once upon a time there lived an old man and an old woman. They had a little granddaughter called Snow White.

Snow White's playmates went into the forest for berries and they came to ask Snow White to go with them.

Her grandparents were anxious but in the end they let her go, telling her that she must not wander away from her playmates.

The children came to the forest and began to gather berries from tree to tree and bush to bush.

Snow White soon wandered away from her playmates. They called after her but Snow White did not hear them.

Soon it began to get dark and the children went home.

Snow White went on through the forest until she was quite lost.

When she knew that she was all alone she climbed up a tree and sat on a branch.

She began to cry, singing this song:

> Granddad and Granny
> Had a darling little girl
> Hear her cry and moan
> Her playmates took her to the woods
> And left her all alone.

A bear came along and he said:

'What are you crying for, Snow White?'

'Haven't I good cause to cry, Mr Bear?

I'm Snow White and I'm the only grandchild of my granddad and granny. My playmates took me to the woods and left me all alone.'

'Climb down from that tree, and I'll carry you back to your granddad and granny.'

'No, I'm afraid of you. You'll eat me.'

The bear went away and left her.

She began to cry again and to sing her song:

> Poor little Snow White
> Hear her cry and moan
> Her playmates took her to the woods
> And left her all alone.

A wolf came along and said:

'What are you crying for, Snow White?'

She answered him just as she answered the Bear.

'Come down,' said the wolf, 'and I'll carry you home to your granddad and your granny.'

'No, I'm afraid of you. You'll eat me.'

The wolf went away and Snow White began to cry again and sing her song:

> Poor darling Snow White
> Hear her cry and moan
> Her playmates took her to the wood
> And left her all alone.

Mrs Fox came running by.

She heard Snow White's little voice and she said:

'What are you crying for, Snow White?'

'Haven't I good cause to cry, Mrs Fox?

My playmates took me to the woods and left me all alone.'

'Come down and I'll carry you to your granddad and granny.'

Snow White climbed down from the tree, and jumped on Mrs Fox's back.

Off they went at a trot.

The fox soon reached Snow White's home and knocked at the door with her tail.

'Who's there?' said granny and granddad.

'It's Mrs Fox and I've brought your little granddaughter home.'

'Ah! Is that our little darling? Come into the cottage.

Now Mrs Fox, sit down and have something to eat.'

They brought milk and eggs and curds, and served the fox with a grand feast.

Mrs Fox asked if they would give her a hen for reward.

The old folk gave her a white hen, and then they let her go into the forest.

REFERENCES

Evaldsson, A. and Corsaro, W. (1998) 'Play and games in the peer cultures of pre-school and preadolescent children.' *Childhood 5*, 4, 377–402.

Goldman, L. (1998) *Child's Play.* Oxford: Berg.

Hendrick, H. (1990) 'Constructions and reconstructions of British childhood.' In A. James and A. Prout (eds) *Constructing and Reconstructing Childhood.* Basingstoke: The Falmer Press.

Jenks, C. (1996) *Childhood.* London: Routledge.

Matthews, G. (1996) *The Philosophy of Childhood.* Cambridge, MA: Harvard University Press.

Piaget, J. (1992) *Psychology and Epistemology.* Harmondsworth: Penguin.

Prout, A. and James, A. (1990) 'A new paradigm for the sociology of childhood.' In A. James and A. Prout (eds) *Constructing and Reconstructing Childhood.* Basingstoke: The Falmer Press.

PART 2

The Supervisory Relationship
and Dramatherapy

Supervisory Triangles and the Helicopter Ability

Katerina Couroucli-Robertson

In this chapter the supervisory triangle (client/therapist/supervisor) and the helicopter ability (keeping an overview) will be examined. Supervision encompasses many different roles. One role is that of a counsellor giving support to another professional, another role is that of an educator helping a supervisee with his/her therapeutic work and in other cases a supervisor may also be a manager with responsibilities towards both the organization and the supervisees.

In this chapter I will be describing the supervision of a professional playtherapist who consulted a dramatherapist supervisor on her practice. The terms supervisor and supervisee will be used. During supervision the therapeutic process of the supervisee's client is narrated to the supervisor so that an objective understanding of the work can be reached. Thus, in the supervisory session a triangle is formed consisting of the client, the therapist and the supervisor.

In dramatherapy supervision this triangle is affected by another very important component, which is the art form (performance, storytelling, puppets, sand-play and drawing, to mention a few). The art form takes on the role of the all-encompassing container, which can substitute for the roles mentioned in the supervisory triangle and shed light on the therapeutic process. It becomes the catalyst, the joining factor which dispenses with hierarchy. In the arts therapies generally the art process intervenes between the identification and counter-identification of the client and the therapist. It mediates within the transference and may facilitate the journey of a relatively unconscious state, through stages of concrete thinking, to the beginnings of separation and eventually to symbolization (Cassirer 1955; Schaverien 1991). The art form in the following example, the story, contains and helps the dynamics of the client's and the supervisee's processes to emerge. It also reveals the relationship between the supervisor and supervisee which mirrors the relationship between the supervisee and the client.

During supervision the therapy session is reproduced very closely to its original form, but at the same time it takes on a life of its own. This parallel processing is a universal phenomenon. As Doehram (1976) suggests, the failure to observe its presence in supervision may be an indication of a natural resistance on the part of the supervisor and/or supervisee to confronting the full impact of those forces which they are asking the client to face.

The relationship of the supervisor with the supervisee, however, is different from that of the therapist and the client. The former relationship is on a more equal basis and resembles the way Reason (1988, p.11) describes co-operative inquiry. In co-operative inquiry we work with our co-researchers, establishing relationships of authentic collaboration and dialogue; ideally we care for each other, and approach each other with mutual love and concern. While not ignoring the necessity for direction and the role of expertise, we eschew unnecessary hierarchy and compulsive control.

In other words, a supervisory session with a professional is different from a therapy session with a client. The difference can be compared to the relationship between peers versus the relationship between parent and child.

Supervising the work of another therapist is similar to listening to a fairy story. However, unlike fairy stories, which speak the language of symbols, representing unconscious content, the story of the therapist represents the reality of her client, as far as she perceives it. (Throughout this text, I will usually use the female form and mean both sexes. As the supervisee was a female and the client was a male I have used she/he respectively for the account on the supervision sessions.)

When a therapist is telling the story of a session with her client, she is really asking and answering questions about the here and now situation of her client-protagonist. During the process of recalling a session the therapist needs to put the events into some form of perspective so as to gain a better comprehension of what took place. For this reason, in the beginning of a supervisory session, the dramatherapist needs to hear out the supervisee before any form of action or analysing can take place.

The way one listens to other people's stories is also very important. According to Reason and Hawkins (1988, p.100), stories can also change how experience is gathered. Instead of asking 'Tell me about…', which leads to an explanatory account, one can ask, 'Tell me the story…' which invites more expression.

Dramatherapy supervisors listening to these stories can call upon their 'internal roles', as guides to their work. These roles are the 'internal client' the 'internal therapist' and the 'internal supervisor', which mirror the supervisory triangle.

The 'internal client' is the role which co-ordinates with the real client, whether that is the supervisee or her own client(s). Life experiences put us in touch with the experiences the client might be going through. These experiences come from the sphere of feelings, which could include joy, pain, loss and others. Many feelings and thought processes originate from the attitudes of parents, teachers and more broadly the culture in which a person has been brought up. The 'internal client' needs to be the spring from which empathy for the client comes forth. At the same time the 'internal client' needs to be kept at a 'safe' distance, so that she is not in danger of getting lost in personal alleys that would render the supervisor unable to help the supervisee and subsequently the client.

The 'internal therapist' is the role that sets out to face any given situation. The 'internal therapist' has the required training, theory and intellectual capabilities. She possesses the structure, the aim and the methods in order to guide the supervisee. Finally, the 'internal supervisor' is the role which can give direction. It has the ability to remain at a distance from the therapeutic process, while at the same time it is also participating in it. The 'internal supervisor' is the role that can literally step outside the self and observe what is taking place. In this fashion the 'internal supervisor' can support or doubt what the other parts are involved in. The 'internal supervisor' navigates both the 'internal therapist' and the 'internal client' so that a balance can be achieved.

Parallel to these roles the dramatherapeutic technique applied during each session represents the artistic element in the process through which supervision can be inspired. In this chapter I will be referring to the use of a story suggested by the supervisor. The story is used to fuel the imagination and thus bring us closer to a solution. The story becomes the guide through which we comprehend situations which would be difficult to describe in a different way.

During supervision the helicopter ability is put into practice whereby the supervisee, the client and the umbrella organization shift between different levels. The helicopter ability incorporates the three internal resources and could be described as the ability which enables the switching of perspectives between them. It gives the opportunity for a bird's-eye view of a particular situation as well as accessibility to different levels. Hawkins and Shohet mention: 'Unless supervisors are relatively clear about their basic feelings to the supervisee, they cannot notice how these feelings are changed by the import of unconscious material from the supervisee and their clients' (1989, p.71).

To illustrate the supervisory triangle and the helicopter ability I will be presenting some extracts from supervision sessions between a client, Alkis (child), a supervisee, Vera (playtherapist), and a supervisor, Katerina (dramatherapist). The names given have been changed in order to ensure confidentiality.

Vera is a playtherapist I work with professionally, both as a co-trainer and as a dramatherapist. We agreed on a fortnightly supervision contract in order to work together on the case of Alkis. When she came to me Vera had already started working with four-year-old Alkis who was referred to her as a hyperkinetic child with behavioural problems. He had started kindergarten but was having trouble adjusting, with the result that a private carer had been appointed to look after him. Alkis' parents had been to several therapists in the past who were not able to deal with Alkis. In fact often, according to the parents, they had been blamed for Alkis' erratic behaviour. As a result, the parents felt threatened by psychiatrists and other specialists and wanted to believe that there was nothing seriously wrong with Alkis. On a different level, they knew that Alkis was not like other children. There were many reasons which would indicate this fact, one of them being that they were unable to socialize when they had him with them.

Early on in my work with Vera, listening to her tell me about her client Alkis brought to my mind the image of *The Little Prince* (de Saint-Exupéry 1982). As a result, I brought the story into our work and it seemed to run parallel with the unfolding of Alkis' own story. The story of *The Little Prince* was used for twelve sessions consecutively and through it we gained insight into our supervision work. I have the whole story recorded in twelve abbreviated chapters so that I can use extracts which I believe could be helpful to my clients. As Lahad (1998) suggested, the story itself became the guide for the supervisory process, allowing the supervisor to take a back seat. A story allows the supervisee a distance from the immediate facts and through this there is depersonalization of the problem. This results in the supervisee entering into a situation more freely and working on an unconscious level which can provide protection from feelings of exposure (Robertson 1998).

In the supervisory work with Vera, after having chosen the story, I used my abbreviated version from the beginning to the end. During each session, after Vera had related her recent work with Alkis, we listened to one chapter and tried to make connections. I did not choose a specific chapter each time; instead I allowed the story to run its course. Using the story as a guide, we were able to gain insight into the work Vera was doing with Alkis. The fact that each chapter in *The Little Prince* seemed to correspond to Alkis' story can only be ascribed to synchronicity. Similarities in the events of a supervisory session can be found with most stories when the fictional characters are similar to the clients. It is through the development of the story that parallelisms are drawn.

De Saint-Exupéry presented the Little Prince as a child innocent to the ways of the world and preoccupied with his own thoughts. His wisdom was simple and his manners were charming. He appeared to have no parents and lived on a little planet of his own far away from Earth. One day he decided to travel and landed on the planet Earth where he met a pilot who had crash-landed in the desert. He asked the pilot to draw some pictures for him. When the pilot asked him questions, the Little Prince never answered directly.

I could see many similarities with Alkis in this story. Alkis, at the beginning of his life, would also seem to have had no parents as he had been put up for adoption. Alkis also appeared to live in a world of his own; he had his own wisdom and never answered questions. He too had found an adult (the therapist) to draw pictures according to his specifications. Finally, one could say that he had also embarked on a journey like the Little Prince, through his playtherapy sessions.

Perhaps one of the main issues arrived at through Vera's work with Alkis was the painful realization by all parties that he was a child with special needs. Together with the death of the Little Prince in our story came the death of the romantic notion of Alkis as 'a cute little baby'. He wasn't a child with a psychological blockage due to his adoption, as had been assumed until then, but it would appear that he did have a more serious autistic problem, which the family needed to face and accept. Von Franz (1970, p.1), in her book *Puer Aeternus*, analyses the story of *The Little Prince* and says that, in general, the man who is identified with the archetype of the *puer aeternus* remains too long in adolescent psychology; that is, all those characteristics that are normal in a youth of seventeen or eighteen are continued into later life, coupled in most cases with too great a dependence on the mother. She suggests that de Saint-Exupéry was such a personality. I feel there is a parallelism in the personalities of de Saint-Exupéry and Alkis, even though the first was a grown man and the second a child. One image I had of Alkis was that of an all-consuming baby. He depended on his mother to such an extent, that, instead of behaving like a four-and-a-half-year-old he continued to act like a baby. His behaviour, however, was reinforced by his environment. Von Franz (1970, p.59) goes on to say:

> It is clear that Saint-Exupéry's genius is that divine child in him. He would not be such a genius or artist if he had not that capacity of being absolutely naive and absolutely spontaneous; that is the source of his creativeness and at the same time it is a little close to being something worthless, something which devalues his personality.

In the case of Alkis, being a child of four and a half years old, one could not say that his naivety devalued his personality. However, his compulsive and infantile behaviour was very tiring for his parents.

A few words about Alkis and his family. Alkis was an attractive four-and-a-half-year-old boy, of average size, with pale skin, large brown eyes and brown wavy hair. His unmarried natural mother had put him up for adoption a few weeks after his birth. However, he was not adopted officially until he was one year old. The reason for his late adoption was that his mother was not certain she wanted to let him go and visited him at the institution a few times. His new parents celebrated his first birthday with him at the institution and shortly afterwards took him home with them. The couple chose him specifically at that age so that they could be sure of getting a healthy and normal child. Alkis' adoptive mother, Soula, was thirty-seven years old and had wanted a child of her own for many years. She had had one abortion when she was eighteen and after that she had many miscarriages. The doctors said that it would be difficult for her to carry a baby as there was a problem with her womb. Together with her husband they decided to adopt.

Soula came from a family of five siblings, three boys and two girls, where she was the eldest. Two of her brothers died at a young age. Her first brother died from gangrene when he was two and she was four and the second died as a result of a car accident when he was four and she was seven. At the time of the accident Soula and her sister had been in charge of their brother on a highway. They accidentally let go of his hands and the boy was run over. Perhaps owing to this incident Soula was over-protective towards Alkis and always held him firmly by the hand.

Both Soula's parents were alive. Soula worked in her own small business selling sports gear and therefore was busy for many hours in the day. The adoptive father, Giannis, also ran a small business of his own selling car stereos and for this he needed to travel outside town once a month. He had one brother and both parents alive. Three afternoons a week he looked after Alkis, as he finished work at 3.00 p.m., whereas Soula finished at 8.00 p.m. or later, on those days. According to Soula, her husband could even read his newspaper while watching Alkis, whereas she could never relax as she was always anticipating his next destructive move. Soula looked after him during the remaining afternoons and weekends. During the absence of both parents as well as his time at the kindergarten, a rather authoritarian student looked after Alkis.

Generally Alkis was hyperactive and disruptive with the result that their home was very sparsely decorated. Alkis did not hold conversations, he only asked questions. From his behaviour it was apparent that he was not lacking in intelligence. He was fascinated with hairs, strings and materials of interesting textures. He was not toilet-trained.

First extract from a supervision session

During this session I first used the story of *The Little Prince*. Vera began by reporting the following account: 'During our last session Alkis entered the room in a good mood saying, "Mrs. Vera, I have loved an Esmeralda, whom I met in the woods and she gave me a piece of cake with raisins in it."'

I felt that this statement, out of the blue, was typical of Alkis who did not always make much sense to others. Perhaps what he was trying to communicate was that he liked his new Esmeralda doll with the beautiful long hair he had recently been given. Vera told me that Alkis had seen the popular Walt Disney film which featured Esmeralda and recognized her character in his doll even though he had not been able to sit through the whole film. Vera also told me that, according to his mother, Alkis had felt his grandmother's dissatisfaction at his playing with a doll and had enjoyed it (in the grandmother's eyes a doll was a toy only for girls).

Vera continued relating Alkis' activities. After his statement he sat down and started his paper-cutting, which had become more co-ordinated. When he had had enough of that activity he asked Vera to draw him a cow and then a goat. Vera asked him to give her a pencil and to help by leading her hand. He was particularly interested in the legs and the tails. Then he tried to cut out the outline of the animals and managed to keep off the line. When this activity was over Alkis brought out a doll and Vera asked him to become the doll's barber. This he did, giving the doll a fairly even haircut. Through this request Vera was offering him a way in which his compulsion for cutting could become part of their playing. When the hair-cutting was over, he quickly got up, lifted a wooden chair and let it drop. Then he ran to the curtains and wrapped them round himself and finally hit the windowpane with a clothes-hanger. Vera had to physically restrain him and told him that apart from the damage he would cause he could also hurt himself. Alkis then started to kick the door but he calmed down more easily than usual.

In spite of Alkis' erratic behaviour at the end, Vera felt the session went well and commented on how clever she believed Alkis to be. After listening to Vera's description of her session with Alkis, I brought out *The Little Prince* and put on the tape so we could listen to the first chapter. Bettelheim mentions how the client/supervisee can resolve inner conflicts through the implications of a tale: 'The fairy tale is therapeutic because the patient finds his own solutions, through contemplating what the story seems to imply about him and his inner conflicts at this moment in life' (1975, p.25). In this supervisory process one could say that the story acted as a 'guide'. After listening to it, Vera exclaimed, 'It took Exupéry six months to learn how to draw and I reckoned it took me the same amount of time to understand Alkis. After six months' work I feel I can see the sparkle in his eyes. He no longer frightens me and we have begun to communicate.' Robertson (1998) suggests literature would not have the power to affect us if it were not, in the first place, a work of art. As with all art, the deeper meaning will affect each person to a different degree and will affect the same person in varying degrees at different times of her life.

Vera then mentioned that Alkis had started to call her by her first name, which she had asked him to do from the beginning. Storr mentions, 'If I call a patient by his Christian name whilst he continues to call me "Dr Storr" the patient's position as "child" is underlined, and this is degrading.'(1990, p.67) Perhaps in the case of Alkis his referring to Vera by her first name meant that he felt more intimate with her as though the relationship had developed on a more equal basis.

We discussed Alkis' erratic behaviour at the end of the session and decided it may have been his indication to Vera of how an elephant feels having been swallowed by a boa constrictor. De Saint-Exupéry begins his story of the Little Prince with the description of a boa constrictor in the act of swallowing an animal and how later his hero in the story drew a picture of a boa constrictor digesting an elephant. The image of a boa constrictor swallowing an elephant is fantastic, but if we retain it as a picture it can help us on a metaphorical level. As Laing (1969) mentions, our view of the other depends on our willingness to enlist all the powers of every aspect of ourselves in the act of comprehension. *The Little Prince* helped Vera see that even though Alkis lived in his own magic world she had begun to enter it. She could see significance in his drawing with the result that Alkis also began to recognize her as an adult who didn't need to have things explained to her. 'Grown-ups never understand anything by themselves, and it is tiresome for children to have to be always and forever explaining things to them' (de Saint-Exupéry 1982, p.6).

During this supervisory session, through the description of Alkis' behaviour by the supervisee, the supervisor made a connection with the story of the Little Prince. Through this story the relationship between the supervisee and her client became clearer. The helicopter ability could be said to have been instrumental in connecting Alkis with the Little Prince. They both lived in a world of their own but in this session Vera had been asked by Alkis to enter his world, as the story illuminated to her.

Second extract from a supervision session

During this session the theme of moving and leaving others behind was prevalent and it seemed to be taking place on several planes. In the story of the Little Prince it appeared through his leaving his planet together with the migrating birds. This synchronicity inspired deeper meaning into the supervisory process.

Vera began her story:

Alkis ran away from school on Friday and it took them more than an hour to find him. The headmistress, who is an acquaintance of mine, was annoyed both with his mother and me because we hadn't warned her that Alkis could be dangerous. She wanted to expel him from her kindergarten. Alkis' mother telephoned me on Friday evening and she was very angry. She felt that everyone was taking advantage of her through her child. Perhaps she had a point. She was paying for an extra child-minder to look after Alkis while he was at school but the child-minder was often assigned to other jobs.

Vera then told me that the weekend before this incident Alkis' parents had gone away from Saturday evening to Sunday evening, leaving Alkis behind for the second time in his life.

I had my own thoughts and questions about Alkis' behaviour. Was Alkis' parents' weekend connected with his running away from school? Could this have been a mirroring of how he had felt about his parents' behaviour towards him especially when he was not used to it? Or was it simply that Alkis may have been unhappy at school, felt bored and wanted a change?

I feel that there was a connection between his running away and his feeling of abandonment. His parents had only left him behind one other time in his life so he must have felt bewildered and perhaps he felt he was to blame in some way. It can be argued that two days is not very long but for a child of four and a half years the notion of time is felt differently. Another important factor in Alkis' life was that he had been left by his blood mother as a very young baby at an institution from which he did not leave until he was a year old. One could therefore suggest that such a child was much more vulnerable to being left behind and one way of coping with this vulnerability would be to leave first.

During his session with Vera, Alkis worked well. When, however, the session ended and Alkis' father was ten minutes late coming to get him, he was very uneasy and destructive. Did he feel his father had left him behind again?

When Vera had finished her story about Alkis I put on the cassette with the story of the Little Prince. We had reached the part of his migration with the birds from his own planet to others. His first visit was to the planet of the king:

'Ah! Here is a subject!' exclaimed the king, when he saw the little prince coming.

And the Little Prince asked himself:

'How could he recognize me when he had never seen me before?'

He did not know how the world is simplified for kings. To them, all men are subjects.

'Approach, so that I may see you better,' said the king, who felt consumingly proud of being at last a king over somebody...

'It is contrary to etiquette to yawn in the presence of a king,' the monarch said to him. 'I forbid you to do so.'

'I can't help it. I can't stop myself,' replied the Little Prince, thoroughly embarrassed. 'I have come on a long journey, and I have had no sleep...'

'Ah, then', the king said. 'I order you to yawn. It is years since I have seen anyone yawning! Yawns, to me, are objects of curiosity. Come, now! Yawn again! It is an order.'

After listening to that scene Vera felt she resembled the king very much and that she was always giving orders to Alkis. She drew a king with a large cape which hid his body completely and next to him she drew a small prince. Vera said: 'What concerns me is whether I am trying to structure my sessions with Alkis too much. I feel he has reached a stage which is a stepping stone and when he passes that he will fly ahead.' Katerina: 'I feel that Alkis is also taking part in the structuring of the session and perhaps you both need to ackowledge this.'

The episode of Alkis' running away from school was an experience I had had in the past with my daughter when she was the same age as Alkis. She had also run away from school and the supervision session had brought this memory back to me. I had had the same treatment by the teacher, who blamed me for my child's behaviour, so I felt a lot of sympathy for Alkis' mother. I remember feeling guilty about keeping my daughter on so late at school, because I was working, and yet I knew it was the teacher's responsibility to keep the children on school grounds. This memory is a good example of the 'internal client' coming to the surface, thus shedding more understanding on the feelings of Alkis' mother.

During this session it was as though several pebbles had been thrown into the pond simultaneously, causing many ripples.

The helicopter ability can call upon the correlation of different persons and ideas. Alkis' parents, 'the system' could be seen as giving information to the 'internal supervisor', thus giving insight through their reactions towards their child. Alkis himself was able to inform the 'internal therapist' through his action of running away which brought forward a chain of reactions.

On a different level one can see the story as a guide to the supervisory process as a whole. The Little Prince in his story was in charge of the situation. The orders were given by the king so that he could establish his power; however, he had to alter them in order to suit the Little Prince. Vera had felt that she was constantly giving Alkis orders, while in fact he had managed to induce her into giving him the orders which suited him. Perhaps the underlying theme of running away had a cathartic effect. Alkis had taken the initiative this time with the result that he was able to concentrate more fully on his play.

Third extract from a supervision session

Vera: 'I have nothing particularly new. Last time Alkis made a puzzle and then took it to pieces, then he took a second one, which he took to pieces and asked me to put it back into its place, which was an unusual request for him. Then he played with his Plasticine and cut it and finally he drew a peacock and cut round it; all his usual occupations with the difference that when he finished he didn't destroy his work by chewing it but went on to the next job.'

I put on the tape with the scene of the Little Prince and the lamplighter:

When the Little Prince arrived on the planet he respectfully saluted the lamplighter.

'Good morning, sir. Why have you just put out your lamp?'
'Those are the orders' replied the lamplighter. 'Good morning.'
'What are the orders?'
'The orders are that I put out the lamp. Good evening.'
And he lighted his lamp again.
'But why have you lighted it again?'
'Those are the orders,' replied the lamplighter.
'I do not understand,' said the Little Prince.
'There is nothing to understand,' said the lamplighter. 'Orders are orders. Good morning.'

When Vera had listened to it she said: 'It makes me wonder whether I give the wrong orders.'

The story made me think also. What had gone wrong with the orders of the lamplighter was that they had not changed when circumstances changed. From year to year the planet had turned more rapidly, making a day last only one minute. The result was a frantic lamplighter lighting and putting out the lamp every minute, closely resembling the behaviour of a hyperactive child. What were the circumstances in Alkis' life that had changed so rapidly with the result that he also became hyperactive? Could it have been his adoption?

I asked Vera to show me a session with Alkis from the beginning to the end, using finger puppets so that we could gain more insight into his behaviour. The scene with the lamplighter focused largely on the movements of the lamplighter which resulted from the orders he had received and was obeying. Through my request to Vera of using finger puppets the action and movements of the session would become clearer. In order to 'follow my orders' Vera had to think carefully about her session with Alkis and by very simple means indicate how it had taken place. The process went as follows: two puppets entered a room together, one sat down while the other made many movements from here to there and ended up sitting down with his back to the first puppet. In a few seconds Vera had reconstructed their playtherapy session very vividly.

Katerina: 'Would you now like to repeat the scene as you would have liked it to take place?' Vera played out the scene again following the same movements, with the difference that the puppets ended up facing each other.

Thinking over the ideal puppet scene she had created, Vera pointed out: 'In the second scene we were sitting at a greater distance from each other but we were communicating through eye contact.'

This was perhaps the essence of their playtherapy: they needed to face each other in order to work together. The relationship of Alkis and Vera was growing but it took time for a feeling of trust to build up.

After this session I had a thought. The helicopter ability came to my aid again. Usually when Vera entered the supervision room where we worked sitting on the floor, she took her cushion and brought it closer to mine, an action which I followed. Most of my clients like the distance between the two cushions, allowing them to rest against a wall. The distance my clients like to sit from me illuminates Landy's distancing theory (1986, pp.98ff). The over-distanced client remains three metres away quite happily and rarely changes the position of their cushion unless we are doing something specific which requires us to be closer. The under-distanced client always moves their cushion closer to mine. I have noticed that for my part I always follow my client's lead with the result that when they move their cushion I do the same with mine. Similarly, I find that I often unconsciously imitate the body stance of the client sitting in front of me. Obviously distance is something important to Vera. She needs to feel that she is close to the person she is working with. Perhaps, however, the distance she kept from Alkis was not comfortable for him with the result that he had to turn his back to her.

Landy (1986, p.98) suggests that distancing is a key concept in dramatherapy theory. A fuller understanding of distancing is that of an interaction or intrapsychic phenomenon characterized by a range of closeness and separation. The range includes the over-distance of the Brechtian actor as well as the under-distance of the method actor who alters his physical and emotional reality to enter into the role of another.

Co-relating the resources of the supervisor to this supervision session we have both the information gained through the story of the Little Prince as well as the significance of the distance in the sitting arrangements. The theme of distance came up again during the following session in the story of the Little Prince.

Fourth extract from a supervision session

This session began with Vera telling me about Alkis' mother and how she was afraid that there might be something seriously wrong with Alkis. She complained about his behaviour and felt that she was running out of patience with him. It was as though he ruled the household and everyone had to comply to his needs. Vera, for her part, was pleased with Alkis' progress in the playtherapy sessions. What did this discrepancy mean? Was Alkis not pleased with the attention he was getting at home? He no longer needed to give the dolls a haircut at every playtherapy session and his compulsion to cut things generally had eased. During the last session he only cut a bit of Plasticine. This time he played with Plasticine, balloons and the animal bag. He put his head into it and looked at the animals. Vera explained that he didn't actually play with the animals but he took his time examining them, which was unusual as in the past he hardly ever touched the animal bag.

I put on my cassette with *The Little Prince* and we listened to the scene where he meets with the fox.

> It would have been better to come back at the same hour,' said the fox. 'If, for example, you came at four o'clock in the afternoon, then at three o'clock I shall begin to be happy. I shall feel happier as the hour advances. At four o'clock, I shall show you how happy I am! But if you come at just any time, I shall never know at what hour my heart is to be ready to greet you... One must observe the proper rites...'

Listening to these words, Vera was reminded of the 'proper rites' in a session with Alkis – or perhaps the distance which Alkis liked to keep from her.

When Alkis took the bag of animals and put his head in the bag, he had his back turned to her.

Katerina: 'Perhaps we could do that scene together.'

We moved to a different part of the room, where after a short warm-up, I took on the role of Vera and she the role of Alkis. I felt her body shrink. She enacted his various activities and then as she turned her back to me she sat down and put her head in the animal bag. Gradually I eased my cushion closer to hers, remembering her movement with the cushions as we began our supervision work together. She looked at me over her shoulder saying what she intended to do to the animals, hoping to frighten me: 'I will pull his antennae out. His hair is stuck to his leg. I will separate it' (placing the horse into her mouth). Any protrusion on the animals she wanted to remove. I responded as Vera, saying: 'Those animals are for you to play with. If you remove their legs or their antennae they will be left without.' Vera playing the part of Alkis didn't take any notice of me and carried on biting whichever piece of the animal protruded.

As it was Vera impersonating Alkis, she did not actually harm the toy animals, so I was safe. If it had been Alkis the animals would have been mutilated. Would this have made me feel differently? A playtherapist obviously has certain toys which she is prepared to have destroyed; however, this did not alter the fact that Alkis was trying to provoke Vera by being destructive.

Landy (1993) mentions that the most significant aspect of the dramatic paradox concerns the notion that the actor and the role are both separate and merged, and that the non-fictional reality of the actor coexists with the fictional reality of the role. This was how I had felt playing the role of Vera – I was both Vera working with Alkis, as well as Vera's supervisor.

When we deroled, Vera said: 'I get it now. He can only communicate through his destruction. I wonder what his parents do when they are alone with him. Is he trying all the time to gain some attention or does he want to distract them from what they are doing?'

Katerina: 'Maybe he never feels that he has accomplished anything unless it is damage. He is not allowed to dress himself as he is slow. Only recently has he been allowed to feed himself, and that not always. He has very few accomplishments to feel proud of. Perhaps he needs to be allowed to do more things for himself.'

We both felt that Alkis needed to be tamed slowly. Next I told Vera that I believed it would be good for the parents to visit a child psychiatrist in order to have Alkis diagnosed.

Following my original premise of the interior resources of the supervisor, during this extract of the story one can see the following parallelisms: the 'internal supervisor' could be represented as the fox, the 'internal client' could be the Little Prince and the 'internal therapist' could have become the process of the taming. Within the story itself another supervisory triangle was formed, thus moving the process of supervision on to another level.

Between this session and the next, the parents went to visit a child psychiatrist who told them that Alkis had autistic tendencies and advised them on how to handle him. What the child psychiatrist in fact said was that they should go easy on him because certain of his activities were compulsive, and punishing or shouting at him would not bring the response they wanted. The parents were very alarmed and started reading all the books they could find about autism. They began to see that Alkis' behaviour was similar to some of the descriptions of autistic children they read about; this realization both terrified them and calmed them down.

Fifth extract from a supervision session

Vera: 'During our last session Alkis went back to his old destructive behaviour.' Perhaps this was not surprising seeing he had just been diagnosed as a child with 'autistic tendencies'. His parents' reactions to the diagnosis must surely have been influencing their relationship with him. Vera and I discussed Alkis in detail. We wondered how much his behaviour could improve and whether Vera had too high expectations of him. Somehow both of us were reluctant to accept that he had a 'real' problem, mirroring his mother's attitude.

I put on the cassette with the last scene of *The Little Prince:*

This is, to me, the loveliest and saddest landscape in the world. It is here that the Little Prince appeared on Earth, and disappeared. Look at it carefully so that you will be sure to recognize it in case you travel some day to the African desert. And, if you should come upon this spot, please do not hurry on. Wait for a time, exactly under the star. Then, if a little man appears who laughs, who has golden hair and who refuses to answer questions, you will know who he is. If this should happen, please comfort me. Send me word that he has come back.

Alkis was just that, a little man with a great sense of humour who refused to answer questions. The only difference was the colour of his hair!

After Vera had heard the end of *The Little Prince* she said: 'The Little Prince reminds me so much of Alkis.'

Katerina: 'You did well keeping an open mind about Alkis without giving him a label. There is a time however when we need to accept a diagnosis so as to help the child according to his needs. In fact, it might even bring a form of relief.' I felt that the end of *The Little Prince* was like a landmark which fitted the situation well. Alkis could not be a Little Prince all his life. From this death a new person would be born – one that fitted in to Alkis' reality. His reality was that he was a child with special needs who showed distinct autistic characteristics and needed to be accepted as such.

Sixth extract from a supervision session

A new start for Alkis.

Vera: 'Last time Alkis was wonderful. He asked me to draw him a peacock and told me how to make the wings. All during the session he had me working for him and the important thing was that he concentrated the whole time. I feel all the business of meeting with the child psychiatrist may have calmed his mother down. I feel that she has less anxiety when she talks to me. It feels as though we are on a new road.'

Reflection

Vera, I believe, handled the case of Alkis with an open mind and was correctly reluctant to label him. However, there comes a time when parents need more specific information. As Davis (1992, p.2) mentions:

> A proper and useful approach towards explaining behaviour, whether mad or sane, is to define its context or, especially, the part it plays in exchanges between one person and another or others within a system of relationships. The context and associated behaviour shows whether reddening of the face is the blush of modesty or the flush of anger.

In other words, when Alkis' parents heard that he had autistic tendencies they began to understand his behaviour in connection to this diagnosis. They no longer felt that he behaved aggressively towards them without reason. The Little Prince in our story had died or gone back to his own planet but Alkis was still very much alive and needed to be recognized for what he was. The acceptance of his autistic tendencies did not need to interfere on any level with his progress during playtherapy. On the other hand, once the parents were able to accept that he was a child with special needs they became more tolerant. As Landy (1993, pp.135ff) suggests: 'In evaluating the effectiveness of the therapy, the therapist/researcher does not look for a resolution – that is, a victory of one role over the other – but rather a means of living in the ambivalence. In terms of role function, this means an understanding of the complementary purposes of two roles.' In other words Alkis was both a 'normal' child as well as an 'autistic' one. Both components were part of him and both needed to be respected for what they were. For Alkis' parents, having a child with special needs was a great stigma and it was something they were desperately trying to avoid from the very beginning when they chose to adopt a one-year-old in order to be 'safe'. However from the moment they accepted that this was the case their behaviour began to relax towards Alkis. Their worst fears had materialized and this realization brought relief.

According to Storr (1960, p.132) the degree of recovery which takes place in the patient is proportional to the degree of maturity of the relationship which he is enabled to make with the therapist. This recovery, however, cannot change a person's basic characteristics. Vera and Alkis had reached a maturity in their relationship but Alkis was still in control.

By using the story of *The Little Prince* during the difficult time which Alkis and his parents were facing, the supervisory process was given food for thought. Through the parallelisms of the story both Vera and myself were able to make connections between Alkis and the Little Prince which furthered our understanding of Alkis. By fuelling and containing the imagination the story nourished and inspired the 'internal supervisor'.

The internal resources of the dramatherapist supervisor need to operate like a team which is involved in a very complicated relay game. At any moment in time one part is holding the skittle and it needs to hold on for as long as is necessary before passing it on. The length of time the skittle is kept with each part needs to be balanced according to the needs of the client. The helicopter ability makes use of these internal resources and at the same time enables the supervisor to observe the dynamics expressed in the several triangles that form during the supervision process.

Acknowledgement

The material reproduced on pp.104–106, 108, 110 is taken from *The Little Prince* © Gallimard 1944. The first edition was published in 1945 by William Heinemann Ltd. The extract is reproduced by kind permission of Egmount Children's Books Ltd, London, and Harcourt Brace Inc, New York.

References

Bettelheim, B. (1975) *The Uses of Enchantment.* London: Penguin.

Cassirer, E. (1955) *The Philosophy of Symbolic Forms.* New Haven, CT: Yale University Press.

Davis, D. R. (1992) *Scenes of Madness.* London and New York: Routledge.

de Saint-Exupéry, A. (1982)*The Little Prince.* London: Pan Books. (First published 1945.)

Doehram, M.J.G. (1976) 'Parallel processes in supervision and psychotherapy.' *Journal of the American Psychoanalytic Association 17,* 2, 312–332.

Hawkins, P. and Shohet, R. (1989) *Supervision in the Helping Professions.* Milton Keynes and Philadelphia: Open University Press.

Lahad, M. (1998) Lecture given at the 'Herma' Dramatherapy and Playtherapy Supervision Training. Athens.

Laing, R.D. (1969) *The Divided Self.* London: Penguin Books.

Landy, R.J. (1986) *Drama Therapy Concepts and Practices.* Springfield, IL: Charles C Thomas Publishers.

Landy, R. J. (1993) *Persona and Performance.* London: Jessica Kingsley Publishers.

Reason, P. (ed) (1988) *Human Inquiry in Action.* London: Sage Publications.

Reason, P. and Hawkins, P. (1988) 'Storytelling as inquiry.' In P.Reason (ed) *Human Inquiry into Action.* London: Sage Publications.

Robertson, K. (1998) 'The application of myth and stories in dramatherapy.' *The Journal of the British Association for Dramatherapists 20,* 2, 3–10.

Schaverien, J. (1991) *The Revealing Image: Analytic Psychotherapy in Theory and Practice.* London: Routledge.

Storr, A (1960) *The Integrity of the Personality.* Oxford: Oxford University Press.

Storr, A. (1990) *The Art of Psychotherapy.* London: Butterworth-Heinemann. (First published 1979)

Von Franz, M-L. (1970) *Puer Aeternus.* USA: Sigo Press.

CHAPTER 5

Role Model
of Dramatherapy Supervision

Robert J. Landy

On supervision

The process of supervision in any form of psychotherapy implies a relationship among three roles – those of client, therapist and supervisor. On the simplest level, the client reports to the therapist who, in turn, reports to the supervisor. The client and supervisor remain unknown to one another, except as the supervisor hears stories about the client and as the client is (or is not) aware of the fact that the therapist meets with a supervisor to review the client's case. Generally speaking, the three roles are fairly well delineated. The client's function is to seek help from the therapist and to work toward getting better through an extended interaction with the therapist. The therapist's function is to facilitate some form of healing on the part of the client. And the supervisor's function is to help the therapist better serve the client by facilitating a self-reflective, critical process on the part of the therapist.

But this is just part of the story. The clear qualities of each role often shift as the therapist, for example, experiences the role of client as he interacts with the supervisor and as he struggles with his countertransferential reactions, and as the supervisor, identifying with the client, does the same. The client, too, will slip into the role of therapist or supervisor as he discovers his own inner guides. In fact, each role of client, therapist and supervisor can serve as an introject for the others. In many ways, an effective psychotherapeutic process implies that the qualities of therapist, client and supervisor can be held together in a balanced way by each person.

Underlying this perspective is the assumption that an optimal psychotherapeutic experience requires a balance of the three roles of client, therapist and supervisor not only on an interpersonal level, but also on an intrapsychic one. On an intrapsychic level, the client would have available an internal therapist and supervisor to guide and critique his progress. The therapist would have available an internal client and supervisor to measure his own effectiveness as a partner in the healing process and as a self-reflective critic. And the supervisor would have available an internal client and therapist to measure and temper the effectiveness of his guidance. Like the therapist, he also needs an internal supervisor to provide a further self-critique.

The role model in dramatherapy

To better explain the convolutions of this role triangle, I turn to a model I have developed to elucidate the process of dramatherapy. I have previously written (see Landy 1993; 1994; 1996b) that the goal of dramatherapy is to help clients discover ways to live with role ambivalence. I conceptualize role ambivalence as the relationship between a role and its counterpart, which I call the counterrole. An example is the relationship between the part of oneself that feels powerless, the victim, and the part of oneself that feels powerful and competent, the victor. When working with this configuration, the dramatherapist helps the client invoke both victim and victor, work them through and discover ways to integrate the two so that it becomes possible to feel powerful and powerless simultaneously without the overwhelming fear of ultimately succumbing to the most extreme qualities of either one.

In working with role and counterrole in dramatherapy, I began to notice that when seeking integration, many clients required a third piece, standing outside the role and counterrole. I thought of this third piece as a bridge. I reasoned that people sought therapy because they became stuck in a single role, too much the victim, for example, unsure what qualities lay on the other side of their sense of powerlessness. Before they could even consider integration, I reasoned, they needed to know the qualities on the other side of the overpowering role. And, being stuck, they needed a third role as an outside helper to move them along the way. Many children understand this third role as a figure in fairy tales whose magic enables the hero to reach her goals. This magical figure goes by many names – fairy godmother, genie, wizard, good fairy and various gods and goddesses. In my clinical work, I came to understand this figure as the guide.

The figure of the guide became most clear to me in my extensive work with a middle-aged alcoholic woman who had been severely abused by her mother. I will call her Fay. Feeling very much the victim in her adult life, wandering from job to job, finding victimizers at every desk, in every attempted intimate relationship, Fay was unable to locate the qualities existing on the other side of the victim. Intellectually, she knew of the existence of love and care, and she knew that she wanted to feel these qualities. But because of a history of sustained abuse, Fay didn't know how to get to them. She needed a guide.

For several years, in our transferential dance, Fay struggled with me. Rather than a guide, I became her tormentor each time I went on vacation or misrepresented a story told. Each time I could not properly hold her pain or anger, I was her victimizer. I knew, at least unconsciously, that I had to be the guide in order to steer her through the powerful storm of re-victimization. But at times I wavered and discussed her case with my supervisor, revisiting old territory in my psyche concerning, especially, my difficulties holding excessive pain and anger.

Then, one day, Fay brought in a photograph of herself as a young girl. She was in the town of her childhood, outside her mother's house, poorly dressed, without shoes, faking a smile for the camera. I asked her to describe the town as she saw it in the picture. The background was a blur except for a distant house. When I questioned her about it, she told me it was Mrs Smith's house. Fay became very emotional and upon further questioning, she identified Mrs Smith's house as one of love and care, of comfort and protection. Mrs Smith was the only example of a good mother that Fay had ever known.

From that session onward, Fay had discovered a guide, one very different from me, the wounded healer who could still re-traumatize, who needed further supervision to still my own countertransferential fears. Mrs Smith was a fiction based in part on a real character who once lived in a town very long ago and far away. As fiction, she was safe and magical. As such, she could help Fay safely reach the other side of the victim, the side that was powerful because she was worthy of love and care and attention. Mrs Smith, the guide, would ultimately help Fay discover a way to live in the ambivalence of feeling despised and unworthy, on the one hand, and feeling worthy of love and care, on the other. Fay's discovery was, for me, a relief, taking away some of the burden of holding her anger. But it was more than that for me – it was a revelation. I saw clearly what I had been intuiting – that in the model of role and counterrole, a piece was missing. This was it – the guide.

During the past several years, I have applied the model of role–counterrole–guide to clinical treatment. In doing so, I attempt first to help clients identify a single problematic role and work with it until it becomes clear. To clarify the role, I ask the client to identify its qualities, function and style. By qualities I mean its distinguishing features in terms of six domains: somatic, cognitive, affective, social, spiritual and aesthetic. Over several years, Fay came to see the victim part of herself as physically weak and exhausted, as ignorant and learning impaired, as lifeless and unlovable, as socially isolated, as spiritually separated from God and as uncreative and unplayful.

I also ask the client to speak about the function of the role in their lives, that is, what does the playing of a particular role give them. This victim part of Fay was very large and functioned to keep her asleep and safe from further trauma and abuse. At the same time, it caused her great distress outside the home as she met the world with the expectation that she would fail and that they would be the cause of her failure.

By style, I mean the form of role playing, whether reality-based and emotional, more abstract and distant or a mix of affect and cognition. Over several years, Fay would play the victim in a realistic, overtly emotional way, with little style and distance. When able to abstract the role qualities and depict the victim as a character in a story, a picture on a piece of paper, a figure in a sandbox, Fay would move away from the profound pain of the victim and slowly discover its other side, eventually locating the house of Mrs Smith which led to a further dis-identification with the role of victim.

Once ready to locate the counterrole or counter-qualities of the primary role, and once able to identify a guide, the process of treatment is well under way. In working with counterrole and guide, the client is also asked to specify qualities, function and style. As the client is able to integrate role and counterrole with the help of the guide, the therapy moves toward its final stages.

I have applied the model of role–counterrole–guide not only to treatment, but also to assessment and evaluation. In testing one's ability to invoke these three figures and to attribute qualities, functions and levels of distance to them, I am able to assess one's suitability for dramatherapy treatment and/or one's present level of functioning. Further, in analyzing the ability of the client to integrate role, counterrole and guide I am able to evaluate the effectiveness of the treatment.

Application of the role model to supervision: four focal points

In applying the role model to supervision, the supervisor helps the therapist focus upon several role relationships:

1. that of role–counterrole–guide within the therapist

2. that of role–counterrole–guide within the client

3. that of the client in relationship to the therapist

4. that of role–counterrole–guide in the relationship among client, therapist and supervisor.

To better see how this model works, I have constructed dialogues based upon actual supervisory sessions between supervisor and dramatherapist discussing the case of Fay. Each dialogue corresponds to one of the four focal points of the role model. To reflect upon the dialogues and attempt to clarify some of the ambiguities, I offer a running commentary. In doing so, I aim to play guide for the reader. As guide and commentator, I retain a first person point of view. As therapist, I move into the more distanced stance of the third person.

First dialogue, concerning the therapist

The therapist brought into supervision the following scenario.

I recently returned from an extended vacation and met with Fay. I see her individually and in group. We had been working together for five years and this was the longest sustained time I had ever been inaccessible to her. She was very quiet and withdrawn. She told me a story about being passed over for a promotion at work and about how a new colleague had been behaving abusively toward her. Toward the end of the session, which was primarily verbal, she told me in a tearful way how much she missed me and how much it hurt to admit to this feeling. I felt it was important that Fay verbalized these difficult feelings and I told her so. I was full of feeling, myself. On the one hand I was bored by Fay's account of being victimized at work. I had heard dozens of similar stories from her and found myself turning off. On another level, when Fay spoke of missing me, I immediately saw myself as a love object and felt a mixture of guilt for abandoning her for so long and fear that I could not hold the ambivalence of the dual roles of therapist/lover. I shared none of this with her.

The session ended as I praised Fay for her openness and reminded her of our group meeting in several days. We ended with a hug, as is our custom following each session. The hug felt safe and containing to me.

During group, however, things went awry. Ruth, going through a confusing divorce, remained withdrawn. Jim, depressed and highly self-critical, went on a talking jag. It was difficult for anyone else to intercede. I felt a mixture of delight, in that Jim was working through some important material, and loss of control, in that I didn't know if I should or how I should shift the focus to others in the group. At some point, Fay shared a story about being ten and having to take care of her younger siblings all by herself while her mother was in the hospital giving birth. During this time, her father was home only long enough to criticize her for her shoddy caretaking. To make matters worse, the youngest baby was sick and there was no money in the house to buy proper food. All the tasks of caring for the baby and siblings, of shopping for and preparing food, of keeping the house clean and neat, fell upon ten-year-old Fay. She felt inadequate and angry, and having nowhere to go with these feelings, she kept them inside.

The group did not dwell upon Fay's story. In fact, without missing a beat, Jim continued his saga. At the end of the group, Fay was angry but could not express it. I could feel her anger but decided it was up to her to express her feelings. I was not going to rescue her. I would see her in several days privately and perhaps we could work with this particular issue.

When I met her next, she was so quiet that I could hardly hear her. Whatever she said made little sense to me. She spoke more about abuse from her work colleague, then said: 'I really have nothing to say.' I asked her to express her feelings non-verbally and she chose to draw a picture. She took a large piece of paper from my shelf, one she had drawn on before, and turned it over. She drew a large face in the centre and began to construct colourful concentric circles all around the face. She spoke as she drew, accusing me of abandonment and caring for Jim much more than her. As she drew more and more circles, her accusations deepened. I became her abuser and she became flooded with feeling. I tried to hold on to the feelings of abuse and abandonment and to draw her attention back to the drawing, but she was far away, back to her abusive family of origin with little ability to return and little trust that I could ever be a worthy guide. I sat with her and felt the pain and the distance. I experienced my own fear of such accusations by intimates in my life. And I was also aware of a certain feeling of helplessness. There was nothing for me to do, I thought. I could neither reassure her nor could I take away her pain. All my skills as a creative arts therapist seemed lost. Yes, she was focused on the art work, but it took her too far away to an unreachable point and I could do nothing to get her back. All I could do was to sit there and wait. At the end of the session, she walked out. No hug, no goodbye.

During the next group session, Jim was unaware that Fay was angry at him. Ruth could feel Fay's anger and acknowledged it. In response, Fay told Jim she was not angry at him but at me. She verbally attacked Ruth who defended herself by saying: 'I'm tired of taking care of people and I'm not going to take care of you.' Jim expressed guilt and immediately thought he was the root of the problem. The session was rough and again I felt unable to contain all the anger and pain. At the end, Fay refused a hug or consoling word from anyone in the group.

Having listened attentively to the description, the supervisor asked: 'What do you feel like doing?'

'I want her to leave me alone,' the therapist cried. 'I want her to break off our relationship. I need so much less anger in my life. I want easier, gentler, less wounded clients. I feel pushed to my limits, all the pieces of my peaceful vacation blowing up in my face.'

'She seems very powerful,' said the supervisor.

'Who?' asked the therapist.

'Fay. Your client.'

'She is.'

'Who is she?' questioned the supervisor.

'She's all the stuff on the other side of my peace. She's the demands, the threats, the double binds, the female,' answered the therapist.

Commentary

At this point, the therapist appeared to be as needy as the client. In working through the countertransference, the supervisor pointed out that Fay serves an important purpose for the therapist. When he returns from vacation in a peaceful role, she is there to remind him to heed the other side. She is the counterrole, the one he tries so hard to push away. If he does not heed the part of himself that is wounded and demanding, the peace that he so greatly desires is truly threatened. If he cannot integrate the female part of himself that is so much a dark, demanding figure (see Landy 1996a), he cannot find a way to play out the lighter quality of his male being.

'I know all this yin/yang stuff,' the therapist told his supervisor, a woman.

She responded, 'In your head, yes. You know how Fay plays out the counterrole and how you will predictably react by fantasizing that she will break off the therapeutic relationship. You know how this scenario has been played out many times in your life, particularly with wounded and abused women who demand too much of you. You are thrust in the role of victim who needs so desperately to escape, and she is your tormentor who can rip you apart like a mythological maenad. All this you know – your role, her counterrole. You even know of this struggle internally. But where is your helper? Where is the guide?'

'I think you are my guide,' said the therapist tentatively.

'You think?' she responded.

'Yes.'

'But you are not sure?' asked the supervisor.

'I am not sure.'

This dialogue continued for a while until the supervisor asked the therapist: 'What do you need in a guide?'

Even though the therapist recognized this as a question about qualities of roles, he tried to answer from his heart: 'I need wisdom. Wisdom above all. But it has to go along with something else ... Care, I think, the ability to see the other person and to be there with him, to accept him uncritically. I need tolerance and patience and I need presence.'

'Presence?' questioned the supervisor.

'The ability to be present with me,' said the therapist, 'without distraction.'

'Is there such a figure inside you?' she continued.

'There is a wise part of me to whom I can turn for understanding. And there is a caring part of me that is able to help others and to be there for them. Sometimes I even allow this part to care for me. But it is hard to integrate the two qualities into one guide.'

'Is that what you'd like your guide to be – wise and caring?' asked the supervisor.

'Oh, yes, definitely,' responded the therapist.

'How does the wise, caring guide go along with the other two roles – victim and tormentor?' she asked.

The therapist responded: 'The wise part of the guide understands that the wounded part of me brought me into the healing profession in the first place. It helps me empathize with my wounded clients. The wise part also understands that I am my own tormentor, especially when I feel most wounded. This part, in its wisdom, could help me better understand the dynamics between the roles of victim and tormentor. But understanding isn't enough. That's where the caring part comes in. I understand my issues well enough. But I need to know what to do with that understanding. The caring guide, I think, helps transform the dynamic. Because I can learn to care for myself, I don't have to identify so deeply with my wounded clients. They are threats to themselves, not to me. If I can care more for myself, I will acknowledge the presence of the self-tormentor who loves to feed upon the wounded, vulnerable part of my psyche. But I will not allow it to cloud my sense of self-worth and power. I am powerful because I care for myself and trust that my clients can learn to take care of themselves. The caring guide leads me to that awareness just as the wise guide helps me understand the interplay of role and counterrole. When I can put the two qualities together, I feel pretty integrated.'

Commentary

This dialogue addresses an application of the first part of the role model, that concerning role–counterrole–guide within the therapist. The therapist struggles to work through an internal process as it parallels the internal process of his client. The supervisor functions to help the therapist understand and perhaps transform his intrapsychic dynamics even as she points out the parallels with the dilemma of the client. As the therapist becomes stronger, he is able to better trust the strength of his client. Ultimately, it is not necessary for him to care for her, but to trust that she can care for herself. With this trust, she then becomes a mirror in which the therapist sees himself as strong, as capable of taking care of himself. Through this mirror, the therapist can discover another way to integrate the scary, out-of-control female part of his psyche. Normally, one thinks of the therapist as a mirror for the client. In this instance, we see that the client can also become a mirror for the therapist. The therapist presents the guide as a fairly intact structure within his personality. But in the tangles of the therapeutic process, will it hold up?

Second dialogue, concerning the client

The following dialogue addresses an application of the second part of the role model, that which pertains to an understanding of the client's internal dynamics of role–counterrole–guide.

'Tell me about Fay,' said the supervisor.

'In which way?' asked the therapist.

'Subjectively. How is she like you?'

'Well, I think it has to do with trying to live with feelings of unworthiness and being afraid that the other side is not available,' said the therapist.

'What is the other side?' asked the supervisor.

'It's what I said before – the side that feels worthy of love and care.'

The supervisor continued, 'Is that side available to her?'

'It is,' said the therapist. 'I have worked long and hard with her to find that side. She has played it out expressively in dozens of ways – verbally, in movement, drawing. But she loses it so easily. The primary role of victim is so big.'

'And you become the victimizer?'

'I do,' responded the therapist. 'I have to be very careful. There are predictable periods like when I go on vacation.'

'Who do you then become for her?' she asked.

'Her tormentor. Her mother and father and siblings and all those who have humiliated her and robbed her of her self-respect and worth. I become the counterrole.'

The supervisor then asked, 'Can you help her when you are cast in the counterrole?'

'I had thought so,' responded the therapist, 'through playing out some of the issues with her and helping her hold on to her role of worthy and lovable adult. I have even tried to do this in a distanced way – through fictional stories, through sand-play and drawing. She enjoys drawing most of all. But often it doesn't work. She needs to stay on a more direct emotional level. She needs more of reality, less of fantasy. She gets confused when I take on the qualities of the counterrole. She needs me to be the guide, the same kind of guide that I need for myself – wise and caring. I would reverse the formula in her case – caring and wise.'

'But can you always be the guide for her?'

'Not always, of course not,' replied the therapist. 'I get caught up in my own inabilities to guide myself through her cycles of pain and anger.'

'What happens then?' asked the supervisor.

'I try to bring her back to her guide,' he responded.

'Her inner guide?' she asked.

'It can be hard to get her there,' said the therapist. 'When the wounded victim part of herself is very large and all possible helpers are seen as tormentors, that guide becomes quite small. I remind her about Mrs Smith, the good mother in her childhood.'

'Does that help?' asked the supervisor.

'It usually does,' said the therapist. 'She is such a grounding figure. She is a reminder that a good mother can exist, has existed. It gives her hope. And it turns her inward, because she remembers that she can be kinder to herself. She can do for herself what Mrs Smith had done for her.'

'What did Mrs Smith do for her?' asked the supervisor.

'It's not clear,' responded the therapist. 'Maybe when she was abandoned by her father and mother and forced to care for the family, maybe she turned to Mrs Smith. And maybe Mrs Smith took her in or gave her some extra cash or said a kind word. Maybe when her mother beat her or humiliated her, Mrs Smith would bring her home in the afternoon and feed her cakes as she sat quietly in the living room. And maybe Mrs Smith never actually did these things at all. But she was there as an antidote to the pain, somewhere across the street, treating her own children kindly. This, in itself, might have been enough.'

'So,' continued the supervisor, 'you have come home from a long vacation, and Fay is angry at you. Her life is not going well. Her hurt and anger spills out not only on you, but also on members of her dramatherapy group. You have the opportunity to help facilitate some action in group and in individual sessions. You are aware that her behaviour affects your own sense of stability. What do you do?'

'I come to you,' said the therapist, with a touch of irony.

'Am I the wise and caring guide?' asked the supervisor.

'I wish you were,' replied the therapist.

'Then I am not?' she asked.

'You are wise enough not to tell me what to do, and you are caring enough to believe that I can find the answer myself. I guess I have to do the same for her, right?'

'What do you mean?' asked the supervisor.

'I mean,' said the therapist, 'not telling her what to do or interpreting what she is feeling, and caring enough to believe that she is capable of solving her own problem.'

The supervisor continued: 'Is she capable of this?'

'She knows,' answered the therapist, 'the parts of herself that need to be put together – the wounded victim, the adult worthy of love and care, and the caring, loving guide. She loses the last two when she feels most abandoned.

When I go away for more than a week, it must feel like a terrible abandonment. Maybe I just have to remind her that the good counterrole and the good guide are not lost at all. Even though I go away, even though the actual Mrs Smith may have died years ago or may be more fantasy than reality, Fay still has internalized both figures of good therapist and good mother. I need to reinforce the idea that she is not one thing – a mass of pain and suffering, a tormented soul who has been abused and who will always be abused. She is also all the things on the other side, and she is someone capable of negotiating the voyage from one side to the other. She is capable of holding the three together.'

Commentary

In the above dialogue, I have demonstrated some of the issues involved in helping the therapist view the intrapsychic dynamics of role– counterrole– guide within the client. In applying the role model, it should be noted that the therapist also becomes entangled in the interplay of roles and needs to draw upon his own internal cast of characters for guidance, even as he turns to an outside supervisor. I note that the therapist does not respond in a direct way to the supervisor's question: 'Is she (the client) capable of this (solving her own problem)?' He seems to be too focused upon what he can do for her rather than trusting that she can move toward a more independent position. The therapist has not fully incorporated the words of the wise and caring guide as clearly articulated by the supervisor. Without the tacit understanding between therapist and client that independent decisions are possible, further entanglement is inevitable.

Third dialogue, concerning the relationship of client and therapist

Having looked at ways of conceiving the inner dynamics of the therapist and the client, we turn more specifically to their interpersonal relationship. Given that the therapist understands many of the intrapsychic dynamics, what should be his next steps?

The supervisor continued: 'Let's get back to the group. The session has ended badly and you feel unable to contain the pain and anger. You feel like breaking off from Fay, but recognize that she has provoked many of your own issues. In reality, you will stay with the process and try to move it forward. You have not lost the ability to guide but fear that Fay has lost a positive and hopeful vision. What do you do?'

'I am worried about her,' responded the therapist. 'I call Fay on the phone, urging her to stay with her feelings, assuring her that I will not abandon her no matter how hard she pushes.'

'And who do you become for her when you do this?' asked the supervisor.

'The good mother, maybe, or, in Winnicott's (1971) terms, the *good enough* guide.'

'How does she respond?' asked the supervisor.

'In silence at first,' said the therapist. 'I just let it be. We make another appointment. At the end of the conversation she thanks me for calling.'

'How do you explain her thanks?' asked the supervisor.

'Well,' said the therapist, 'I have done something that her mother never would have done. She wants to believe me.'

'Are you being honest?' pressed the supervisor.

'With Fay?' responded the therapist.

'And with yourself,' said the supervisor.

'Yes. I'm committed to her as long as it takes,' said the therapist. 'And yes, I am also committed to making peace with the part of me that pushes away painful feelings.'

'Can Fay help you discover that peace?' asked the supervisor.

'Yes. In that way she becomes my guide. It's complex. When she is in the role of the needy one, I become the helper, a counterrole. When she is in the role of the angry one, I sometimes take on the counterrole of victim and want the whole relationship to end. But as you suggest, her anger also guides me back to my own pain.'

'It seems like your roles are dependent upon hers,' observed the supervisor.

'To some extent, yes. But that's the nature of this relationship. We are dependent upon one another. We give each other another perspective, another side. Isn't this what you mean by role and counterrole?' asked the therapist.

'Yes, but I am concerned about the dependency,' said the supervisor.

'Why? I think it happens all the time in therapy. Fay is dependent upon my absence and presence, my holding and withholding, and when she touches on my issues, I become dependent upon her. I need her to find a way out of the cycle of pain and anger, of the victim role, so I can then be more of a guide for her.'

'Or should it be the other way around?' asked the supervisor.

'What do you mean?' asked the therapist, genuinely baffled.

'She needs you to find a way out of your own problems. She is the client. She pays you for your services. When a patient with an infection goes to the doctor, should she have to wait for the doctor to cure his own illness before prescribing effective medication?'

'I am not a doctor with magic pills,' said the therapist.

'What are you?' asked the supervisor.

'A different kind of healer,' said the therapist. 'I bear my own wounds and they sometimes get entangled in the treatment of others who have similar wounds.'

'And when your wounds get entangled with Fay's?' asked the supervisor.

'We both get lost,' said the therapist, 'no counterroles, no guides, just the loss.'

The supervisor pressed on: 'And then what happens?'

'Dependency. I worry about her and call her up frantically to assure her that I will be there for her for ever and ever. I push away my revulsion at her acting out and her endless boring stories of violation. I succumb to her cries for help. I will not allow her to guide her own destiny or to solve her own problems. "I am there," I tell her, "I will rescue you. You do not have to do it for yourself." And so I fail Fay and in doing so, I fail myself. We guide each other into the dependency of victim and victimizer.'

'And which role do you play?' asked the supervisor.

'Both,' answered the therapist.

'And Fay?'

'Both,' said the therapist again.

'And the guide?' questioned the supervisor.

'In the moments of dependency, there is no guide,' answered the therapist. 'He or she, or whomever it is, can only appear when I can say to Fay: "That's it! No more. I will no longer agree to endlessly support the wounded parts of you." Then maybe I can find that guide of mine – not quite the same one as the wise and caring guide. Maybe more of the kind that is tough and independent. Maybe more of the kind that feels worthwhile, valuable, intact.'

'And when you've found it?' asked the supervisor.

'When I've found it and taken it on,' said the therapist, 'I can model those qualities for Fay, just as you try to model them for me.'

'Which qualities?' asked the supervisor. 'Can you tell me again?'

'Independence and self worth – those are the main ones,' responded the therapist. 'That's what I want my guide to have. That's what I want Fay to discover from her own guide.'

Commentary

Throughout this dialogue client and therapist are locked into a dependent relationship, based upon a mutual fear of being unworthy of love and care. One's counterrole is dependent upon another's taking on of a particular role. This dynamic is played out in many ways. When Fay becomes the needy one, the therapist becomes the helper. When Fay is the angry one, the therapist becomes the victim. When the therapist becomes fearful or frustrated, Fay becomes the victim. When Fay becomes the victim, the therapist becomes the victimizer.

It could be that whenever client and therapist work on a deep level, a degree of dependency is unavoidable. In dramatic terms, every protagonist requires an antagonist. In most dramatic struggles, some form of conflict is present. And therapy is such a struggle. However, an effective psychotherapeutic process is noted by the shift from dependency to independence and, finally, interdependence, a state where each person feels intact and committed to dialoguing with the other.

In terms of the role model, there needs to be a point, after struggling with the role confusions of transference and countertransference, when the client and therapist recognize their independent qualities and are able to play them out in a balanced way. Beyond that is a further goal. Once both recognize their separateness, they can envision a connection based upon their difference. In their interdependence, the client and therapist create a meaningful dyad, a protagonist and antagonist, a role and counterrole. At this moment, both are able to experience an internal balance between discrepant parts of themselves that can be held together with the help of a guide.

One way of conceptualizing the function of the guide is to help move the therapist and client from a state of dependence to independence to interdependence. As we have seen in the above dialogue, each at times guides the other. Each, too, turns to an inner guide for the strength needed to move beyond a dependent relationship. In seeking further guidance, the therapist turns to the supervisor. In examining this relationship and connecting it back to the client, we move to the final piece of the role model.

Fourth dialogue, concerning the relationship of client, therapist and supervisor

At some point in the supervisory sessions, still focused upon the theme of dependency, the therapist portrayed himself as servant of three masters – his client, himself and his supervisor. In response, the supervisor asked: 'How do you serve me?'

'I come to you in humility and ignorance,' replied the therapist. 'You are strong and wise. I come to you with questions.'

'But,' countered the supervisor, 'I am the one who has been asking the questions.'

'Yes,' replied the therapist. 'So I serve the questioner.'

'If I am the questioner,' asked the supervisor, 'how do you serve me?'

'By taking on the counterrole and trying to answer your questions,' said the therapist.

'Is that servile?' continued the supervisor.

'The kind of servant I play is not servile,' said the therapist. 'It is more obedient.'

'And what is it about me that you obey?' she asked.

'I obey your game of question and answer,' he responded. 'I obey your power. You are a "supervisor", one who has a superior kind of vision. I accept that.'

'Do you?' she pressed.

'Not always,' he answered. 'Sometimes I see you as vulnerable as myself and as ignorant. Sometimes I see you as judgemental.'

'How?' asked the supervisor.

'Like judging me for becoming so entangled with Fay, for not foreseeing her pain when I returned from vacation and buckling at the knees at her anger, for not containing her feelings better in a dramatic form, for calling her up on the phone and being too weak to resist her cries for help and for a thousand other reasons.'

'You don't tell me this,' said the supervisor.

'Right,' responded the therapist. 'Because sometimes I don't trust you enough to hold my negative feelings.'

'You sound a bit like Fay,' countered the supervisor.

'How do you mean?' asked the therapist.

'Fay might say the same thing to you,' she said.

'Yes,' he said.

'When does she doubt your power of super vision?' asked the supervisor.

'When she feels most vulnerable,' replied the therapist, 'and I represent another of her tormentors.'

'Yes. So who am I for you?' asked the supervisor.

'Many things,' responded the therapist. 'Not really a master. And as you are not a master, I am not a servant. You feel more like my therapist. Or when I question your care and suspect your judgement, you feel like my mother. But you are not really any of these things – master, mother, therapist. I guess guide would be the most accurate. Your questions guide me.'

'Where do you need to be guided?' she asked.

'Back to my role as therapist,' he replied. 'Back to my client who needs my guidance to help her find a way to become more independent. Back to my own sense of worthiness and independence, to those parts of myself that can help a client and that can be helped by a supervisor.'

The supervisor then added, uncharacteristically: 'I think the guide is the key part. It is the piece that ultimately connects us all.'

'How do you mean?' questioned the therapist.

'On one level, I guide you and you guide your client,' she said.

'Who guides you?' asked the therapist.

'Well, you do and even Fay does in a more distanced way,' she replied.

'How?' asked the therapist.

'You guide me into the messy territory of pain and anger which is hard to deal with for all of us – clients, therapists, supervisors.'

'Isn't a guide supposed to help you out of the mess?' asked the therapist.

'Before you can get out,' she replied, 'I think you need to get in pretty deep. A guide also leads you to the muck. By bringing me rich material and being brave enough to look at your part in the drama, you lead me to invest a lot of myself. I get my hands dirty and when it all seems overwhelming to me, I speak to my own supervisor. Fay has become so vivid to me. In understanding her, I learn to serve you better.'

'Then you are my servant?' asked the therapist.

'We all reverse roles,' responded the supervisor.

'Role and counterrole and guide?' said the therapist.

'Yes,' responded the supervisor. 'Client and therapist and supervisor playing all the parts of role, counterrole and guide. We are linked, held together by the pain and searching for a way to move beyond it, for a way to help one another even as we experience our own inability to help ourselves. I think we are all looking for the same thing – connection, integration, acceptance, the ability to hold contraries together – call them female and male, darkness and light, powerlessness and power, role and counterrole. And I think we are all in need of a guide to help us make that connection.'

'The guide as supervisor,' added the therapist.

'Yes, one with super vision,' responded the supervisor, a touch of irony in her voice.

'A god,' offered the therapist, tentatively.

'Not a god. A person of this time and place, a vulnerable person …'

'What about Mrs Smith?' the therapist asked.

'… And a persona,' added the supervisor, 'one who is not necessarily flesh and blood, but who stands in for someone real and corrects the real person's painful ways. Mrs Smith, as guide, gives Fay the corrective for growing up with an abusive mother. You give her the same when you are able to find your sense of independence. Maybe I give you some sort of corrective, too.'

'I think our time is up,' said the therapist playfully, as if he were the one in charge.

'Yes,' said the supervisor, 'for now our time is up.'

'Thank you for allowing me to ask you some questions,' the therapist said. 'I liked listening for a change to someone outside myself.'

Commentary

At the end of their dialogue, the supervisor becomes more philosophical, reminding the therapist of the complexities of the role relationships. Also, she subtly draws his attention to a primary goal of dramatherapy (see Landy 1993), which is to hold contraries together. Throughout this chapter, I have emphasized that all players in the therapeutic drama need to do the same, that is, to discover a way to live within their contradictions of role and counterrole, and to enlist a guide figure to help reach that goal.

And at the end of the dialogue, therapist and supervisor become more playful with one another, the therapist even taking on the role of supervisor and calling the time. Their connection seems quite intact at this point. Each has said his/her piece and each sees the other as an independent person. In fact, they exist in an interdependent relationship as they end their work. Neither has unrealistic expectations of the other – the supervisor will not play god, the therapist will not play servant. They are separate yet connected. They have shared a meaningful experience around the case of Fay. They are aware of their separateness and also aware enough of their feelings to play with each other. This interdependence serves as a good model for the therapeutic bond of Fay and the therapist.

Conclusions

Through the supervision process the therapist recognizes that he needs to listen to those persons outside and those personae inside that will help him better understand the dynamics of the healing process. In this chapter, I have conceptualized the dynamics in terms of a model of role–counterrole–guide. As we have seen, this is an interactive model on two levels, interpersonal and intrapsychic. Within the process of supervision, each participant – client, therapist and supervisor – aims to integrate qualities of the others. And each participant does so by activating a particular part of the psyche, a role, discovering its other side, a counterrole, and locating a guide that can hold the two together in a meaningful way.

Although all participants in the supervisory process are defined by their specific qualities and functions, they engage often in role reversals. Their role definitions are both fixed and fluid. They are fixed in the sense that the client seeks help from a therapist who, in turn, seeks help from a supervisor. They are fluid in the sense that all aim toward the interdependence of role, counterrole and guide, and any participant can assume the status of role, causing the others to regroup as counterrole and guide.

Supervision from a dramatherapy role perspective, like supervision from a psychodynamic perspective, takes into consideration the many inevitabilities and consequences of transference and countertransference. Transference and countertransference are therefore viewed as dramatic phenomena in that a person is as much defined by his personae as by his self. In untangling the complexity of perceptions and accepting the separate qualities and functions of each role, all are then able to move toward the goal of integrating the three. In the end, if the treatment has been successful, the client will see himself as the one who needed help and was willing to accept help from a guide. And he will see himself, finally, as one who can ultimately help himself even when his countertendencies to feel helpless arise. In the end, the therapist will see himself as a helper who also needs help when he feels helpless. And in the end, the supervisor will see himself as a guide whose wisdom is based upon his ability not to know the answers, but to ask good enough questions that can lead all three role-players back to themselves. In the end, all three are separate but interconnected. That which has been transferred onto the other is taken back without diminishing the power of the other.

At the end of Shakespeare's play, Lear takes back the role of father to mourn the loss of his daughter, Cordelia. In giving her the love she deserved all along, he has, finally but tragically, undone the twisted transference. Over and above the physical destruction lies the spiritual power of redemption.

Few human beings in their lifetimes will play out the scope of a Shakespearian drama, but many will seek ways to make sense of their lives and discover the territory that lies on the other side of pain. The fortunate ones will do so with the help of a guide who will surely lack super vision but may well possess a modicum of wisdom and care.

Throughout this chapter, I have offered an example of one searcher, Fay, whose journey required the help of several guides. Fay's story is emblematic of the tragic consequences of the human condition that once abused requires the skill of many to repair. Fay's story has a happy ending. With the help of her guides, she was able to integrate role and counterrole effectively enough and proceed, however cautiously, with her life. As for the therapist and supervisor, their stories are unfinished. Like Pirandello's characters in search of an author, they await other clients to provide meaning. They await other guides.

References

Landy, R. (1993) *Persona and Performance – The Meaning of Role in Drama, Therapy and Everyday Life.* New York: The Guilford Press, and London: Jessica Kingsley Publishers.

Landy, R. (1994) *Drama Therapy: Concepts, Theories and Practices.* 2nd edition. Springfield, IL: Charles C. Thomas.

Landy, R. (1996a) 'In search of the muse.' In R. Landy (ed) *Essays in Drama Therapy: The Double Life.* London: Jessica Kingsley Publishers.

Landy, R. (ed) (1996b) *Essays in Drama Therapy: The Double Life.* London: Jessica Kingsley Publishers.

Winnicott, D.W. (1971) *Playing and Reality.* London: Tavistock.

PART III

Supervision with Dramatherapy in Different Fields

CHAPTER 6

Supervision of Crisis Intervention Teams

The Myth of the Saviour

Mooli Lahad

Introduction

In the present chapter, I attempt to document observations from my experience in crisis intervention and in the supervision of professional helpers who are involved in intervention immediately after and following a disaster with victims of emotional trauma. 'Helpers' in this chapter refers to psychological team members intervening in a crisis/disaster.

The purpose of the chapter is to offer new understanding to the phenomena, looking at them from a dramatherapeutic perspective. What I will discuss is what results from the lack of differentiation rituals, protection and initiation ceremonies and metaphoric myths. I shall also apply psychosocial and anthropological explanations to the understanding of these phenomena. These reflections are based on my observations as a supervisor of professional helpers soon after their contact with victims and survivors of disaster and their family members, as well as my personal involvement in such incidents. In a further step, I will present ways of working in supervision with ritual, story and myth in order to restore the affected helper's balance.

Let us first look at the term 'compassion fatigue' and its meaning. The term was suggested by Figley (1995) as an alternative to the earlier concept of secondary traumatic stress disorder (McCann 1990). Both terms describe the influence on mental health professionals of the therapeutic encounter or intervention with victims of disaster suffering post-traumatic stress disorder

(PTSD). In compassion fatigue, symptoms resembling the physiological, emotional and cognitive symptoms of victims appear among those who administer help to them. In 3 per cent to 7 per cent of cases, these may be so severe that the professionals themselves develop PTSD, with all its long-term implications (Hodgkinson and Stewart 1991).

The subject of emotional burnout among mental health professionals has been widely researched (Freudenbeyer 1974; Maslach 1982; Maslach and Jackson 1981; Pines 1993). This literature describes a continuous process of burnout, composed of three principal components: emotional, physiological, and mental (Pines and Aronson 1988). However, burnout develops gradually, though there are advance warnings expressed in emotional fatigue, irritability, difficulty in concentrating, and other physiological and mental phenomena. In contrast, compassion fatigue may appear suddenly, with no previous signs (Figley 1995). In addition, Figley (1995) notes that, unlike with mental burnout, here there is a strong sense of helplessness, confusion, a feeling of being cut off from support and psychosomatic symptoms similar to those of survivors or victims. However, recovery is also usually very speedy.

The term 'compassion fatigue' was first coined by Joinson (1992) and later adopted by Figley. *Webster's Encyclopedic Unabridged Dictionary of the English Language* (1989) defines 'compassion' as 'sympathetic consciousness of others' distress together with a desire to alleviate it'.

Who are likely victims of compassion fatigue?

Figley (1995) indicates two major components that lead to compassion fatigue: empathy and exposure. Without both empathy and exposure, there is a low probability of developing compassion fatigue. In principle, according to Figley and other researchers, work with trauma victims (survivors, family relatives and the injured) subjects helpers and those engaged in intervention to extremely forceful exposure to trauma-inducing factors. This vulnerability is attributed to several causes:

1. Empathy is a central instrument in helping and assessing injury and planning the intervention programme. Harris (1995) claims that empathy is the key factor in the 'penetration' of a traumatic event among crisis counsellors.

2. Most of those involved in intervention have experienced traumatic events in their lives. Because those who administer help after trauma

cope with a variety of events, at some time they inevitably encounter some that are similar to the trauma in their own lives.

3.   The helpers may have unresolved traumas of their own.

4.   The encounter with children in trauma has a particularly strong effect on the helpers (Beaton and Murphy 1995).

Understanding the context of disaster and the vulnerability of the helpers

The following discussion is based on my own observations as supervisor and interventionist and on discussions held with professional helpers, who offer psychosocial intervention in Israel (Tel Aviv, Jerusalem, Kiryat Shemona), the states of former Yugoslavia and Northern Ireland.

Inability to prepare or to set the stage

Disasters take place without prior warning. They can happen at any moment, anywhere, and to anyone. In light of the lack of warning, on the one hand, and the massive, intense penetration of the event into our lives (including direct television broadcasts from the disaster site, voices and primary witnesses), helpers today are immediately exposed to the disasters that they are meant to go to. Their daily ability to control the setting and the staging is shattered as they are being called to act without appropriate 'warm-up'.

TELECOMMUNICATIONS AND THE ROLE OF MENTAL HEALTH PROFESSIONALS:
AN ANTHROPOLOGICAL APPROACH TO THE MYTH
SURROUNDING CALAMITIES TODAY

Until the Gulf War in 1991, civilian mental health professionals did not have much direct and immediate exposure to real-time disaster situations. First of all, the approach was that psychosocial helpers met the victims at emergency relief centres, or in the clinic. Only in rare situations were they asked to help families at the cemetery or in their homes. In other words, there was a physical distance from the site of the disaster. Second, as telecommunications technology required a studio, it took time to broadcast a disaster, not to mention print a paper, and thus helpers were spared some of the most upsetting immediate sights. Ethical limitations adopted by the journalists' associations, as well as government control over electronic media, also prevented some of the pictures from being broadcast. Thus professional helpers working with trauma victims were exposed at a distance of both time and place, almost exclusively to descriptions of the horrors by the victims with whom they worked or to the written reports in newspapers or photographs on television and in the movies.

After the Gulf War, it was decided, in Israel, that civilian mental health professionals (social workers and psychologists) would also come to the scenes of disaster and work according to Salmon's (1919) proximity, immediacy and expectancy (PIE) model, which had been adopted many years earlier by Israel's defence forces' mental health units (Solomon 1993). The idea was that immediate intervention, close to the site of the event, including conveyance of expectations for recovery, would reduce the incidence of post-traumatic stress disorder among victims, survivors, witnesses and family relatives. The psychosocial team was also expected to support the rescue workers, whom research indicates as prone to develop PTSD (Hodgkinson and Stewart 1991).

This intervention, which is meant to take place alongside or at the end of the rescue operation, exposes psychosocial helpers to the horrific sights of a disaster on a much greater scale. Furthermore, the CNN model of electronic media, of reaching the site of the event, quickly setting up equipment, and broadcasting live without editing (made possible by modern technology) also became prevalent.

Thus the care-giver who comes into contact with victims in proximity – both physical and temporal – to the disaster is exposed, even before reaching the area, to the sights and sounds of the horror. He or she has often 'seen' and 'knows' more than the victims themselves. This almost 'real' exposure of the helpers, prior to even being on site, makes even minimal distancing difficult and leads to an immediate identification with the survivors' descriptions not as a listener but as an equal and sometimes more informed partner, with pictures of the event bringing arousal of strong emotions. This increases the degree of empathy, identification and assimilation of the event by the helper. The fact that these scenes are being broadcast over and over again are often described by helpers as having a semi-hypnotic effect on them, drawing them to look at them over and over again; much like a nightmare that keeps coming at them, making them feel as if 'they were actors/participants and sometimes "invisible" survivors' of the same incident.

LACK OF RITUALS OF ADMISSION AS BOUNDARY SETTING PROVISION

In the daily routine of a mental health professional, there are several rituals that enable differentiation and protection against the penetration of loaded or morbid information into his or her life. These rituals are very helpful in the process of 'getting into role'. An important ritual is the 'intake', the first stage of contact with the client. In this ritual, the care-giver informs the client that he or she will do the interviewing, in order to collect data that will help the helpers and the client to understand his or her own situation/condition. The therapist records the client's answers. Thus a boundary is drawn between the two. The ritual of acquaintance may or may not be limited in time; it may spread over one or more intake meetings. However, even if there is only one such meeting, the study of the material (after the client has gone home) by the helper helps him or her conceptualize the client's problems and thus differentiate between the helper and the client.

No less important is the ritual of setting the time – an element that is usually in the sole control of the helper even if the needs of the client are taken into account when determining the time. In this ritual, the helper controls a central component, namely the length and time of the meeting. A related ritual is that of '50 sacred minutes'.

Of the same importance is the ritual of the place. This is totally in the control of the helper. It is usually his office and is designed or at least partially decorated by him, thus making it his or her territory. And there are also other rituals such as greeting, saying goodbye, etc.

Immediate intervention in a disaster site precludes the use of these rituals. There is no time for an in-depth anamnesis; on the contrary, the professional literature indicates that historic connection with the immediate distress (acute stress reaction – ASR) and post-traumatic (PTSD) situations are counterindications of recovery (Witstom 1989). Thus a central mechanism of the differentiation process is eliminated.

Neither does the helper decide where the intervention will take place. Today, secondary interventions may begin near the incident site, at the mortuary as has happened in Israel since 1995 and lately in Northern Ireland following the Omagh massacre in August 1998. It may include visits to grieving families in their home, neighbourhood, or in the victims' school.

Even the length of the 'performance', which is a crucial aspect of every play, is undefined. The work shift can be 18 and more hours. Sometimes the intervention takes days, with meetings every day or even several times during the day, and the work is always very intensive.

In the time close to the event, Kfir (1990) recomends daily encounters with the victim(s), sometimes for several hours. Thus availability of helpers and intensity of contact without the appropriate rituals exposes them more forcefully to the intensity of the disaster.

GEOGRAPHIC PROXIMITY AND PSYCHOSOCIAL PROXIMITY
(THE LACK OF DISTANCING)

Psychosocial crisis helpers are often called upon to provide intervention at locations that are geographically close to their place of work or residence. This proximity creates immediate identification and a sense of being a 'near miss' – they could have been the victims, yet they are called to help. This makes it very difficult for the helpers to maintain distance from the event and its immediate threatening meaning to themselves and the well-being of their dear ones. Because the site is the helper's natural setting, going home may expose the helper time and again (that is even when the event has ended) to the scene and experience, and thus may weaken the defence mechanism by continuously reminding him that 'this could have happened to me'. This is called geographic proximity.

Similarity between the victims or their relatives to the helper's life and sometimes to his or her peer group or family is called psychosocial proximity and can also create great difficulty. For instance, the disaster at Dizengoff Shopping Center (Tel Aviv, Israel, April 1996) and the disaster at Apropos café (Tel Aviv, Israel, March 1997) occurred in areas that were familiar to most of the helpers. The victims were similar in age and socioeconomic status to those who came to help them (in the Dizengoff Shopping Center disaster the aspect of injury and death of children increased vulnerability and in the Apropos café disaster the victims were three social workers – friends of the helpers).

Thus the possible similarity between the helper and the victim, considering the random and chance occurrence of the disasters and the geographic proximity noted above, reduces the important aspect of distance and creates greater chance of identification with the victims, and absorption of their story as 'part of me'.

Identification and countertransference: the imprint of death

Identification and countertransference are well-known aspects of the therapeutic process which have been discussed widely, both in training and supervision of therapists in general and with crisis interventionists. However, as explained here, when the care-givers come into contact with disaster victims these two phenomena arise with particular intensity and take a heavy toll on those providing intervention.

In their work routine, mental health professionals make a point of coping directly with transference either by direct confrontation with the client or through other ways of processing it. However, when helpers meet with a survivor (or family members) who say, 'you remind me so much of my son', or 'you are like a relative of mine', it is difficult for them to deal with it or work through it as transference. In fact, it is typically reported that this is like 'a blow at the soft spot of my stomach; it makes me feel significant to them, on the one hand, and places a tremendous emotional burden on me, on the other hand.' And the helper goes along with it, trying to fulfil an imaginary (countertransferential) role of family member or friend.

The emotional burden of identifying with the victim is often expressed in the development of intense, deep relations with the survivors, victims and their families. It is expressed in frequent home visits and telephone calls beyond the scope of the intervention or therapy; the helpers explain that 'it is so important to them; they need me so much.'

This phenomenon is related to a concept which I call 'the imprint of death' of the disaster. The survivor, victim or family member becomes very attached, like an imprint, to the image of the first 'lifesaver' they happen to meet. The helper goes through a similar process of clinging to the victim. It is often expressed in undertaking tasks that he or she does not usually do for clients, thus deviating from work definition. S/he spends irregular work hours with the victim, calls all sorts of agencies on behalf of the client. S/he has great difficulty parting from the victims, family members and survivors and does many 'little services' for them.

Other expressions of the identification process are the development of physical symptoms similar to those suffered by the victims, such as physical pain or intense anger toward institutions, organizations and service providers with whom these professionals usually co-operate. Some helpers report dreams about the event or about the victims and their families, as well as difficulty in concentrating and apathy toward daily life (all phenomena similar to grieving and mild depression).

How soon does compassion fatigue develop? I have seen it developing within hours. Helpers are exhausted yet refuse to go home saying, 'I can't leave these people now I am so significant to them. They will not be able to make contact with someone else.' Or helpers will find themselves calling the families on the phone to see how they are, despite the fact that they have just seen them for a few hours and the regular worker has already taken over the 'case'. On other occasions helpers disclosed to me that they became so attached to the family there wasn't one day without them visiting the family 'just passing by to say hello'.

In one incident the helper, a very experienced social worker, learned at the mortuary that the family had just moved house and as it happened did not have any furniture in their living room. When she discovered their new place was near her son's flat, she took her son's furniture and brought it to the family 'just for the seven days of mourning'.

But the most common symptoms are those of physical aches, pains and changes in appetite, sleep disturbances, moods, loss of interest in daily activities and most of all the routine workload of the office.

These symptoms resemble very much the phenomenon of 'combat fatigue'. That is, it develops quickly and the physical and emotional symptoms generally pass after three to four days, although the full return to routine often takes a longer time. We shall discuss what may help the process of recovery later. The next part of this chapter suggests another perspective to this phenomenon based on a poetic and metaphoric approach.

Humpty Dumpty, the saviour myth; or understanding the compelling urges to put all the pieces together again

Humpty Dumpty sat on a wall
Humpty Dumpty had a great fall
All the king's horses and all the king's men
Couldn't put Humpty together again.

Figure 6.1 Humpty Dumpty

The wish to put Humpty together again is a great example of the hero's or saviour's urge to help – not just to intervene but to reassemble the pieces and put them exactly as they were when new. This wish definitely plays a major role in the development of compassion fatigue. But what is the interplay between Humpty and the king's men, the helpers?

Disaster creates a sudden break in our continuities (Omer and Inbar 1991; Winnicott 1971). These continuities are the bridges that we build for ourselves in order to ensure that yesterday will predict tomorrow, that we are stable, that life is coherent, that the world is a decent, logical, safe place, and that people who are good have good things happen to them.

Disaster breaks our faith in a good world and confronts us suddenly with chaos. Typical reactions are: 'I don't understand what is happening' (cognitive discontinuity); 'I don't know myself' (historical discontinuity); 'I don't know what to do, how to act here, what it is to be a bereaved person/an injured and wounded person' (role discontinuity); 'Where is everyone, I am so alone, where are my loved ones?' (social discontinuity).

In my experience, I have found that two contradicting thoughts run through the minds of victims: (1) 'This is a nightmare – any minute now I'll wake up and see that everything is as it was'; and (2) 'This will only get worse; this is the end, it is horrible, it is a disaster, it hurts more than any pain.' Because the disaster is real and actually occurred, the first thought fades quite

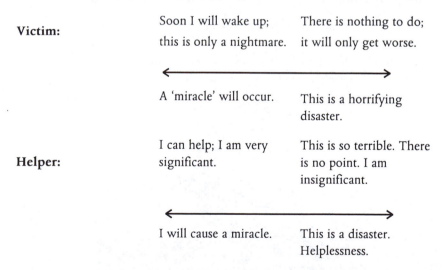

Figure 6.2

quickly and the victim often enters catastrophic thinking entertaining the idea that everything will become worse.

The tremendous need for someone from outside to organize the person, to anchor him or her in reality, to ensure that it didn't happen, who will take him or her somewhere safe, often leads some victims to cling to the care-givers with very strong emotional and physical force (the death imprint) and like Humpty to project this verbal and non-verbal existential message: 'Help me, tell me it is not true, put things together again'.

In parallel, the helper has a similar experience. On the one hand, there is tremendous commitment, with a sense of mission and a desire to help, based on the belief in his or her ability and power 'to put things together again – to stitch it up' (omnipotence); on the other hand, there is a feeling of worthlessness. This can be graphically represented as shown in Figure 6.2. The victim projects expectations of omnipotence on the helper, who is a sort of parent figure, and this meets the helper's fantasy of being an omnipotent parent.

Valent (1995) uses the term 'attachment'. I call it the parental 'magic touch', comparing the contact with survivors to a parent's calming of a small child who has been hurt. An 'adaptive attachment', crying and a call for help, lead to calming down the need for help by satisfying needs (hugging, kissing, physical contact). The unification with the attachment figure creates a sense of security, satisfaction and relief. Rutter (1991) claims that ethological theory correctly predicts that stress should enhance attachment behaviour.

According to Valent, attachment can also be directed to a father or any member of a group, and it operates among adults who too feel their vulnerability. It is the universal experience of the parental 'magic touch', the pain-relieving kiss and hug of a small child, that in my view trigger the helpers' fantasy of omnipotence. Devora Omer, an author of Hebrew children's books, describes this phenomenon in a poetic way. She called her story *The Kiss that Got Lost*. She tells about the phenomenon that once a mother's kiss was found it was like magic for the crying child and pacified him. This experience is closely connected to attachment and in my mind is at the basis of many helpers' fantasy of the ability to bring things back to where they were. Unfortunately, this phenomenon disappears when the magic of childhood ends and even then, when facing trauma or disaster, it does not often work.

The victim who projects such great helplessness, pain, and suffering 'looks' to us as helpless as a small child. The fierce desire to protect activates the fantasy of omnipotence related to the experience of the parent's 'magic touch' and makes the helper feel omnipotent. However, the failure of the 'magic' in the encounter with the victim of disaster is liable to make the helper feel helpless, empty and self-doubting. In the literature, this experience is referred to as 'impotence vs. omnipotence'. For years I had been involved in emergency intervention and this term did not seem adequate to me. One day I realized why.

Darkness over abyss: a metaphoric understanding of the helper–victim interplay.

In his recent book on traumatic stress, Van Der Kolk (1996) includes a chapter on the 'black hole of trauma', in which he presents the description of the experience of exposure to traumatic incident as being pulled into a black hole. In my encounters and observations of disaster victims and their family members, I have also often heard metaphoric descriptions, such as 'I am falling into a black hole', 'I feel as though I am diving into a black abyss', 'I am surrounded by black', or 'It is like an endless hole.'

Several years ago, in reading the Book of Genesis I had a very profound experience. I suddenly had an insight into what darkness over abyss is, the darkness experience that so many victims of traumatic incidents describe along with their plea for a glimpse of light, hope and recovery.

Let us look for a minute at the description of the experience of the encounter with 'chaos' as described in Genesis:

> And the earth was without form, and void; and the darkness was upon the face of the deep … (Genesis 1:2)

> And God said, let there be light. (Genesis 1:3)

The experience of chaos described by so many victims is well depicted by the encounter with abyss and darkness. The sudden break in the continuities that disaster victims experience increases the feeling of the destruction of order, called chaos in Genesis. This is the experience of the victim, the survivor and family members described earlier. The helpers are not at a distance, as they are 'standing' at the edge of the abyss, 'peeking into the eyes of darkness'.

Peeking into the darkness at the abyss not only involves a sense of impotence. I believe that it is also an existential confrontation with mortality, fear of death, fear of injury, and concern for your loved ones, your values and beliefs.

Further study of Genesis tells us about the establishment of order and the elimination of chaos, lending further insights into the dynamics between the helper and the victim. According to Genesis 1:3, in the confrontation of darkness and the abyss, there is a need of an omnipotent entity to bring the light. In other words, it is the encounter of the victim with chaos that triggers his/her plea for the omnipotent and to beg for light. And, in my view, vice versa. Helplessness and chaos nurture the urge for omnipotence in the helper. There is a fascinating dynamic of the 'omnipotence' of the helper, which grows stronger through the needs of the victim, a dynamic that makes the helper want to bring light, however weak and dim it might be.

However, according to the Book of Genesis, the ability to create light within darkness requires a superhuman entity. Furthermore, the process of creating order out of the chaos is gradual:

light (and the stars)
water
plants
animals
man.

Because the task of creating light is a task for the Almighty, the omnipotent (and therefore not possible for a helper), the question arises what, then, is the role of intervention?

Study of the process of the biblical creation of order led me to the realization that since the creation of light is beyond our power, perhaps to 'restore order' by reversing the sequence described in Genesis is a task possible for humans. That is, for us to be 'human'. It seems to me that this may be a clue to the help that we can give the victim. In the beginning you need to bring your 'humaneness'. Unfortunately, that has a toll. The price for being human in an impossible situation and that is in my mind what 'compassion' fatigue is.

It is interesting that when the term PTSD was first introduced in *Diagnostic and Statistic Manual of Mental Disorders*, 3rd Edition (American Psychiatric Association 1980) the authors used the concept of 'disorder', which is parallel to the Greek term 'chaos'. Therefore, perhaps inadvertently, they coined a concept that describes the chaos that arises as a result of the encounter with a traumatic event. Sometimes it remains with the victim, his/her family or survivors forever. And so I believe that we are talking not only about impotence vs. omnipotence but rather in a much broader sense about the experience of our human vulnerability.

Supervising the 'king's men'; or how can helpers be helped?

Let us now return to the hero's or saviour's urge to help and to the interplay between Humpty and the king's men, the helpers.

Literature from throughout the world – from Harris (1995), McCammon and Allison (1995), Perlman and Saakvinte (1995), Mitchell (1985), Dunning (1988), Dyregrov and Mitchell (1993), Hodgkinson and Shepherd (1994) – and from Israel – Lahad and Cohen (1997), Klingman (1991) – a number of approaches to helping helpers to protect themselves. Most of these propose either structured procedures like the CISD (Mitchell 1985), supervision or spontaneous recovery. (The CISD is a verbal/cognitive structured procedure aimed at helping professionals who have been exposed to critical incidents to process their thoughts, feelings and symptoms and teach them what is expected and how to cope with it.)

These approaches or recommendations can be classified according to the multidimensional BASIC Ph Model (Lahad 1993):

B   Belief – belief system, hope, self-esteem, locus of control

A   Affect – direct or indirect emotional expression

S   Social – friends, role, family

I   Imagination – improvisation, creativity

C   Cognition – logic, realism and cognitive techniques

Ph   Physical – physical activity, relaxation and activity.

Of course, some of the recommendations relate to more than one category.

Let us look more closely at the application of the model to this context. The beliefs and value system is related to giving the event a new meaning, cultivating the belief system that has been injured, finding meaning in suffering (Ayalon and Lahad 1990; Frankel 1970; Lahad and Ayalon 1994; Perlman and Saakvinte 1995; White 1990).

Affect refers here to encouraging speaking, ventilation, and legit-imization of direct and indirect emotional expression after the event (Dyregrov and Mitchell 1993; Lahad and Ayalon 1994; Mitchell and Bary 1990).

The social aspect includes social support, taking a role, belonging to the organization (Ayalon and Lahad 1990; Dyregrov and Mitchell 1993; Elraz and Ozami 1994; Hodgkinson and Stewart 1991). It emphasizes one particular role and that is the role of the team leader as manager of the event, the one responsible for the emotional health and physical needs of the team.

This is also the person responsible for work schedules, referrals and for rest, the organization of briefings, the provision of official recognition of the effort and helping create distance.

Imagination refers to the use of creativity, acting, guided imagery, relief and diversion of attention (Ayalon and Lahad 1990; Ayalon and Shacham 1997; Breznitz 1983; Moran and Collers 1995).

The cognitive aspect refers to the preparation of the staff in advance for what may happen, updating them in the course of the process, guidance and problem solving, the use of prepared programmes and the CISD (Binyamini 1984; Cherney 1995).

In the physical aspect, the focus is on physical activity as a stress reliever, resting, sleeping, and using relaxation and proper diet (Lahad and Ayalon 1994; Mitchell and Bary 1990; Figley 1995; Kfir 1990).

Multidimensional supervision *in vivo*: accepting the fact that the pieces cannot be put together again

I met these nine helpers a few days after they had been involved in a disaster. That was their third incident in the past five months. All of them have been through CISD sessions, but the group showed signs of fatalism, tiredness and apathy. Some were in constant contact with individuals and families of previous disasters, despite the fact that it was not their official role. Some were manifesting anger and discomfort, but all were very dedicated to their role as helpers and continued to report at any incident. I was offered three supervision sessions with them.

The atmosphere at the start of our meeting was a combination of 'He (me, the supervisor) will solve all our problems' and 'What can really be done? – it is a hopeless situation.' I immediately registered in my head the parallel processes between them and their clients moving on the scale between despair and omnipotence.

I decided to start with movement (as they had talked enough through the CISD sessions). I put the words: Hope, Despair, Fear, and Courage on the different sides of the room. The instructions were to move around the room and whenever they got near the signs either to stop or reflect, to write or draw anything, or make a movement or a sound.

I then asked each of them to choose one of the corners and meet the other members that chose the same place. (If anyone found it difficult to choose a place s/he was encouraged to find a position between the two signs depicting the feeling at that moment.) Everyone found a corner except one who positioned himself between 'courage' and 'despair'.

The next step was to communicate for about five minutes without words but with signs, sounds and movements the feelings, thoughts and sensations that this corner brought up. They then were to share two to four sentences each, making a joint lyric or prose and stage it as a choir. They had to decide on the rhythm, tempo or use a known melody. This took about half an hour.

Then, they were asked to perform the outcome and the listeners/ observers were asked to write down anything that came to mind or any image or sentence they liked from that performance.

The mood in the group shifted to the 'Ph', 'S' and 'I', that is 'physical', 'social' and 'imaginative' but still many shed tears even at that stage (A).

When they were asked to share what happened some said that the poems, and more than them the melody or rhythm, put them in touch with their impotence. Dark, darkness and dark colours were very apparent in the images and words. A few members were in tears, talking about the permission to grieve. They said that the poems, and more than that the time they were by themselves but still with others, for the first time gave them permission to express sorrow and grief publicly. The helper who was in between the signs talked about impotence and an inability to choose; he cried and laughed at the same time and when asked to share that, he said: 'Crying is about my own losses in life, laughing is the relief to be able to share that without fear.'

The next supervision session was opened by reading the poem from *Alice in Wonderland*. They all knew Humpty Dumpty but did not connect it to their experience. The purpose of bringing the poem (a distancing technique) was to look into their need to put all the pieces together, how frustrating and impossible a task this is, and all their anger towards the 'king' who in their minds expected them to put Humpty together again.

They were now encouraged to take different roles and experiment with different inner and outer dialogues. For most of them it was the first time they had realized the impossible role they were putting themselves in, the need to fix things for others, their fantasy of replacing the irreplaceable and the enormous pressure this puts on them. The 'king' was demystified and there followed heavy attacks and expressions of anger and frustrations toward the 'king' who expects so much of them. The last part of the session was a guided imagery leading to a meeting with Humpty Dumpty and sharing with him 'what I can and what I can't do for him'. Sharing these thoughts in the form of a letter was the end of the session.

The third supervision session was dedicated to re-entry; that is to the sharing of skills or activities they do in order to reduce symptoms, uncomfortable feelings or other distressing issues. We put a huge basket in the middle of the room and asked each one to write on a separate piece of paper one thing that is still distressful. Each one could put as many papers in the basket as s/he wanted. Than I asked them to randomly take a paper from the basket and react to it, passing it then to the next person to add ideas. If anyone took out their own paper they could either respond to it or put it back. However, when the paper they had drawn reached them again they kept it.

This was a very busy session, but at the end many of the 'problems' got some ideas and answers, some in the form of cognitive advice, others with practical ideas, and yet others 'just' with words of comfort and support.

Finally, the participants were encouraged to either keep the 'answer' or 'get rid' of it by symbolically throwing it in the garbage or destroying it and saying goodbye to it.

Only three out of the nine participants opted for the second option. We concluded the session by talking about 'compassion fatigue' and how to prevent it. Training the participants in self-relaxation ended the last supervision session.

Conclusion and summary

Through using dramatherapeutic – creative and distancing – means in supervision the 'king's men' or helpers were allowed to express their vulnerability. Drawing on their physical, social and imaginative resources – as those were expressed through the use of the BASIC Ph – they were reconnected to their humanness. They acknowledged the fact of being human, thus putting the dichotomy of feeling omnipotent/impotent into perspective. The helpers were also supported through their emotional insights and the practical and/or comforting input they received from each other on how to deal with the incidence of compassion fatigue.

In this chapter I have discussed what happens to helpers who are involved in intervention at times of disaster. The thoughts presented here are based upon my personal experience, observations, and discussions with professionals whom I supervise and guide.

I have indicated two components related to the absence of professional defence rituals, the event's penetration into consciousness through media exposure; and geographic and psychological similarity between those performing intervention and their clients. I have also noted the phenomenon of the death imprint and its influence on the helper.

By studying Chapter 1 of the Book of Genesis, and considering the concept of chaos, I suggested another way of understanding the experience of the victim and that of the helper. I looked at the fantasy of omnipotence related to the 'magic touch' of parenting evoked by the interrelationship of helper–parent/victim–child. Understanding the experience of the encounter with the 'darkness in the face of abyss' may help explain the powerful psychological effect on the helper, once they get in contact with the abyss and the dark.

Finally, I have used the multidimensional BASIC Ph model to classify the methods that have been found effective in helping care-givers to reduce compassion fatigue and I have demonstrated its application with an example of group supervision.

Naturally, these are only initial suggestions, and to the best of my knowledge it is the first attempt to use creative methods in supervising crisis intervention teams and to use a dramatherapy approach in the formation of new concepts of understanding of this phenomenon. As such they need to be followed up and further researched. However, they do provide insights that I believe give us a direction for understanding and coping with the incidence of compassion fatigue and serve as a milestone in the ongoing endeavour of the creative therapies to find a recognized status within the family of psychotherapy.

Dedication

This chapter is dedicated to the memory of the late Professor Kalman Binyamini.

References

American Psychiatric Association (1980) *Diagnostic and Statistic Manual of Mental Disorders*, 3rd edition. Washington DC: APA.

Ayalon, A. and Lahad, M. (1990) *Life on the Edge*. Haifa: Nord Publishers. (Hebrew)

Ayalon, A. and Shacham Y. (1997) 'Who will help the helper?' In A. Klingman and B. Stein (eds) *The Binyamini Memorial Book*. (Hebrew)

Beaton, D.R. and Murphy, S.A. (1995) 'Working with people in crisis: research implications.' In C. Figley (ed) *Compassion Fatigue*. New York: Brunner/Mazel.

Binyamini, K. (1984) 'The psychologist in the field tent: Introduction to professional camping.' *Israeli Journal of Psychology and Counseling in Education*, 35–54. (Hebrew)

Breznitz, S. (1983) *The Denial of Stress*. New York: New York University Press.

Cherney, M. (1995) 'Treating the "Heroic Treater".' In C. Figley (ed) *Compassion Fatigue*. New York: Brunner/Mazel.

Dunning, C. (1988) 'Intervention strategies for emergency workers'. In M. Lystad (ed) *Mental Health Response to Mass Emergencies*. New York: Brunner/Mazel.

Dyregrov, A. and Mitchell, J. (1993) 'Traumatic stress in disaster workers and emergency personnel.' In J. Wilson and B. Raphael (eds) *The International Handbook of Traumatic Stress Syndromes*. New York: Plenum Press.

Elraz, I. and Ozami R. (1994) 'Use of supporting resources: During a progressive war incident.' *Psychology 4*, 1–2. (Hebrew)

Figley, C. (ed)(1995) *Compassion Fatigue*. New York: Brunner/Mazel.

Frankel, V. (trans) (1970) *Man in Search for Meaning*. Tel Aviv: Dvir. (Hebrew)

Freudenbeyer, H.J. (1974) 'Staff burnout.' *Journal of Social Issues 30*, 1, 159–165.

Harris, C.J. (1995) 'Sensory based therapy for crisis counselors.' In C. Figley (ed) *Compassion Fatigue*. New York: Brunner/Mazel.

Hodgkinson, P. and Shepherd, M. (1994) 'The impact of disaster support work.' *Journal of Traumatic Stress 7*, 4.

Hodgkinson, P. and Stewart, M. (1991) *Coping with Catastrophes*. London: Routledge.

Joinson, C. (1992) 'Coping with compassion fatigue.' *Nursing 22*, 4, 116–122.

Kfir, N. (1990) *Like Ripples in the Water*. Tel Aviv: Am Oved. (Hebrew)

Klingman, A. (1991) *Psychological and Educational Intervention in Disaster*. Jerusalem: Ministry of Education. (Hebrew)

Lahad M. (1993) 'The six pieces story making – the story of survival and the BASIC Ph model.' In S. Jennings (ed) *Dramatherapy Theory and Practice 2*. London: Routledge.

Lahad, M. (1995) 'Masking the gas mask: brief intervention using metaphor, imagery, movement and enactment.' In A. Gersie (ed) *Dramatic Approaches to Brief Therapy*. London: Jessica Kingsley Publishers.

Lahad, M. and Ayalon, A. (1994) *On Life and Death*. Haifa: Nord. (Hebrew).

Lahad, M. and Cohen, A. (1997) (eds) *Community Stress Prevention 1 and 2*. Kiryat Shemona: Community Stress Prevention Centre.

Maslach, C. (1982) *The Burnout: The Cost of Caring*. Englewood Cliffs, NJ: Prentice Hall.

Maslach, C. and Jackson, S.E. (1981) 'The measurement of experienced burnout.' *Journal of Occupational Behaviour 2*, 2, 99–113.

McCammon, S.L. and Allison, E.J. (1995) 'Debriefing and treating emergency workers.' In C. Figley (ed) *Compassion Fatigue*. New York: Brunner/Mazel.

McCann, L. (1990) 'Vicarious traumatization: A framework for understanding the psychological effects of working with victims.' *Journal of Traumatic Stress 3*, 1, 131–149.

Mitchell, J. (1985) 'When disaster strikes … the critical incident stress debriefing process.' *Journal of Emergency Medical Services*, 36–39.

Mitchell, J. and Bary, G. (1990) *Emergency Services Stress.* Englewood Cliffs, NJ: Prentice Hall.

Moran, C. and Collers, E. (1995) 'Positive reactions following emergency and disaster responses.' *Disaster, Prevention and Management 4,* 1, 55–60.

Omer, D. (1978) *The Kiss that Got Lost.* Tel Aviv: Sherbrak.

Omer, H. and Inbar, H. (1991) 'Mass disasters: the role of the emergency team. *Sichot* 2, 3, 157–170. (Hebrew)

Perlman, L. and Saakvinte, K. (1995) 'Treating therapists with vicarious traumatization and secondary traumatic stress disorders.' In C. Figley (ed) *Compassion Fatigue.* New York: Brunner/Mazel.

Pines, A.M. (1993) 'Burnout.' In L. Goldberger and S. Breznitz (eds) *Handbook of Stress, 2nd edition.* New York: Free Press.

Pines, A.M. and Aronson, E. (1988) *Career Burnout Causes and Cures.* New York: Free Press.

Rutter, M. (1991) *Maternal Deprivation Reassessed.* London: Penguin.

Salmon, T.W. (1919) 'The war neuroses and their lessons.' *New York Journal of Medicine,* 109.

Solomon, Z. (1993) *Combat Stress Reaction, The Enduring Toll of War.* New York: Plenum Press.

Valent, P. (1995) 'Survival strategies: A framework for understanding secondary traumatic stress and coping in helpers.' In C. Figley (ed) *Compassion Fatigue.* New York: Brunner/Mazel.

Van Der Kolk, B.A. (1996) 'The black hole of trauma.' In B.A. Van Der Kolk, A.C. McFarlane and L. Weisaeth (eds) *Traumatic Stress.* New York: The Guilford Press.

Webster's Encyclopedic Unabridged Dictionary of the English Language. (1989) New York: Grainevay.

White, M. (1990) *Narrative Means to Therapeutic Ends.* New York: Norton.

Winnicott, D.W. (1971) *Play and Reality.* London: Tavistock Publications.

Witstom, A. (1989) 'Crisis intervention and short-term psychotherapy.' In H. Desberg, I. Isaacson and G. Shepler (eds) *Short-term Psychotherapy.* Jerusalem: Magnes. (Hebrew)

CHAPTER 7

Supervision and Coaching of Teams in Business

Reinhard Tötschinger

Introduction

The current methods of activating and encouraging processes of change within organizations are manifold. The market of counselling and training is flooded with concepts of restructuring and reorientation, which are either new or pretend to be new. Many participants in team development projects, management training and management coaching courses think: 'A new method? What's this? Not *again!*' Against the background of global economic and social changes, however, there are good reasons for all of these projects: every day we can read about business firms having noticed too late that formerly successful concepts do not work any more, about cases of insolvency, mergers, radical changes of organizations and their management structures, but also about new companies establishing themselves successfully on the marketplace with innovative ideas and products. How can such 'new' methods (among which I also count drama, though it is several thousand years old) be used in practical work? How can processes of awareness and change be reasonably integrated into an enterprise? How can the development and the formation of processes within organizations be described and modified so that those who are involved can visualize inner scenes and images of their organization, their roles in the working process, their products, their communicative concepts, and their visions, all of which are indispensable for real adaptation and change? 'Ideas about organization are always based upon mental conceptions, implicit mages or metaphors,

which make us see, understand and manage situations in a specific way.'
(Morgan 1998, p.16; translated from the German)

One of my answers to these questions is drama. Drama, as a vehicle for
'detecting' answers that are not planned or premeditated, allows an approach
which is both careful and intensive, holistic and very precise, which pays
respect to people and organizations and yet keeps in mind their objectives.
The systemic, process-oriented approach is, so to speak, inherent to drama.
To prevent being bogged down in the individual processes, the processes are
directed towards an objective, the 'performance', which is process, product
and vision of the future at the same time. By bringing situations, images and
metaphors to life, the flesh is, so to speak, added to the bones, and the work
becomes more related to practice and everyday life, 'Besides the obvious
usefulness of system theory and systemic thinking in the work with
organizations, a number of difficulties also become apparent … One
difficulty lies in the fact that systemic ways of seeing and understanding are
often abstract and hard to translate into concrete intervention.' (Fatzer 1996,
as quoted by Storch and Rösner 1995, p.78).

'Never judge a man before you have danced in his moccasins for a month'

This Native American saying tells a lot about our subject. The idea it
expresses is put into practice in various ways in psychotherapy: the empty
chair in gestalt therapy; the role reversal in psychodrama; role-plays as
commonly used methods in supervision, coaching, team development and
organization counselling. (In contrast to the term 'supervisor' – in
connection with the internal control of profit-oriented enterprises – the term
'supervision' is used in German-speaking countries above all for non-profit
organizations in the field of social work and health care and refers to external
supervisors helping professionals reflect on the quality of their working
practice and communication in the working place. In profit-oriented
organizations the term 'coaching' is mostly used, though the term
'supervision' is becoming more frequent.)

This slipping into the role of someone else, in order to understand him or
her better and to learn to feel the way he or she feels, is a form of early drama.
From numerous cultures we know rites of healing, animal dances and the
like. In roles that were not yet fixed the actors, clad in animal hides, danced
around a centre (altar, fire, etc.). In these conjuring dances of hybrid figures
(both animal and human) the figures are, as Elias Canetti says, still:

free figures, in which both aspects are equivalent, none of them is superior to the other, none of them is hidden behind the other. The figure appears to us as complex and, contrary to what we understand by the terms of figure or dramatic character, the process of transformation is at the same time its result. The process of transformation expresses itself simultaneously with its result ... The process of transformation thus becomes the oldest figure or character. (Canetti 1960)

The metaphor of drama as a mirror of the world we live in is as old as mankind. The connection, or similarity, between a theatre performance (the play itself, the rehearsal, the performance, the reviews) and a business firm, a team, an organization and its existence on the market is so self-evident and banal that it may be the reason why this approach is only slowly being accepted in enterprises and organizations. One of the difficulties seems to be that managers and personnel developers cannot 'grasp' such an approach, that drama is not provided by the usual training methods and, therefore, is not a 'thing' but a concrete experience of learning, which only evolves in the interaction between the persons involved as they work together.

I was commissioned by an institute, which, housed on the premises of a hospital, specialized in the rehabilitation of victims of sports accidents. It was run as a profit-oriented enterprise and was very successful. Part of my task was to keep the team together (obviously there was the fear it might fall apart, and this indeed proved a danger even later on). The team was made up of highly qualified physicians, therapists, masseurs, nurses, etc. The pressure for success was felt very strongly, as the institute, unlike hospitals, was not financed by the state, the province or the district. The immediate cause for consulting me was the emergence of problems of relationship in the team (in which there were two married couples), and the fact that the turnover had fallen with respect to the previous year. The request that I should make use of theatrical methods ('because they would be faster and more effective') was consistent with the overall culture prevailing in the institute. One of the principles was to 'finish first' – just like the athletes who were cured there – and it found its expression in the motto 'one way, one destination', which they used to exclaim jointly over and again (like in a soccer or volleyball team). So my position was regarded as that of a coach not in the usual (though inaccurate) psychological meaning of the word, but in the meaning it has in sports, with the only difference that I was concerned with drama and not with basketball or boxing. The team was very open to the idea of theatre playing, and so it was possible to play very demanding improvisations from *commedia dell'arte* (which satisfied their love for competition and efficiency) as well as scenes in between, in which personal contact was in the foreground (drama exercises), which encouraged self-perception and communication and ended up in joint improvisations. By admitting both extremes (efficiency/competition/pleasure and contact/meeting) and working up the problems with dramatic means, the team was able to find a common rhythm of learning and development, which could be put into relation and brought into line with their competitive situation in regard to other hospitals. They experienced their objective or vision as coming from within and no longer needed to be motivated from outside ('one way, one destination'), which made itself felt in a considerable reduction of pressure.

'There is no such thing as a learning organization' (Peter Senge)

Modern enterprises are challenged to react to changes of the environment in a flexible way, to check their state of health (de Geus 1998), and to recognize developments beforehand. The market has, in the past few years, increasingly demanded qualities like flexibility and customer orientation and maximization of profit as well as quality, strict observation of deadlines and much more. It is, however, very difficult to respond to new realities (it is hard enough for the individual, how much harder is it for a company!). The 'classical' descriptions and the isolated dealing with particular areas within an enterprise often generate false views and realities, as many of these companies seek advice in the hope that the employment of 'specialists' will help prevent imminent or actual crises. These specialists then deal only with specialized areas, taking apart the generally complex situations and phenomena and then putting them together again. But organizations are more than the collection of their individual elements and live through the people who work in them (Morgan 1998, p.15).

> A cosmetics wholesaler with about 15 employees asked me for conflict moderation. The commission was given to me by the chief. The atmosphere within the staff, above all between the field service (sales agents, all of them male, who were constantly travelling through all of Austria) and the chief in Vienna, was very bad, which was reflected in the weekly meetings by the fact that discussions centred almost exclusively on sales figures, profit and market shares, and frustration prevailed. It came to a point where especially the agents met the chief with hidden or

overt condescension, and he, in his turn, reacted with cynicism and withdrawal (he was an intellectual and a man of philosophic and artistic interests, who was on the one hand sometimes the butt of derision for his whimsical ways of behaving and dressing, on the other hand esteemed for his competence and correctitude). We (the chief, the staff and I) agreed upon five days of team coaching in the course of three months (two days with the agents, two with the internal service, one day with both teams and the chief). First we worked on images and their dramatic representation. Most men had the idea of the enterprise as a machine (a frequent image) which turns out as much money as possible (the sales agents worked on a commission basis). The chief, on the contrary, had in mind images and scenes from an expedition into the jungle (he was also the founder of the firm). After many of these scenes had been enacted, which by the way was a lot of fun for the participants, the background became clear. Before the company was founded, almost all of the agents, and the chief, too, had been employed in one of the country's biggest cosmetics wholesalers, and from there they had transferred a good deal of the strategies, visions and behavioural patterns to their present, smaller team. We could then work out strategies, visions, roles, communication patterns, etc. which were in line with the small size of the team and finally presented a very cheerful outlook to the future in the form of a theatre performance.

In most organizations, the 'knowledge' of all the persons involved is not exploited to its full extent, thus forestalling a continuous development. Moreover, leading managers generally do not have adequate tools for recognizing hidden contents, movements and motivations within the enterprise so as to integrate them into their planning and thus create a 'learning enterprise' (Senge 1997). Consequences of actions in bigger organizations generally appear at a certain distance in time and space and are therefore hardly felt and not easily and unequivocally recognized as such. The images and scenes in the minds of the people employed in the organization must, however, be modified from time to time, if the firm is to survive in the long run. Drama as a medium offers various possibilities to understand the relationships between people, the images they have in mind and their meanings. Greek drama knew how to operate with the images and the conceptions people had of the world as long as 2000 years ago. Theatre is learning by doing, and this – as Peter Senge (1998) writes in his well-known book *The Fifth Discipline* – requires not only the observation of the consequences of our actions and the subsequent adaptation of our behaviour, but above all prompt and unequivocal feedback. In the MIT Center for Organizational Learning a group of sociologists, businessmen and journalists dealt with the question of how the staff of a company can collectively reflect upon their experiences and how they can be made to concentrate more on the essential in their thinking and acting and to mobilize themselves (Kleiner and Roth 1998). They developed a method of 'story telling' and of writing down these stories to make them workable. It is similar with theatrical methods. The simultaneity of the narrated representation, together with the physical experience (as author, stage director, actor, audience), creates a sense of concern, which leads to a more profound understanding and therefore a higher degree of responsibility. Of the manifold uses of dramatherapy in companies, I want to mention the most important ones and subsequently describe one of many possible approaches.

Use of theatrical methods

The use of theatrical methods in coaching, supervision and team development enables the persons involved:

- to participate actively
- to assume responsibility for oneself and simultaneously for the team and its development
- to keep in mind the targets
- to develop a common awareness of problems
- to settle problems related to relationships (both factual and personal)
- to deal with taboos without hurting anyone
- to clear up unconscious motivations and rules
- to develop visions.

They promote:

- perception
- growth of the personality
- courage
- clearing up of roles
- motivation
- creativity
- clearing up of organizational structures
- preservation of and restoration to health (prevention of the burnout syndrome, reduction of sick leaves, etc.).

Steps and phases of the process

I want to present the following four steps:

1. defining the job
2. diagnosis of the situation/finding the themes
3. the play phase (methods/techniques)
4. working up and transfer.

Defining the job

To make sure that the process, which, unlike traditional training methods, does not convey cognitive contents, proceeds in correspondence with the needs and objectives of the organization, it must be made clear from the start (and at all further stages of the process) that the job is clearly defined, that the management (particularly the top management) is well informed about the method and supports the project. Especially with the use of drama there is the constant danger that whenever the state of mind of the participants changes, the project is considered a luxury or some kind of talk show and is dissolved. The use of drama in supervision, coaching and team development in business requires endurance, safety and a certain degree of personal development and reorientation, which are always connected with crises. These problems must be addressed in advance with all the persons involved and especially with the leading managers, and the necessary measures of crisis management must be agreed upon. The importance of a clear contract is fundamental.

> A big Austrian government enterprise commissioned me, together with two colleagues I hardly knew, but who had previously worked with that organization, to carry out a team development project (10 teams with about 150 members) which was scheduled for one year. It was my method of working with drama that had drawn the attention of the enterprise and of the two other counsellors to me. One of them was the contact man with the enterprise and at the same time the project manager, although he and the other colleague had no or almost no experience with my method. The head of the department which was in charge of the teams supported the project and he wanted 'the circus' to be the theme of the project. During the first stage, when the contract was negotiated and the working procedure was discussed, it turned out that the executive board of the company was only informed about the team

development project, but not that theatre would be at the centre of the activities. As I always make clear arrangements with all the people involved beforehand, I discussed this with the project management, too, which, however, did not think it necessary to inform the executive board directly and comprehensively about us and to include us in the contract. (After all, there was a high fee at stake.) As there were not enough agreements between project management, head of the department, executive board and, as it turned out later, also the personnel development department, and as it was not possible to bring about such agreements, I saw no way to start the project and declined the job.

Diagnosis of the situation/finding the themes

From the gestalt cycle of experience (Figure 7.1) we can learn where there are deficiencies and disturbances but also resources in the person, the team or the organization supervised. In order to perform an action in line with oneself and one's environment, one must reach and pass each of the areas described in the gestalt cycle.

For each of these areas the drama offers methods which help the person supervised to activate them.

Mr Seiler, a leading manager of a big bank, was coached by me. He felt exposed to a high degree of stress because of a merger with another bank, its different culture and history and the short time at his disposal. During the negotiations, his high qualification and his tendency to proceed straight away to questions of implementation (area: action, see Figure 7.2) got him more and more into the role of an impatient know-all, and consequently into the position of an outsider, even within his own bank. He neglected the area of contact with his partners in the negotiations and became increasingly unpopular. When we worked on the aspect of contact, it became clear that one of the 'new' ones was Mr Müller, whom Mr Seiler knew well, since Mr Müller had been his superior before, and the two had often quarrelled because of serious factual and personal differences. We developed and played the scenes which arose from the history and the culture of the two banks. After Mr Seiler had gained an insight into the similarities to the scenes with his former bank and Mr Müller in the play, he was able to recognize the differences in his present position. Mr Seiler's position was now on the same level as Mr Müller's, and the bank for which he worked was even more important. After we had staged his visions and objectives he could

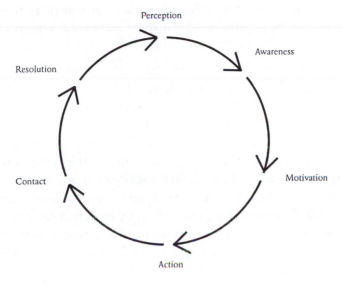

Figure 7.1 The gestalt cycle of experience

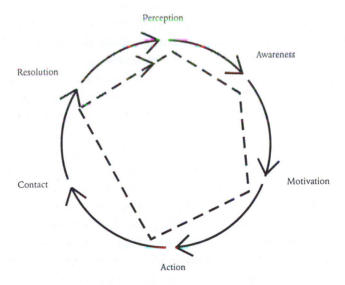

Figure 7.2 Mr Seiler's strategy

react in the decisive moments of the negotiations more slowly and more considerately, but more efficiently, and adapt himself to the overall rhythm of the negotiations. Soon afterwards he was offered a higher position.

If, as in the example described above, the given objective does not correspond with the image that colleagues have of their jobs, then there is an empty space (Brook 1988), which, however, can be filled at the level of dramatic reality and in which it is possible to discover information relevant to the person supervised and the enterprise. 'Empty space' can be interpreted as space with 'nothing (= no thing) in it'. But in the background we find atmospheres, scenes and images (in the above example: what Mr Seiler had left out and what he did not dare to imagine). These atmospheres, scenes and images, which are not or are only indirectly expressed can take a concrete shape in the dramatic space and by means of theatrical methods. In contrast to lengthy analyses, the empty space can be shaped by means of drama and the gestalt circle quite easily and within a short time. By entering the dramatic reality and enacting such 'interspaces' new ways become visible and perceptible – new solutions are found that were not thought of before.

The play phase (methods/techniques)

Elements like stage, scene, text and history, means like décor, make-up and costume, and contents like images, conflicts, moods, modes of comm-unication and feelings, can be represented in manifold ways. The selection of the method and the performance requires a certain delicacy of feeling on the part of the project manager (e.g. which style is best suited to the atmosphere of the system that is to be supervised). As theatre has always a high potential of change and is fast in bringing repressed elements as well as new, daring and creative elements into focus, I recommend to proceed slowly and carefully, to support the process by frequent checkbacks. Moreover, the coach or supervisor will choose those methods and styles which he gets fun out of (and this is already a significant criterion of selection). If one uses drama exercises and styles too often one may easily become the team's showmaster and the theatre may become something like the company's entertainment radio station. In this case, of course, the coach or supervisor, if he does not notice the danger in time, loses his function and becomes part of the routine of the system (this of course can be an important diagnosis which the coach can bring to the stage, too). Suitable elements for the play phase are:

- all kinds of improvisation
- role-plays
- development of plays
- using existing plays or scenes as models
- mask play
- clown and circus
- melodrama
- Greek tragedy
- sensory awareness exercises
- forum theatre
- action theatre
- movie sequences
- any other element the creativity of the coach or the coached persons may introduce.

As a coach and supervisor, my role is on the one hand that of the stage director committed to the 'actor', who on the other hand must keep in mind the whole play, the subject, the collaborators and the organization. In line with the client's potentials and actual possibilities, I try to achieve the optimum balance between environment and objectives of the person advised and the organization (as we know, for an enterprise only those events are important which meet or affect their goals). It seems important to me to mention that one should not deal too much with the client's personal affairs, as this might hurt him and, in most of the cases, is not part of the job (this is a temptation that psychotherapists are likely to succumb to). The condensation of space and time in the stage situation makes it possible to live everyday situations either retrospectively or in anticipation, and thus enables one to gain time and to avoid mistakes one has already made or expects to make.

Working up and transfer

In the course of such a coaching, seemingly paradoxical team capabilities, like individual, independent acting and adaptation, capabilities for conflict and feedback, orientation towards an objective and empathy are so to speak by-products which come out of the dramatic paradox, i.e. the 'actor' being at the same time involved in the play and looking at it from a distance. The possibility of feedback following the play as described above enables learning by doing with simultaneous control of action. Together the players become participants and the meaning becomes apparent in a social context. Social changes only take place, if those who are concerned are turned into active participants. Drama presents what the players have in common and what differentiates them in a simultaneous, holistic and precise representation. An image of the organization (Morgan 1998) becomes visible, audible and tangible, i.e. it can be experienced through the senses, which promotes the transfer of learning. It is a basic assumption that facts, sensual perception, behaviour and phenomena are defined and get their independent and specific meaning through the way they are organized and not through their individual elements.

If teams and groups make the experience of good communication and recognize its advantages, they will almost automatically try to achieve the same quality of communication again. The members become aware of the manifold realities they live in and will act accordingly. In the laboratory situation of the play, these realities unfold simultaneously and with a speed that meets the demands of enterprises and their employees. We see that 'the whole is more than the collection of its elements', as the old thesis of gestalt psychology says, and that the whole is contained in every part of it. On this basis change is made possible, as in the play individual roles can be singled out and limits can be drawn and, paradoxically, expanded. ('The meaning of limits is in the limitation of meaning' – Willke 1996, p.53.)

'Nothing that is vast enters into the life of mortals without a curse' (Sophocles, *Antigone*)

Unfortunately, this maxim, which is more than 2000 years old, still holds true. Do we stop at the theoretical positions of Henry Ford (man as a machine) and Frederick Taylor (everything can be measured)? Or do we slowly learn, at an early stage, when the 'curse' is not yet threatening us, to look at the way we act from a different angle and to develop new ways of thinking about organizations and management (Morgan 1998)? The problem of most enterprises is, as Peter Senge writes in the *Fieldbook of the Fifth Discipline*, that they lack good ideas, that the objective of the enterprise as determined by the managers consists in 'maximizing the investors' profits' and the employees let themselves be guided by the maxim, 'Climb up the career ladder' or 'Mind your personal advantage'. No wonder that people in such organizations lack commitment, that they find their work profane and boring and do not feel any deeper loyalty to the organization (Senge 1997). Changes cannot be stimulated by a static *weltanschauung* and encouraged with static tools. The theatre with its spontaneous, creative and dynamic possibilities shapes a creative future and this will become a more and more urgent necessity in the next few years.

References

Brook, P. (1988) *Der leere Raum (The Empty Space)*. Berlin: Alexander Verlag

Canetti, E. (1960) *Masse und Macht (Crowds and Power)*. Duesseldorf: Fischer.

de Geus, A. (1998) *Jenseits der Ökonomie: Die Verantwortung der Unternehmen (The Living Company)*. Stuttgart: Klett-Cotta.

Fatzer, G. (ed) (1996) *Supervision und Beratung (Organisational Process and Supervision)*. Cologne: Edition Humanistische Psychologie.

Kleiner, A. and Roth, G. (1998) 'Wie sich Erfahrungen in der Firma besser nutzen lassen.' ('How to make experience your company's best teacher.') *Harvard Business Manager 5*, 9–15

Morgan, G. (1998) *Loewe, Qualle, Pinguin – Imaginieren als Kunst der Veraenderung (Imaginization. The Art of Creative Management)*. Stuttgart: Klett-Cotta.

Senge, P.M. (1997) *Das Fieldbook der fuenften Disziplin (The Fieldbook of the Fifth Discipline)*. Stuttgart: Klett-Cotta.

Senge, P.M. (1998) *Die fünfte Disziplin: Kunst und Praxis der lernenden Organisation (The Fifth Discipline)*. Stuttgart: Klett-Cotta

Storch, M. and Rösner, D. (1995) 'Soziodrama und Moderation als Methoden der Organizationsentwicklung.' ('Sociodrama and visualized moderation-techniques for organizational process consultancy.') *Psychodrama 1, 2*,

Willke, H. (1996) *Systemtheorie I: Grundlagen. (Theory of Systems 1, Basics)* Stuttgart: Lucius and Lucius.

CHAPTER 8

Supervision and Consultancy of Art-Based Research

Roger Grainger

Art-based research opens up new possibilities for dramatherapy research. This chapter draws attention to some possibilities for its supervision.

First of all, what is art-based research? Dramatherapy research itself may be defined as systematic investigation undertaken to discover whether or not a dramatherapeutic approach has a successful outcome – and if so, why? It depends, of course, on what 'therapeutic success' means in a particular situation. Art-based research was first identified by Shaun McNiff (1998). It equates success with healing mediated by and occurring in terms of the world of artistic experience. Investigation into the kind of therapy that takes place via artistic experience is to be taken as congruent with research into ways of actually producing art. Other kinds of research have depended on the kind of awareness represented by mathematical measurement, which is very different from artistic experience. Whereas quantitative research produces mathematical results, art-based research gives rise to artistic ones – the assumption being that artistic results are signs, or 'proofs', of the presence of healing that cannot be scientifically determined.

From the point of view of 'hardline' scientific research procedures this may not appear to be an acceptable way of going about things; so far as arts therapists are concerned, however, it may immediately be recognized as the only authentic way in which they can learn more about the ways that their profession really works.

Before looking at art-based research more closely and attempting to draw some conclusions about its implications for supervision, it would be advisable to glance briefly at some of the processes of consultation which are involved in the selection of an appropriate research model for dramatherapists.

Consultation

Many dramatherapists are interested in the possibility of carrying out some kind of research, but are by no means certain what would be the best way of doing this; the best way for them, that is. If they are well versed in research procedures and have taken part in this kind of activity before, they will obviously be in a better position than those who come into it without any previous experience. Even they, however, will need to spend a good deal of time thinking about the kind of research they want to carry out and the advantages and disadvantages of various ways of trying to solve the problems, theoretical, technical and procedural, that they will certainly encounter in the course of their journey between deciding what it is that they want to discover and being able to say with any confidence that they have discovered it. If, on the other hand, they have no research experience at all, they are likely to think twice before venturing into an area widely believed to hold dangers for the uninitiated, and will probably decide against becoming involved – in which case both they and dramatherapy will be the losers, because research into the arts therapies can be excitingly creative and dramatherapy needs as much of it as it can get.

Either way, however, there is always the demand for advice and consultation. No researcher works entirely alone. Newcomers obviously need help, but even seasoned researchers depend on opportunities to discuss work in progress with others who have had experience in the particular field they are investigating. Creative research largely depends on this kind of interchange of experiences and ideas (Robson 1993). The growth of practitioner-research, in which those engaged in investigating an interpersonal phenomenon are themselves involved as members of the social context they are researching, has led to an even greater tendency to share expertise and insights than used to be the case when experimenters stood professionally apart and spoke only with members of their 'team' in order to try to preserve the objectivity of their scientific approach. Nowadays phenomenological authenticity is largely preferred to artificially imposed distance within the human situation being investigated; and collaborative discussion and consultation work together to achieve a kind of distance that manages not to distort the relational truth it is concerned to understand.

Research approaches are ways of using certain very definite procedural strategies, each of which has been devised with a particular aim in view. As with any kind of tool their action is defined by, and consequently limited to, their purpose. A particular research strategy will produce a particular kind of result. New researchers frequently need advice about the kind of results they want to obtain. They want their results to be as definite as possible so that their questions can be seen to have been answered in a way that is convincing and authoritative. Because of this, they run the risk of the questions not actually being answered at all; not, at least, by the research strategy they have chosen which, despite its efficiency in producing results within its own parameters, turns out to be quite unable to deal with the sorts of questions they would like it to handle on their behalf. It is possible to abandon one strategy in favour of another, more appropriate one, of course. Here again, however, newcomers are likely to need advice (if not actual encouragement and support!) (King, Keohane and Verba 1994; Robson 1993).

Clarification is the principal aim of consultation, as it is of research itself. Some things are obviously easier to clarify than others. Distortions occur wherever there is a mismatch between method and theory. Dramatherapy research chooses to concern itself with the attempt to be precise about a sphere of life which, like pure mathematics, speaks its own language and resists being translated into any other; one in which the degree of mistranslation will vary according to the rigour of our attempts at accuracy. To the extent that dramatherapy is a therapeutic art, dramatherapists will be drawn to approaches that are artistically well-defined and expressive, but scientifically imprecise or even inaccurate: to the extent that research is an attempt to demonstrate phenomena in ways that underline their relevance to areas of life that society considers (and has probably always considered) more important than art, they need to pay attention to research strategies that will lead to the kind of results that it can allow itself to take seriously – to the obvious advantage of dramatherapy and dramatherapy research!

Research strategies are about ways of demonstrating process. This can be done by *measurement*, *description* or *exploration*, according to whether research is quantitative, qualitative or experiential in orientation. All these approaches are useful and relevant for dramatherapy research but each of them applies to it in a different way. Before starting a piece of research a dramatherapist needs to know something about the differences and similarities between and among them. This is particularly important because of the doctrinaire attitudes researchers sometimes take up with regard to any position other than their own. Part of the responsibility attached to acting as a consultant is that of trying to present as balanced a picture as possible.

Here, in brief, are the main orientations available to those embarking on dramatherapy research (Grainger 1998):

1.   *Quantitative*

     If the main purpose of a piece of research is to decide whether or not a certain course of action has an effect on a particular state of affairs which would not occur if that course of action were not followed, the answer is only likely to be convincing if it invites some kind of measurement. Quantitative research is basically *outcome* research: its use is to establish cause and effect relationships so that a reasonable claim may be made as to whether something 'works' or not. Obviously this is important information for those whose job is to cost particular programmes of action; they are likely to take this kind of research seriously because it is in their interest to do so.

2.   *Qualitative*

     Whereas quantitative research concentrates on looking for evidence that something has a measurable effect upon something else, qualitative research extends this by wanting to know *how* this happens. This is sure to increase the researcher's understanding of processes of change, but often can only be achieved at the cost of being willing to be less precise about *why*. Qualitative research is *process* research, recommended to those who are concerned to examine complex situations in the reality of their complexity. It is possible to do this in ways that respect the rules governing cause and effect linkages, however.

3.   *Practitioner-oriented*

     In practitioner research the qualitative approach is extended and deepened by the researchers' refusal to leave themselves out of the research equation, both as researcher and researched, and their consequent willingness to use their own experiences as valid experiential data. This is *action* research. It is an effective way of gaining in-depth experiential knowledge of a research context.

4.   *Art-based*

     Art-based research could be called *creativity* or *creation* research. Because of its unwillingness to translate the language of artistic experience into any other kind of code, claiming that the loss of meaning involved in doing this actually destroys the whole purpose of research, art-based research explores experiential transformations without quantifying them. In this sense, it is a work of art in itself – but one that is recognizably different from its original form, and aesthetically unique.

Each of these models of research is designed to produce a different type of result. Quantitative strategy aims at observing and measuring specific effects, while qualitative approaches concentrate on examining experiences rather than results; action research, which involves the researcher herself or himself in the situation being investigated, is concerned to examine processes of change and development; while art-based projects explore by developing awareness in terms of the artistic medium itself. You could say, in fact, that they all do this, each according to the medium it chooses as its research tool. In the case of quantitative research this is mathematics; qualitative research adopts a phenomenological approach to personal experience; action/ participation concentrates on group theory. Art, of course, remains firmly artistic. The models are distinguished from one another by different ways of knowing, and consequently evaluating, the state of affairs that they are trying to understand.

The search for human understanding – understanding about being human – is never simple nor straightforward. Dramatherapy research, like research of any kind, involves a degree of compromise. As I have written elsewhere:

> Research always involves a trade-off between two kinds of inaccuracy, numerical and existential, corresponding to the way we think about life itself. This is the case whether we are scientists or artists. It is our own fault if we confine ourselves to being one or the other, refusing to see the world otherwise than in its capacity to provide certain kinds of evidence in certain well-defined ways. (Grainger 1998 p.139)

One of the most important tasks of research consultancy is to communicate this to those who are immediately involved in the actual business of carrying out research.

Supervision

> The generative powers of a creative expression need to be fed with a corresponding consciousness which appreciates and keeps their mysteries. (McNiff 1998, p.28)

Taking on the responsibility of supervising research in the arts therapies calls for a particular attitude of mind. First of all, the supervisor or supervising body needs to be aware of the aims and intentions of the researcher(s); in other words, to know what kind of research is being undertaken. Second, he or she should be in sympathy with this. Supervisors who are not in tune with their supervisees' understanding of what arts therapies research should really be are wasting their own and their supervisees' time, if not actually getting in the way of the research they are trying to carry out.

The principle holds true for any kind of research supervision. It is, however, particularly important for research in the arts therapies, where there is a good deal of disagreement – or plain, simple confusion – about what kind of research strategies are appropriate. Writing about his own experience as a research supervisor, Shaun McNiff describes how he saw a process at work in his students' researching that cut across his own current understanding of research:

> I was intrigued by what my students had done, but I was still encouraging thesis writers to follow research procedures that corresponded to my own experiences ... Why not simply let them choose from amongst different ways of conducting research?' (McNiff 1998, pp.27, 30)

McNiff is certainly right to suggest that the supervisor should stand back and survey the landscape so as to be in a position to draw conclusions about what the researchers are doing and also what they think they are doing. Research, like therapy itself, is all-absorbing. Supervisors are necessary to provide a source of clarity that will be less powerfully affected by the special pleading associated with enthusiasm. Researchers need a way of looking at themselves as well as at the objects of their enquiry and supervisors are there to help them do this. Because of the prestige attached to the experimental paradigm developed for quantitative research, there is an endemic tendency for the reflective nature of all human enquiry to be ignored – in other words, for researchers to claim an 'objectivity' that human beings are just not capable of. It can be the supervisor's role in research to supply greater objectivity simply by being at one remove from the actual research procedures.

The process of 'enquiring into inquiry' is made more complicated by art therapy research because the arts therapies are involved in carrying out their own inquiry simply by being themselves. Art therapy, music therapy, drama – and dance movement therapy – are all explorations and consequently may be seen as kinds of research. They are research of the most immediate, hands-on kind. Research supervision itself is, consequently, two stages away from whatever it is that is being researched in the therapeutic context. It is this actively investigative, consciously creative identity of the arts therapies that led McNiff to opt so decisively for what is now becoming known as art-based research. McNiff claims that the only appropriate kind of research for arts therapists is research carried out by the process of art therapy itself. Only when the arts therapies are used to *explore themselves by being themselves* can they be said to be being true to themselves. Art itself is a kinetic and unpredictable force. Research associated with it, in order to be genuine, must be 'in synchrony with the transformative nature of the creative process' (McNiff 1998, p.47).

In *Art-Based Research* McNiff (1998) describes how one of his research students 'used art to understand art'. This student was engaged in an attempt to understand the experience of a young girl's daily life in terms of a series of mythological pictures giving rise to psychological insight on the part of the beholders. Attempts to interpret the paintings by providing some kind of psychological commentary were rejected as inadequate ways of embodying what was actually happening between the student and the work she was producing; some other way had to be found:

> In our next meeting it occurred to the student she could give voice to the young girl who was protagonist in her story. The first person voice allowed the thesis student literally to 'get inside' the thesis process and access insights that would not have resulted from an external analysis. Art was used to interpret art. (McNiff 1998, p.27)

This is to see the arts therapies supervisor as sharing much the same basic perspective as an art critic – albeit an art critic who is also an artist. He or she has a foot in both camps, knowing what it is like to be involved in the process of creation (i.e. therapy) and the supervising role of an informed observer. To this extent art critics share in the kind of insight that produces art itself – otherwise they could never comment meaningfully upon it. The work itself, as a work of art, combines the immediate expression or exploration of encounter with the formal structure required for understanding and assimilating an experience; like all works of art it is an embodiment of the 'I-Thou, I-It' principle of perception described by Martin Buber (1966). This is the kind of awareness the arts therapies communicate; they communicate it in two directions, to the client and to the supervisor who, *as an artist*, is able to reflect it back upon the therapist/researcher and so complete the cycle in a creative way. The difference lies in the way art mediates meaning, resonating 'between-ness' rather than imposing its conclusions as 'interpretations'. The artefact *remains*. It is not explained away. As Herman Hesse says about literature, we enter not only into relationship with a book, but also with the book *itself*.

It must be said, however, that not everybody engaged in art therapy research, or research into the arts therapies, sees it in quite this way. Some investigators take the pragmatic view that the arts therapies, in order to survive as identifiable professions, must allow themselves to be assessed according to the same validatory criteria as everything else that comes under the general heading of 'scientific medicine'. This is an influential view; to some extent it affects most arts therapists' attitudes towards research, even those whose main concern is qualitative rather than quantitative, or participatory rather than clinical/experimental. Research is seen as being 'the scientific end' of art therapy practice: scientific in the sense of intending to make statements about the nature and function of the arts therapies that represent as high a degree of sustainable agreement about them as possible. In other words, arts therapies research is about being as scientific as possible about the arts therapies.

It is around this area – that of *the possibility of being scientific about dramatherapy* – that most discussions of dramatherapy research revolve. There seems to be an almost automatic assumption, however, that research must be quantitative to be scientific. This is the point of view usually taken by arts therapists of all kinds, and I believe it to be a mistaken one. The essence of science lies in an attitude of mind, not an approach to understanding things that is limited to measuring them; it is a way of arguing about reality, not reducing or controlling it. Certainly, research can be qualitative *and* scientific. The fascination of dramatherapy research lies in the attempt to use scientific inference to draw conclusions from things that evade direct mathematical quantification, yet can be made sense of in the way we manage to make communicable sense of the rest of life. This is a conversation that is going on at present on dramatherapy research, and is giving rise to a great deal of creative discussion among researchers themselves and within research supervision settings.

The supervision of dramatherapy research is a very different activity from that of supervising dramatherapy itself. Certainly therapy and research are both things that can be supervised; but some dimensions of relationship between therapist and supervisor are changed in an important way when the primary focus is shifted away from the nature of the therapist's relationship with actual clients to that of his or her involvement in specific research activities *concerning* clients. It becomes necessary to distinguish between two possible meanings of the phrase 'research supervision' according to which of two activities, therapy or research, is actually being supervised. Or should it be taken to refer to supervision of a kind that involves both?

With regard to supervision of the psychotherapeutic process itself, it should be remembered that the supervisor's primary responsibility is always to the therapeutic interaction between client and therapist. It could be argued from this basic premise that *supervision of any part of the therapeutic process,* including all research activities associated with it, is principally concerned with this relationship, so that supervisors should concentrate upon observing how the research situation is experienced by the client – who, in this case, happens to be an 'experimental subject', perhaps along with the experimenter herself or himself. This makes sense, of course, if researchers see themselves, and are regarded by their client-subjects, as still engaged in a therapeutic process; in other words, to be carrying out what Robson (1993) calls 'practitioner- research'. Certainly the dramatherapeutic process which the researcher is examining itself depends upon a quality of interpersonal relationship in order to be therapeutic and to function as dramatherapy. Consequently it must itself be subject to the influence of any other relationships it becomes involved in – including the critically focused research awareness being brought to bear upon it. These two sets of interactions, 'researcher–client and therapist–client' on the one hand and 'supervisor–supervisee and supervisor–researcher' on the other, both have to be taken into account in any attempt to understand the task facing those who attempt to supervise research into psychotherapy (Figure 8.1).

In the language of art-based research these relationships fit naturally into the kind of scenario which can be explored dramatically and not simply understood in theory.

The basic supervisory relationship, however, is that between functions and persons. This can be seen as a two-level operation. At the first level, supervisor and therapist are concerned with the latter's actual performance as researcher; that is, her or his ability to solve the strategic and tactical problems involved in designing and carrying out a particular piece of work as effectively as possible. This is the technical component in research supervision: the need to take account of the structure of an investigation in order to be able to make statements about what appears to be happening and draw conclusions as to why this is so. The variety of research approaches and

Figure 8.1

methods currently available makes choosing which of them to use a major difficulty. This is an area in which the supervisor's experience may turn out to be extremely valuable. Whatever kind of research is decided upon, however, whether it is experimentally rigorous or creatively expressive or an ingenious harmonization of both, it will always need to be designed and carried out as thoughtfully and skilfully as possible in order to be recognizable as an authentic research operation.

The second level is equally important, however, and not quite so obvious. This concerns relationships rather than expertise. Specifically it involves the interaction between therapist-researcher and supervisor *as people rather than functionaries*, which is the heart of the supervision process. Research into dramatherapy is a way of trying to find out what is happening among a group of people (or sometimes a pair of individuals) involved in a particular kind of social structure; and the only way we can understand such things is by reference to our own experience of such structures – our personal life as beings-in-relation. So much is obvious, but it is easy to overlook its special relevance to any kind of research involving people. Research into relationship depends upon the kind of knowledge and experience of relationship which is ours at the most personal level; it is always knowledge that refers to ourselves which we use to explain others (and explain ourselves *to* others!). In research supervision we are provided with a source of relational experience which is immediately useful and relevant because it is already focused on the relationship we are trying so hard to understand. In dramatherapy research supervision we are in a position to use one relationship in order to study another in a way that is particularly illuminating for both of them. For dramatherapists, any kind of enquiry into social behaviour (i.e. human relationships) is allowed to stand forth in dramatic form as a kind of scenario, recognizable and recognized as such by those involved. Researcher and supervisor discover their role relationships in small dramas about being 'myself as researcher' and 'myself as supervisor', with all the opportunities and openings presented for role-reversal and the embodiment of ideas and feelings. In this way, the business of carrying out research, and the complementary experiences of supervising and being supervised, become part of a unified relational event – a drama of human interaction, not simply a set of abstract principles and precepts. (Research is being carried out at present by Madeline Andersen-Warren and Lorraine Fox into the effects of different kinds of focus in dramatherapy supervision as this reflects theoretical orientation and specific client groups. This research is art-based. See Appendix I for further information.)

The idea that the supervisory relationship can itself be an occasion for studying client/therapist interaction has been explored in some depth by writers on psychotherapeutic supervision. Searles, for instance, points out that

> the supervisor experiences, over the course of a supervisory relationship, as broad a spectrum of emotional phenomena as does the therapist, or even the patient himself – although, to be sure, the supervisor's emotions are rarely as intense as those of the therapist, and usually much less intense than those of the patient. (Searles 1965, p.158)

The existence of a decreasing scale of emotional intensity is crucial, in fact. In order to understand what is actually happening between and among people we must be able not only to engage with them directly but to stand back from them as well. Intense involvement and critical distance alternate in any kind of knowing that is human and personal. Diane Shainberg (1983) has written eloquently about the need for counsellors to give their clients space to 'be' themselves. In order to know somebody we are trying to help, she said, we must be willing to allow them to be their own subject as well as the object of our attention and expertise. There is a tendency for counsellors to protect themselves by closing off the anxiety of openness by using the patient or client as a kind of embodiment of their own theoretical understanding – an object to be worked on, not a person to be met. Real persons create their own personal space, and it is this that is resisted by a process of professional reification. The supervisor, however, is able to confront these tendencies by bringing them to the counsellor's attention within a context which the counsellor experiences as less threatening because it is less emotionally intense. Within the supervision relationship, says Shainberg (1983, p.175), 'the supervisee becomes aware of how his lifetime conditioning to accomplish, to get better, to get more, to please, to be liked, to be thought of in a certain way, to avoid anger, terror, hopelessness, block genuinely letting be what is with the patient and himself in the treatment.' Supervisees can do this because the supervisor encourages them to stand back and recollect their emotions within a more tranquil context before returning to the treatment situation in order to meet (and re-meet) the patient and re-experience the reality of the relationship. This is, of course, the heart of the wider supervision context. In their six-part analysis of the supervision process, this is where Shohet and Hawkins (1989) look first; the supervisor's purpose is to help the therapist pay attention to the client so as to gain a living sense of another person's experience of being alive. (After this Shohet and Hawkins move on to focus on 'Exploration of strategies and interventions used by the therapist' and 'Exploration of the therapy process and relationship'. Only then do they turn to the therapist's and supervisor's analysis of their own reactions to the supervision process itself.)

Shainberg is writing about the state of affairs that exists in straight-forward therapy supervision, where the lessening of emotional intensity permits a potentially threatening and psychologically distorting relationship to be examined in a more realistic way. The special circumstances involved in research supervision go a step beyond this, however. The research situation permits two other kinds of relationship to be studied in terms of, or as mirrored by, the supervisory relationship itself: the interaction within the group (i.e. the object of the research) and the researcher's own relationship with the group. Both these stages in the process represent a distancing of the supervision event from the original object of attention, in other words, the relationship between therapist and client; both of them allow a greater measure of freedom to think more clearly about the emotionality which is always a component of genuine relationships between and among human beings. This is not freedom to escape from feelings, however. A dramatherapist's obligation to approach social experience of any kind in the awareness that she or he is participating in a human drama is as powerful here as in the researcher/supervisor relationship we have been considering. In fact, the art-based nature of the proceedings stands out even more clearly within a setting dramatically designed to provide circumstances which are favourable to the attempt to discover what those feelings were really about: the point being, of course, that they are only really understood when they can be re-experienced.

Certainly the history of research supervision in dramatherapy suggests awareness of the significance of this kind of monitoring. In this case, it has usually been expressed in the collaborative, exploratory ways of thinking, feeling and proceeding among those taking part in the research process, as this finds an echo in the way that the Arts Therapies Research Committee has interacted within itself. A committee structure organized for the sharing of expertise and insights within an atmosphere of mutual support and encouragement corresponds to the kind of research design that has been found to be most appropriate for arts therapies research. The newly formed Dramatherapy Research Subcommittee of the British Association for Dramatherapy has taken upon itself supervisory responsibility for the research activities of its members, whether they are working as individuals or groups. Although each member of the group has her or his own therapy supervisor, the process of carrying out research seems to call for the kind of open-ended, purposeful and effective structure provided by the research committee, either by consultation with individual members or specially convened groups of interested people, or at workshops organized by the whole committee. The experience of being supervised by and among one's peers often seems to give rise to insights of a less conventional, more spontaneous kind than those likely to surface in orthodox, one-to-one supervision, where the supervisor's awareness of being 'on the spot' – in the sense described above by Shainberg (1983) – may prove fatally inhibiting. From the discussion of possible research areas to taking actual decisions about design, methodology and treatment of results, the committee is there at every step of the way to make suggestions and give support, reproducing in its own creative action the kind of interchange embodied in the research activity it is engaged in commenting on, to which it contributes something of its own brand of involved detachment.

The Arts Therapies Research Committee

In dramatherapy research, consultation and supervision tend to overlap. This is because consultation develops into the kind of involvement in the research process that is usually associated with supervision, whilst supervision, in its group or shared form, comes to resemble the exchange of insight and expertise associated with consultancy. In fact, research supervision tends characteristically towards consultation, as the actual structure of the research serves as a focus for examination and discussion apart from the researcher's personal experience of involvement in the human situation under scrutiny –

which characteristically takes centre stage in other kinds of supervision. As we have seen, however, this distancing effect sometimes actually permits a greater degree of engagement with interpersonal reality because it is able to disarm some of the therapist-researcher's natural defensiveness in the real presence of the client.

From the formation of the Arts Therapies Research Committee in 1988, an important source of research supervision and consultancy has always been the research seminar, in which a small group of interested people, some of whom are actively involved in ongoing research projects, meet and discuss work in progress. Out of this way of working came a series of Arts Therapies Research Conferences, notably those held at the City University in London in 1989 and 1990. The research projects themselves, of course, are now carried out under the auspices of universities (or other institutions having university status and facilities), which provide supervision for investigating dramatherapy as they would normally do for any kind of research activity. The benefit of the seminar system lies mainly within the area of training in research methodology – and the opportunity this provides for students to reflect on the underlying theories and philosophies of research. Because dramatherapy research is still a comparatively new field, however, people setting out to do it are likely to find more help outside their parent institution than within it, and this is where research seminars are particularly valuable. Individual supervision may sometimes be hard to find; although, as Payne points out, 'Those arts therapists who have conducted research may be willing to act as academic and clinical supervisors to those beginning projects' (Payne 1993, p.232).

Among the Aims and Objectives of the Research Subcommittee, which attempt to provide a forum for discussion in dramatherapy research, are:

1. To collate details of research undertaken by dramatherapists and other information relevant to dramatherapy research.

2. To be a point of contact for those interested in dramatherapy research.

3. To provide guidance for undertaking and writing up research. The committee will also have other members outside the Sub-committee Council ... so that it will be large enough to function as a point of contact and forum for discussion. (BADTh Research Subcommittee *Aims and Objectives* 1998)

The Arts Therapies Research Committee may be contacted at the Birmingham Centre for Arts Therapies, The Friends Institute, 220 Moseley Road, Highgate, Birmingham B12 0DG (e-mail BCAT.office @Binternet.com Internet:http://wkweb5.cableinetco.uk/ccc)

References

Buber, M. (1966) *I and Thou.* Edinburgh: T & T Clark.

Grainger, R. (1999) *Researching the Arts Therapies: A Dramatherapist's Perspective.* London: Jessica Kingsley Publishers.

Jones, R. (1989) 'Supervision – a choice between equals.' *British Journal of Psychotherapy,* 505–511.

King, G., Keohane, R.O. and Verba, S. (1994) *Designing Social Enquiry.* Princeton, NJ: Princeton University Press.

McNiff, S. (1998) *Art-Based Research.* London: Jessica Kingsley Publishers.

Payne, H. (ed) (1993) *Handbook of Enquiry in the Arts Therapies: One River, Many Currents.* London: Jessica Kingsley Publishers.

Robson, C. (1993) *Real World Research.* Oxford: Blackwell.

Searles, H. (1965) 'The informational value of the supervisor's emotional experiences.' In H. Searles (ed) *Collected Papers on Schizophrenia and Related Subjects.* London: Hogarth Press.

Shainberg, D. (1983) 'Teaching therapists how to be with their clients.' In J. Welwood (ed) *Awakening the Heart.* New York: Random House.

Shohet, R. and Hawkins, P. (1989) *Supervision in the Helping Professions.* Milton Keynes: Open University Press.

PART IV

Supervisor Training with Dramatherapy

CHAPTER 9

Training the Supervisor-Dramatherapist I

A Psychodynamic Approach

Marina Jenkyns

Introduction

There are many models of supervision and a variety of trends and views of what supervision is, what it covers and with whom. Carroll (1996) has done extensive research in the field and provides a helpful overview of the literature. His work is related to counselling, as indeed is much of the writing on process supervision of clinical practice. Langs (1994) provides a much-needed perspective on psychoanalytic supervision and Martindale *et al.* (1997), also coming from that area, most stimulatingly apply their thinking to a range of different clinical situations and health care workers. Pritchard (1995), writing of supervision in social work, includes a helpful chapter entitled, 'Supervision – taking account of feelings' but the main thrust of this book is a focus on task or management supervision. The therapist working within an organization can learn much from these approaches to supervision used in allied fields. However, the supervision of therapy work, whilst it may be undertaken within a management structure of a large organization, requires that the affective and unconscious processes indicated by behaviour and feeling are brought from the wings into centre stage. The seminal work of Mattison (1975) which came from social work via the Institute of Marital Studies brought a psychoanalytic perspective and introduced the importance of recognizing the now widely accepted concept of parallel process or mirroring in supervision for anyone working in the area of interpersonal relationships. Hawkins and Shohet (1989), to whom we shall return in this chapter, usefully bring together some of these approaches which had gradually been disseminated through a growing interest – reflected largely through articles rather than books – on supervision in the field over the last twenty years or so. It is against this background that I shall consider the training of dramatherapist supervisors. Very little has been written as yet about the supervision of arts therapists, so how do we find our way in training dramatherapists when the only costumes we have for them appear to be borrowed from other plays?

The course which I run in Britain for the training of dramatherapy supervisors will form the basis for this chapter. Within dramatherapy supervision we are forging our own ways, working within what is important to us in our theoretical development so far but also using models, methods and ways of thinking from work already existing within the fields of psychoanalyis, counselling and the care professions. In my work as a trainer of supervisors I try to achieve a balance between the essence of dramatherapy and models of reflective practice used in those other fields. As a teacher I have always believed in the effectiveness of the enthusiasm of the teacher for the subject taught. In training at such an advanced level a thereotical perspective is important and as trainer I can only offer a theoretical base which speaks to me. We best remember stories that have a particular resonance for us and so it is with theory. Theory is a way of thinking about something, it is not an absolute truth; other people's ways may be different from mine, others may teach supervision differently. I see my task as offering my trainees a way of thinking about supervision which makes sense to me of the roles to be undertaken and the tasks to be performed. I can also offer room within the structure of the course for people to develop their own ways. Thus the trainee does not become a clone of the trainer but is enabled to find their own way of working from a firm base of an initial theoretical framework.

My own influences are the importance of the work of both Winnicott and Klein from the psychoanalytic object relations field to the theories of dramatherapy. (For a fuller exposition of this see Jenkyns 1996.) Winnicott is especially helpful in relation to our consideration of the environment provided by the dramatherapist through his understanding of the importance of play and creativity in therapy. His notion of the 'good-enough' mother is also highly relevant to the work of supervision. Klein has much to offer the dramatherapist on the concepts of projection and introjection which are central to dramatherapy. I also believe that these theoreticians provide a rigour and holding framework for the therapist to think about and work with some of the more difficult and painful areas, the avoidance of which is often expressed through resistance, idealization and denial and which the supervisor must continually be on the alert for. What follows is an attempt to show how theory and practice come together in the particular supervisor training which I have designed and run.

Supervision as support

Supervision is often spoken of as support. But what do we mean by support? And who is being supported? Hawkins and Shohet (1989) quote the British Association of Counselling thus, 'The primary purpose of supervision is to protect the best interests of the client.' The British Association of Dramatherapists' statement on the supervision of Dramatherapy practice (1997) defines supervision as a:

> formal arrangement for dramatherapists to discuss and explore their work regularly ... through the supervision process the supervisor can ensure the dramatherapist is addressing the needs of the client. (p.41)

The client, then, is the final focus of the work. The BADTh statement also points out that:

> Dramatherapy makes considerable demands upon dramatherapists who may become over-involved, overlook some important point or have undermining doubts about their own usefulness. It is difficult, if not impossible, at times to to be objective about one's work and the opportunity to explore it regularly in confidence with an appropriate person is an invaluable and essential component of good practice ... Through the supervision process the supervisor can ensure that the dramatherapist is addressing the needs of the client. (p.5)

Thus the message is that in order to carry out the task of therapy responsibly the therapist must have a structure within which to examine his or her practice. Support does not therefore mean having a space simply to talk and be heard, to offload and be replenished, or to be reassured, though all of these things might happen within supervision. Supervision is, rather, a place to rigorously explore one's work and gain insight into it in the service of the clients; the word 'support' must therefore be interpreted within this context.

The tasks of supervision

If the central aim of supervision is to support in the ways outlined above we need to be clear what are tasks which will enable that to be achieved. Hawkins and Shohet (1989) summarize Kadushin's (1976) proposal that supervision has three main functions: educative, supportive and managerial. Although written in the context of social work I think these can be particularly helpful when thinking about the stage of professional development and work context of the supervisee. A newly qualified therapist, although having had supervision whilst training, may still need the supervisor to provide an educative function, not simply by modelling but by adopting more of a teaching role in relation to the acquisition of skills, particularly where the use of the art form is concerned, reinforcing the importance of boundaries and helping the supervisee with difficulties arising out of their new role as a dramatherapist. These functions operate alongside the consultative process which is the exploration of the session and ongoing therapy work and the understanding of transference and countertransference phenomena. The skill of the supervisor is to move within these functions according to the overall aim of supervision in the context of the individual supervisee.

Supervision: a question of authority

The aim of the supervisor training is to extend the skills, expertise and experience of the dramatherapist into that of the supervisor. The image conjured up by the word supervisor is in many ways an unfortunate one with the connotations of 'super' being altogether better. I think of the image it can create in the mind of a vertical line with the therapist somewhere near the bottom and the supervisor somewhere near the top. I think the image of a horizontal line is a more accurate and more helpful one. In this image the supervisor is not projected into an elevated position. What is reflected by this image is the fact that they have travelled further along the line in some aspect of therapeutic work and training and have acquired the skills necessary to perform the task of supervision. The training course automatically engages trainees with the struggle as they are caught on the cross between those two lines: the struggle with projections of judge and judgement, with inner judgemental objects which get projected onto the concept of 'supervisor' with its connotations of superior power, all-seeingness and looking over one's shoulder. As accomplished professionals the very fact of being in training again can provoke feelings of being deskilled, or be manifest in an omnipotent defence; these may also echo other times in training. They can, too, be a mirror of the dynamics which will enter the supervisory space especially with student or newly qualified therapists.

The course is a part-time course which takes place over two years. To proceed along the horizontal line paying attention to both the conscious and unconscious processes which are involved in this kind of learning takes time. Where conscious learning is concerned new skills are being learned and time is needed for them to be practised. I shall return to this when discussing the course structure in more detail. Where learning by enabling unconscious aspects related to the work of supervision is concerned, one of the most fundamental is the need to pay attention to the inner parental objects which are activated in such a training. These can, over time, be worked with in such a way that allows shifts in an individual's sense of their own authority to occur. Only then is it possible to take on fully the authority inherent in the role. This is crucial in supervision work, for if the supervisor is not comfortable with the authority invested in the role, the therapist will find it harder to take the authority of the supervisee's role. If we cannot fully occupy our roles then the performance of the task will be less effective. The concept of authority derived from group relations training can be particularly useful in thinking about the role of supervisor. Related to this Obholzer (1994), whilst discussing authority in relation to organizations, refers to authority from above, from below and from within. I would suggest that the supervisor (who might or might not be in a management role) needs a good-enough sense of the 'authority within' in order to inhabit his or her role and carry out the task of supervision. This means that trainee supervisors need time to become aware of their own patterns related to authority figures. The process of facing issues of good-enoughness, and issues of projection and denial in relation to one's own authority can be painful and difficult. The training aims to provide a context in which this journey can be made.

The idea that the supervisee also has authority is sometimes met with surprise. As long as the notion of authority implies an 'authoritarian' rather than an 'authoritative' stance it is difficult to begin to think of each role as having its own authority within it which enables one to fully occupy it and work within the tasks it exists to accomplish. Obholzer (1994, p.41) distinguishes the two stances within the frame of reference of object relations theory, positing that the term 'authoritative' denotes 'a depressive position state of mind in which the persons managing authority are in touch both

with the roots and sanctioning of their authority and with their limitations.'
'Authoritarian', on the other hand, he places within the paranoid schizoid
state, 'manifested by being cut off from roots of authority and process of
sanction, the whole being fuelled by an omnipotent inner world process'.
The supervisee is a therapist; he or she has their own authority as a therapist.
Therapists are the ones in ongoing contact with their clients, they have the
authority designated to them by the therapeutic contract and relationship. As
supervisees they also have an authority in that role; the role requires that they
discuss their work honestly and are open to the process which takes place in
the consultation space of the supervision session to the end of furthering
their understanding of the client's difficulties and the nature of the work
being undertaken in the therapy. The task also therefore gives authority to
the role. I suggest that the more the supervisor and the supervisee can operate
from their own authority within their respective roles the more the client will
be enabled to take up his or her role as client. It is a rigorous task. The
supervisor has continually to operate within this depressive position process,
tolerating ambivalence which is a characteristic of this state, in order to be
truly authoritative in role. In being able to do so he or she can hold the
potential space of supervision in which something truly creative can occur.
In this space the fantasy is dispelled that the supervisor knows all the answers
and can tell the supervisee what to do – which is often what the supervisee
would like as a way of avoiding staying within their own depressive position
state of mind and tolerating ambivalence, not knowing, being aware of
limitations, which are painful and difficult places to inhabit.

Supervision's subtext: envy, rivalry and competition

Related to these issues of authority are those of envy, rivalry and competition.
Since they are part of the dynamic of supervisor–supervisee relationships
anyway they cannot be ignored in the training and since the training involves
a small group of people who are all working towards completing a training
course which entitles them to be approved supervisors, these issues which
echo earlier sibling relationships will inevitably arise in overt or covert ways
or both. And since the training by definition means that there are trainers,
unresolved difficulties with authority figures and paranoid schizoid ways of
dealing with issues of envy, rivalry and competition in relation to staff
quickly become apparent if the trainers are idealized or denigrated. Again the
process of two years allows time for these issues to emerge and be worked
with at some depth within the context of the task of the course; movement

towards the depressive position state of mind is given room to grow. I believe it is crucial that these issues are addressed because the supervisor has to be alert to the part they play in the relationship between supervisor and supervisee, in the client's material and therapy relationship that are being brought to supervision.

Supervisor training: a potential space

The context

I have already suggested elsewhere (Jenkyns 1997) that it can be helpful to look at supervision as a potential space, described by Winnicott as a place in which the unconscious of client and therapist can play (Winnicott 1971). But we must also remember that any training course takes place within a wider context, another 'space' to which it has a conscious relationship and which must also be remembered when unconscious dynamics surface. This course takes place within the context of the British Association of Dramatherapists which has stipulated certain requirements of its members related to supervision and who can supervise. It also takes place within the context of a variety of postgraduate dramatherapy courses which each have their own particular emphasis whilst sharing a broad agreed basis for training laid down by the Association. Trainees on a further course, such as supervisor training, will have different ways of practising and thinking about dramatherapy, and a rich variety of skills. The trainer has to be alert to this wider context particularly when processing the activities and dynamics of the group and when planning content.

The second aspect of context which is important to consider is that of the workplaces which trainees are in, since the particular dynamics of that workplace, and the difficulties of a particular client group, can be carried by the therapist into the course. Helping trainees to understand these dynamics are important in their learning to be able to recognize what supervisees might be bringing with them into the supervisory relationship. Lloyd-Owen (1997) points out, for example, that those working with forensic patients may initially experience the supervisor as 'a persecuting superego'.

If we return to Winnicott's notion of potential space we can find it helpful when thinking about supervisor training and the most beneficial course design. Given that a central aim of the training is to enable the therapist to move along the continuum to occupy the role of supervisor and inhabit it with authority, conditions must be provided in the course structure for that shift to take place. Winnicottian approaches to conditions for growth and development sit very comfortably with dramatherapy. If the training of dramatherapy supervisors is to be related to the root discipline of dramatherapy then the way in which such training is thought about can helpfully echo the theories which underpin dramatherapy. The emphasis is therefore to provide a space which has clear boundaries of organization, role and tasks, and clear aims, but which allows enough freedom for the trainee supervisor to 'play' within the structure to find his or her own authority as a supervisor. It must be a place where knowing and not knowing can be equally balanced since part of the supervisor's task must always be to manage that balance and to help the therapist manage it and therefore enable the therapist to help the client with that aspect of the therapeutic journey.

Containment

The concept of containment is key to therapy. It must therefore be modelled in a training which relates to therapy. Langs (1994) makes clear the unconscious train of events which can affect the work with the analytic patient if what he calls the 'frame' of the supervision becomes muddied. Unconscious material is leaked and it is the patient who suffers from lack of a boundaried frame within which supervision can be practised. He comments with concern on the loose frameworks within which much analytic supervision of trainees has hitherto taken place, where blurring of role boundaries, as well as those of time and place and conduct of the supervisor, lead to the inability to correctly interpret the patient's material or the interventions of the therapist. Containment is achieved by clear aims, task setting, task and role boundaries and the maintenance of these in spite of difficulties which might occur. In the training setting this is achieved by regularity of time, adherence to time boundaries, and the perpetual reference of the trainers in their own processing to the aims and purpose of the training. This mirrors the constant checking a therapist must do to remain on task when confusions abound and the way seems unclear in a therapeutic relationship. Since the training is not therapy, however, this is particularly vital, because there are times when the conscious learning agenda and the unconscious learning agenda become either too split or too merged rather than in balance. By constantly referencing the aims and purpose of the course, staff continue to provide containment through the choice of intervention, task execution and course management.

Boundary management

A timetable which contains times for clearly defined tasks and also provides structured time for activities which are not pre-determined is a good way of catering for and managing the different thrusts of the course. With a course which meets on average every two months for two days' intensive work the way in which the process is allowed to develop and both conscious and unconscious learning needs are revealed, is by adherence to well-structured learning provision. One of the most frequent comments in course evaluation forms has been the positive experience related to the way the learning has been structured. But the partnership of structured learning with attention to boundaries is crucial. Thus the stage a group is at by the end of any one weekend must be respected. To put in extra time, extend the discussions, etc. would simply dissipate the emotional charge of the group and disallow the truthful development of the process. Thus a collusive relationship between trainers and trainees could develop which implicitly states that painful material can be avoided, that unknowing cannot be tolerated, or that projections and transferences are not able to be held, reflected upon and appropriately interpreted. This would subvert the experience from staying in touch with an essential part of the overall supervisory process. The course must model the boundaries from the beginning and if the group tries to flout them then that is material for the trainers to be aware of and ponder on its meaning in the context of the aims and purpose of the course. Only then will group members be able truly to be free to play within the space, explore their own behaviour and eventually take responsibility for it.

Structure

The course is structured over two years with trainees meeting for six weekends in each year. During the weekends the group works intensively combining theoretical study with experiential learning structures, both staff led and trainee led. Between the weekends a peer partnership operates with trainees meeting and/or communicating in other ways to focus on aspects of the course. This peer-pair substructure also provides the opportunity for practising supervision skills in the first year. It also helps continuity of learning and relationship within the course.

Between weekend meetings detailed process recordings of supervisory work are written and sent for comment to tutors who provide written feedback designed to help the trainee supervisor reflect on their work and provide pointers for learning. In each year short tutorials to clarify points arising from the comments are built into the course, as are more substantial tutorials mid-year and end of year.

On a course where a group meets weekly, course members can build up acquaintance with one another much more rapidly than a group which meets, on average, every eight weeks. In that situation the dynamics of the group can be harnessed for learning in a different way to those on a course such as I am describing where anxiety must be both recognized yet contained sufficiently to enable the group to cohere and bond together in the common task. If trainees become overwhelmed by anxiety there can be the temptation to revise the decision to train. Given that the nature of supervision means that the supervisor must be able to tolerate unknowing there must be a balance between holding to that part of the task on the part of the trainers and providing access to enough 'knowing' to make the anxiety manageable and constructive to the learning process. This is where the relationship between structure and content is crucial.

Content
YEAR ONE

In the first year the emphasis is on the trainees acquiring a method of working in supervision. They explore what supervision means from their experience thus far in their career. They become acquainted with different ideas as to what supervision is and acquire an understanding of categories such as Kadushin's, mentioned earlier. This is where the 'knowing' comes in. Trainees are required to get to know a method of working, understand its theoretical base and experiment with applying it in practice. The model used on the course is that evolved by Hawkins and Shohet (1989). In this the supervisor works with six modes of reflection which can guide the supervisor in his or her thinking at any moment in the session and provide choices for intervention. The authors divide these into two groups; modes 1–3 *The therapy session is reported upon in the supervision* and modes 4 – 6, *Focus on the therapy session as it is reflected in the supervision process.* The modes are described as (Hawkins and Shohet 1989, pp.56–58):

1. Reflection on the content of the therapy session.

2. Exploration of the strategies and interventions used by the therapist.

3. Exploration of the therapy process and relationship.

4. Focus on the therapist's countertransference.

5.   Focus on the here-and-now process as a mirror or parallel of the there-and-then process.

6.   Focus on the supervisor's countertransference.

Acquiring an ability to work with the first three modes means developing the trainees' powers of listening and making accurate observations of what is actually told them by the supervisee; they are having to listen to two stories simultaneously: the therapist's story of the session and the client's story as revealed in the session. They also have to hold in mind the other stories that have formed the history of the work so far. Working within the second three modes they must have the ability to be able both to be present in and simultaneously observe the story which is being woven between therapist and supervisor and to think about the relationship between those two stories in the here-and-now.

In order to work within this method a sound understanding of notions of projection, transference and countertransference is essential. The reading and way in which these aspects of theory are taught will depend on the kind of training and experience the course members already have because the course will consist of trainees from initial therapist trainings which have different theoretical bases. The learning structure for acquiring an understanding of this method is four-tiered:

1.   The theoretical underpinning mentioned above is worked with through prescribed reading, seminar discussions and workshops.

2.   A staff-led workshop approach is used to introduce the concept near the beginning of the course. Here the essential formula of client/therapist/supervisor is introduced which will inform all future work on the course. After that trainees are responsible for taking each of the modes and designing a workshop to explore it using dramatherapy methods with their fellow trainees during the first year.

3.   Throughout the year the trainees in their peer pairs are supervising each other using the six modes; they also use the pair structure to discuss and explore them and their related theoretical concepts and application.

4.   Process recordings are written in which trainees are required to define the modes used in their thinking at different stages of the reported session. As the year proceeds increasing emphasis is laid on the use of the process recording to reflect retrospectively on the interventions made. For example the trainee can ask himself or herself, 'Why did I

work from mode 2 at this point rather than mode 4?' or 'Was the fact that I worked within a framework of mode 6 at this point, while being useful for me as a way of untangling what was going on, not as useful to the supervisee as if I had led her straight back by focusing my mind on the need for a mode 1 intervention?' As the trainee gets more used to the modes as tools for thinking and acting, these kinds of questions can deepen the understanding of the way the mode method can be both a holding structure for the supervisor and a rigorous system for both intervention and reflection on the process of the work.

Whilst this aspect of the 'knowing' is in place, it provides containment for the trainees to struggle with the difficulties of the other areas of work which are just as important. Without the struggle in the here-and-now with their own process the work with the six modes would not be possible, for a focus in the supervision session on the supervisor's own process is integral to that way of working.

Throughout the course I find it useful to bear in mind Bion's basic assumption theory (Bion 1961). Here the apparently irrational behaviour of groups can be understood in terms of what he calls three basic assumptions, that of dependency, pairing or fight–flight. (For excellent expositions of Bion's ideas see Rioch 1975 and Stokes 1994.) Whilst a group is in the grip of any one or all of these basic assumptions it will not be able to function on task as a work group. However, he goes on to illustrate how these basic assumptions can also be usefully harnessed to further the work of an organization for which dependency, pairing or fight–flight are useful or indeed essential to achieving the aims of the organization.

Thus, on the supervisors' training course the question for the tutors is how to harness this in a helpful way rather than collude with it as an anti-task activity. For example, at the beginning it is likely that the dependency basic assumption is operating. Recognizing that this is occurring at the very beginning when anxiety is high and group cohesion needs to develop, it would be unhelpful for the staff to hand over the running of sessions to the trainees; a certain amount of dependency is helpful at that stage in a way which it would not be later on in the course when trainees are struggling to gain a sense of their own authority.

The pair structure is built into the course; again the ways in which this is worked with can enhance or impede the progress of both individual and group. Fight–flight is most common in this context as a basic assumption activity which cannot be usefully harnessed, for when it occurs it is as a defence against the anxiety of dealing with such issues as envy, rivalry and competition or engaging with the painful aspects of the task.

In the light of basic assumption theory the link between the group itself and learning about supervising groups can helpfully be made, for the group can draw on its own experience of itself and, with staff input on group theory linking with reflective group processing, implications for working with supervisory groups can be addressed.

YEAR TWO

Whilst the awareness of the group and its process continues throughout the course, in the second year a major shift in content is that each trainee must supervise a therapist in the field. This work forms the cornerstone of the course and is brought to the course in formal presentations, seminar discussions and peer pair work as well as providing the material for detailed process recording. Finding a supervisee and setting up supervision is not always an easy process; practical reasons such as geographical location may mingle with less tangible unconscious forces within the individual and the group. Great attention is paid to this in the course with trainees working experientially and in seminars on issues of setting up supervision both on a practical level and on a dynamic level. Here work on contracts, legal and ethical issues, reviewing, evaluating and ending are issues to which attention is given. If a trainee finds difficulty in finding a supervisee the process is deemed as valuable in itself both for the individual concerned and for the whole group in terms of the learning which is gained from this situation. In the second year the aim is to encourage a more integrated way of working and for trainees to experience other teaching styles provided by the input of high-calibre guest lecturers whose known expertise in particular fields interests the course members of that particular intake.

The other difference between Year 1 and Year 2 is that more of the timetable is without the prescription of precise content. This is to allow trainees to begin to define their own learning needs more clearly and take responsibility for those. It is in this year that organizational issues are addressed: Hawkins' and Shohet's seventh mode where the six modes are seen in wider context of organizational issues comes into focus here. It is in this year also that issues of ending, leaving and moving away from both peers and staff can be both addressed in themselves in terms of the group's experience and also related to the supervision process and the development of the supervisee and the supervisory relationship.

The dramatic muse at the heart of supervision

'Paradox is at the heart of the dramatic experience. The individual as actor or group as chorus lives simultaneously in two realities' (Landy 1993, p.11). How close the words of a dramatherapist are to those of a psychoanalyst writing of the therapeutic relationship. Casement (1985, p.35) writes 'the capacity to be in two places at once, in the patient's shoes and in one's own, can only be encompassed if therapists can develop a capacity to synthesize these apparently paradoxical ego-states.' Casement coined the term 'trial identification' where the therapist tries out in his own mind receiving the interpretation he is about to give his patient. By putting himself in the shoes of the patient he can feelingly judge how the patient will hear what he says and therefore try to connect empathically with the patient. He first developed the technique of trial identification from trying out identifying with the patients his supervisees brought to supervision sessions. He created a kind of internal drama for himself in order to arrive at a greater understanding of the patient. 'The observing ego' and the 'experiencing ego' of which Casement speaks are states of relationship within the self which are essential to understanding the practice of dramatherapy. The dramatherapist, infinitely adept at working in role and enabling others to do so, has automatically, I would suggest, an invaluable tool for use in supervision and this informs all the work a trainee dramatherapy supervisor does in extending his or her dramatherapist self into a supervisor self. In this respect the deep understanding of the dramatic form informs the training. Whilst it is actualized in training sessions, presentation of supervisory material, or workshops where trainees continue to practise their art-form, it is also central to working the concept of supervision in the way that Casement suggests when he writes of developing the internal supervisor in the therapist.

The dramatic element is also crucial when it comes to interpreting the theories and methods I have outlined, exploring and internalizing them. The setting up of a client/therapist/supervisor matrix with role-play, inner voice, auxiliaries and participant/audience is one of the best ways to engage trainees in the six-mode structure and begin to learn and internalize the concepts. Likewise transference and countertransference is explored theoretically through prepared reading and seminars but this is always in partnership with an experiential workshop which is designed to deepen the learning gained from the cognitive work. Whilst concepts can be explored and internalized more deeply, I believe, by use of dramatherapy methodology, particular skills are taught in this way too. For example, I invented a teaching exercise for this course in order to develop both rigorous discipline of thinking and the ability to hold on rather than jumping in with advice or interpretation, which would also provide an opportunity to acquire proficiency with the diffferent modes. In pairs one trainee presents a piece of work and the partner who plays the role of the supervisor listens. Here the 'supervisor' has different coloured counters for each mode. Each time the 'supervisor' would normally speak they instead put down a counter representing the appropriate mode of intervention which is informing their thinking at that point while they remain silent and continue listening. At the end of a given time the 'supervisor' now tells the presenter what counter represented what they might have said. Together they think about the piece of therapy work, the 'supervisor's' strategies and the implications both for supervision and for their understanding of the modes. A variation on this is for the trainee who is presenting also to have counters which they likewise put down without comment as they proceed through their presentation of material. Sharing afterwards in the same way the two trainees have a perspective on the internal supervisory process and the difference of perception of supervisor and supervisee.

Casement's trial identification can also be worked with in an experiential setting where different members of the group try out responses to a statement given by a member playing either a client or a supervisee. How the words are heard can be closely examined and the emotional effect of the words and tone of voice explored. It is particularly useful when trying out the initial phone call or first meeting of supervisor and supervisee to write dialogues which can be rehearsed and then played to an audience of the rest of the group. The experience can be felt through the role-play and feedback can help the trainee to reassess the original dialogue. The store of teaching techniques is endless if the trainers keep their art-form firmly to the fore while at the same time keeping the therapist and supervisor within themselves alive.

Conclusion

To train in the spirit of supervision is the task I set myself as a trainer. In training dramatherapy supervisors the challenge is to permanently allow the aims, tasks, roles and processes involved in supervision itself to inform those of training, while maintaining a clear distinction between supervision and training for supervision. At the end of the course trainees who have successfully moved through an ongoing process of learning which is self, peer and tutor assessed receive a Statement of Completion. At no stage are marks given, for this is not in the spirit of supervision. Learning to take one's authority and feel oneself able and ready to take up the role is the most important place for a trainee to have arrived at. Held by an understanding of this — the primary task of the course — training supervisors can be a rich experience in which the trainees are by no means the only ones to learn. Just as the paradox of being in two ego-states simultaneously is at the heart of the kind of listening the supervisor needs to do, so two apparently paradoxical statements from two poets seem a fitting way to sum up the task of a trainer of supervisors who work within an art-form:

> ...Negative Capability ... is when a man is capable of being in uncertainties, mysteries and doubts without any irritable reaching after fact and reason. (Keats 1970)

> There are five people in this room
> Who still don't know what I'm saying.
> 'What is she saying?' they're asking.
> 'What is she doing here?'
> It is not enough to be interminable; one must also be precise.'
> (Alice Walker 1985)

Notes and acknowledgements

The course described was originally designed for the training of dramatherapy supervisors. Interest has been shown in it by therapists from other disciplines, especially other arts therapies. The spirit and structure of the course is, I believe, applicable to those working in allied fields who include a psychodynamic approach in their clinical work. In time some changes are envisaged in the teaching provision to embrace the needs of those wishing to take the course who are not dramatherapists but who find that it encapsulates the essentials of training for supervision applicable to their own discipline.

I should like to acknowledge the input of the visiting lecturers on the course and the invaluable contribution of Ditty Dokter. I should also like to thank all those who have trained on the course so far, from whom I have learned much.

References

Bion, W. (1961) *Experiences in Groups*. London: Tavistock.

British Association of Dramatherapists (1997) 'Statement on the supervision of dramatherapy practice.' BADTh, pp.5, 41.

Carroll, M. (1996) *Counselling Supervision*. London: Cassell.

Casement, P. (1985) *On Learning from the Patient*. London: Tavistock.

Hawkins, P. and Shohet, R. (1989) *Supervision in the Helping Professions*. Milton Keynes: Open University Press.

Jenkyns, M. (1996) *The Play's The Thing: Exploring Text in Drama and Therapy*. London: Routledge.

Jenkyns, M. (1997) 'Gender issues in supervision.' In S. Jennings (ed) *Dramatherapy Theory and Practice 3*. London: Routledge.

Kadushin, A. (1976) *Supervision in Social Work*. New York: Columbia University Press.

Keats, J. (1970) 'Letter to George and Tom Keats, December 1817.' In Gittings, R. (ed) *Letters of John Keats*. Oxford: Oxford University Press.

Landy, R. (1993) *Persona and Performance*. London: Jessica Kingsley Publishers.

Langs, R. (1994) *Doing Supervision and Being Supervised*. London: Karnac.

Lloyd-Owen, D. (1997) 'From action to thought: supervising mental health workers with forensic patients.' In B. Martindale, M. Hörner, M. Roderíguez and J.-P. Vidit (eds) *Supervision and Its Vicissitudes*. London: Karnac.

Martindale, B., Hörner, M., Roderíguez, M. and Vidit, J.-P. (eds) (1997) *Supervision and Its Vicissitudes*. London: Karnac.

Mattison, J. (1975) *The Reflection Process in Casework Supervision*. London: The Institute of Marital Studies (Publications).

Obholzer, A. (1994) 'Authority, power and leadership.' In A. Obholzer and V. Zagier Roberts (eds) *The Unconscious at Work*. London: Routledge.

Pritchard, J. (ed) (1995) *Good Practice in Supervision*. London: Jessica Kingsley Publishers.

Rioch, M.J. (1975) 'The work of Wilfred Bion on Groups.' In A.D. Colman and W.H. Bexton (eds) *Group Relations Reader 1*. Washington. A.K. Rice Institute.

Stokes, J. (1994) 'The unconscious at work in groups and teams: Contributions from the work of Wilfred Bion.' In A. Obholzer and V. Zagier Roberts (eds) *The Unconscious at Work*. London: Routledge.

Walker, A. (1985) *Horses Make a Landscape Look More Beautiful*. London: The Women's Press Ltd.

Winnicott, D.W. (1971) *Playing and Reality*. Harmondsworth: Penguin.

CHAPTER 10

Training the Supervisor-Dramatherapist II

The Theatre-Based Approach

Elektra Tselikas-Portmann, Sue Jennings,
Katerina Couroucli-Robertson
and Demys Kyriacou

Introduction

In this chapter we would like to reflect on issues concerning the training of supervisor dramatherapists, making special reference to the theatre-based approach. After discussing the need for supervision training in general and the necessity for dramatherapy supervision training in particular, we will present some principles that underlie the structure of curricula and apply them to the conception of a theatre-based supervision training. Finally, some examples from training sessions will illustrate the effect of theatre-based supervisor training and demonstrate the advantages of this approach. In our arguments we take a position that does not differentiate between theatre and drama. We rather see 'theatre as the direct experience shared when people imagine and behave as if they were other than themselves in some other place and at another time' (Booth 1992, p.1). In that sense all activities that take place in dramatic reality are 'theatre'. We will not enter the debate that creates a dichotomy between 'drama' and 'theatre' here. Maybe 'performance' is a term that could help integrate the two: 'Performance means process as well as final artefact' (Huxley and Witts 1996, p.2) and concerns itself with an artist's creative process (Huxley and Witts 1996). It is the supervisor's, supervisee's or client's creative process that interests us here. A next step could obviously be to introduce the term 'performance' to the debate. But since we will not be explicitly concerned with terminology here, we will leave this for another occasion and merely state that, in the present chapter, we will adopt a definition of theatre that is all-inclusive.

About supervision and dramatherapy supervision

Supervision can be defined as the process whereby two individuals, the supervisor and the supervisee, meet 'to discuss clinical and professional issues as they relate to the professional growth of the supervisee' (Holloway 1995, p.3). The goal of supervision is the enhancement of the supervisee's effective professional functioning (Holloway 1995, p.6).

At a first glance these definitions look simple. Indeed, why should there be a need for a specific training in supervision, and particularly dramatherapy supervision? Before we proceed to looking more closely at the necessity for dramatherapy supervision training, let us look at the necessity for supervision training more generally. What is the task of the supervisor and why would she need special training to perform this task in addition to her professional experience? According to Holloway (1995, p.2), 'articulating the layers of thinking, understanding, conceptualizing, and applying is the task of the supervisor.' Furthermore, in the situation of training (trainee supervision) the supervisor will need to connect science (theory), method and practice, and thus supervision becomes the most complex of all activities associated with the practice of therapy (Holloway 1995). The professional must be assisted to treat each case uniquely, to understand and conceptualize the situation, and then selectively adapt known methods. The professional must be capable, through the process of supervision, of strategically adapting to the needs of the client, using 'interventions through discourse' (Holloway 1995, p.2) on a moment-to-moment basis. As the supervisor identifies and describes the covert processes of this dynamic context, the supervisee is also assisted in the articulation of his or her own process (Holloway 1995). Appropriate training is required in order for the supervisor to satisfactorily complete these tasks by keeping the overview over the supervisory system.

This having been said, several questions now arise. Why should it be necessary to plan and carry out supervision training particularly for dramatherapists or a dramatherapy supervision training? Wouldn't supervision training courses offered generally for professionals working in the counselling and clinical fields also cover the needs of dramatherapy supervision? What is so specific about dramatherapy supervision that it needs specific training and what would then be the advantages of a theatre-based approach within such training?

What is specific about dramatherapy supervision on a theatre-based approach is parallel to what is specific about dramatherapy itself (differentiating it thus from 'drama in therapy'). As Jennings (1998, p.68) points out, in dramatherapy it is 'the relationship between the client and the art form' that is the basis of the therapy. 'The therapist facilitates the relationship with the art form' (Jennings 1998, p.68). In other words, it is not primarily the relationship with the therapist that moves on the process but the relationship with the art form. This 'is a very important difference in philosophy and indeed in belief, concerning the therapeutic outcomes of artistic experience' (Jennings 1998, p.68), which also has important implications regarding the development of the therapeutic process and of the relationship between client and therapist. Accordingly, and with respect to dramatherapy, Jennings (1998) invites us not to succumb to playing the psychotherapist and starting to analyse bits and pieces. Instead, we should imagine that there are alternatives to analytic thinking and through an act of will stay in a different mind-set, that of the dramatic framework. We are not then to make use of different theoretical constructs analytically, but to make use of the drama itself. These same principles would therefore apply for the practice of dramatherapy supervision.

If we compare what has just been said with the statements concerning supervision and supervision training in general as mentioned above, the necessity for a theatre-based supervision training becomes apparent. The supervisor dramatherapist will need the skills of the supervisor as described above. Additionally, she will need to be able to make use of the art form and to differentiate when an analytical attitude is appropriate to the situation and the setting and when a dramatic process will be more helpful in enhancing the supervisee's potential and insight. In this case, the supervisor will need to allow the dramatic process to unfold using her own artistic skills.

Apart from this, the dramatherapy supervisor will need to connect not only science but also art, method and practice. She will model to the supervisee how to apply interventions through art (not only through discourse) on a moment-to-moment basis. The covert processes of the dynamic therapy context will not only be identified and described. Through staying within a dramatic framework, the artistic skills of the supervisee will be enhanced thus enabling her internal guide to emerge, nourishing her and activating her internal supervisor.

Let us now see what could be an appropriate theatre-based curricular structure for the training of dramatherapy supervisors.

A theatre-based curriculum for dramatherapy supervision

The following are defined as general characteristics of curricula (Schreyögg 1994, p.55):

- a consistent and substantiated structure
- explicit and coherent teaching/learning aims and goals according to which the contents will be organized
- a clear time and form structure ...
- ...including forms of evaluation of learning
- openness.

Referring to what we have discussed in the previous section and to the five points mentioned above, we would now like to present the principles of a theatre-based curriculum for dramatherapy supervision.

A consistent and substantiated structure

A curriculum structure should ideally be based on substantiated decisions concerning content and teaching methods. These decisions will be taken according to the value system underlying the curricular concept. An interdependence between the different parts of the curriculum will be prevalent rather than an aims/means relationship (Schreyögg 1994, p.56).

The art of theatre in the sense of dramatic activity is central to dramatherapy and to dramatherapy supervision. In his proposal for a four-part model for the training of the dramatherapist Landy differentiates between theatre art and drama, stating that, 'The performance art of theatre is not necessarily for everyone. The expressive art of spontaneous drama is for all, as we are all performers in everyday life' (Landy 1996, p.8). Yes, we are all performers in everyday life. And our need to perform is even more essential – it is at the very root of our nature. Based on her observations of pregnant women Jennings postulates that humans are already dramatic *in utero* (Jennings 1998, p. 50) and that subsequently the structure of the human mind is essentially dramatic (Jennings 1998, p.124; see also Chapter 2 in this volume). What we should keep in mind then, particularly when designing a dramatherapy curriculum (whether for therapists or supervisors), is the hypothesis about the basically dramatic nature of the human being. This is probably also the feature at the basis of theatre art activity.

It follows from this that we are all by nature potential art performers of theatre, hence our relationship to theatre art will depend on the kind of upbringing and the amount of opportunities we have had to develop this potential. What should be kept in mind here is our basic connection and our potential to theatre-based activity and to artistic dramatic processes.

This having been said, one of the anthropological premises underlying a curriculum for dramatherapy supervision will be the dramatic structure of the human mind. This will need to be taken into consideration when deciding about course content and methodology.

Explicit and coherent teaching/learning aims and goals according to which the contents will be organized

Defining teaching and learning aims as well as goals helps reduce a random selection of contents and methodologies and promotes a systematic organization of the teaching and learning material. The *general aim* of dramatherapy supervision training could be defined as 'promoting qualified, supervisory work building on essentially dramatic premises, as these were defined above.'

The *goals* of training in dramatherapy supervision would be to promote supervisory professional competence, personal and interpersonal competence, and supervisory artistic competence. These competences can be acquired through theory (supervision and dramatherapy), methodology, self-exploration and awareness as a supervisor, practice, and finally supervision of the supervisory practice.

By *professional competence* what is meant is professional knowledge and professional skills for the task of theatre-based dramatherapy supervision. This includes theoretical, artistic and methodological knowledge. In this particular instance this would be covered by the following contents:

- supervision theory (including forms and models of supervision – see also the Introduction to this volume; dramatherapy and playtherapy supervision – see also Chapters 2 and 3 in this volume; supervisory roles and functions – see also Chapter 5 in this volume)
- supervisory triangles (see also Chapter 4 in this volume) (including the supervisory relationship, the client/therapist mirror, accountability and confidentiality)

- supervision settings (see also Chapter 1 in this volume)
- dramatherapy models and their application to the practice of supervision (see also the Introduction to this volume)
- forms of intervention in dramatherapy supervision (see also Chapters 6 and 7 in this volume)
- the dramatherapy supervision bag, which includes artistic materials with which the dramatherapist supervisor works (paints, toys, puppets, clay, props, etc.).

Personal and interpersonal competence can be acquired through an exploration of the qualities of the dramatherapy supervisor, including working with parallel, reflection and artistic processes, contact making, modelling, supporting and encouraging, challenging, giving feedback and guidance, and finally relating theory to practice. An important point here will also be promoting the capacity to perceive complex social situations through different perspectives and reacting to them in a flexible and artistic way. Finally, developing a critical-emancipatory attitude as well as social responsibility will be part of the teaching and learning of personal and interpersonal competence.

As we have defined the facilitation of the relationship between the client and the art form as being central for dramatherapy (and for dramatherapy supervision), the keeping alive and staying aware of the supervisor's *artistic capacity* as well as enhancing the artistic capacity of the supervisee will be central goals through the whole of the teaching and learning processes (we will be giving examples of this later on in this chapter).

A clear time and form structure …

A dramatherapy supervision curriculum will need to have a clear time and form structure. The time and form structure will be related to the goals of the curriculum and will, furthermore, be adapted to the needs of the learning group concerned as well as to their specific context.

A modular structure alternating experiential teaching modules with practice and supervisory modules seems to be most appropriate for a theatre-based dramatherapy supervision curriculum. For example, the curriculum that has been introduced in Greece and recently validated by the British Association of Dramatherapists consists of a) three experiential teaching modules of 30 hours each on theory, methodology and supervisory self-awareness; b) two practice modules of 6 supervision sessions with an individual and 15 supervision sessions with a group or an individual c) written reports of this practice; and d) a total of 12 hours of supervision of practice.

The time and form structure of a dramatherapy supervision curriculum should, finally, be conceived in a way that it can be monitored, evaluated and eventually revised through the initiative of the teaching staff and/or the trainees if necessary.

... Including forms of evaluation of learning

It is obvious that a curriculum should offer the possibility of assessing the learning effects, namely how far the teaching and learning goals have been met. In the dramatherapy supervision curriculum mentioned above, the evaluation of learning (or assessment) took place mainly through written essays, the written supervision reports and case presentations. Furthermore, experiential and creative self and peer assessment taking place during contact time served as a form of learning control. In these assessments, special emphasis is put on the dramatherapy supervisor trainee's understanding of the relationship to the art form within the supervisory system and the insight and empowerment this relationship can enhance. More precisely, at the basis of theatre-based supervision is not only a relationship between client and therapist, and therapist and supervisor, there is also – and this is even more central – the art form and the relationship to the art form. Having faith in the relationship that evolves with and within the art form, as well as maintaining this relationship within the supervisory system, i.e. on all the levels of supervisor, therapist and client, is one of the main tasks of theatre-based supervision (see also the examples stated in the different chapters in this volume).

Openness

Curricula are open concepts, not static institutions, and should be constantly refined and adapted on the basis of a dialogue between teachers and learners. As the formulation of aims and goals depends not only on the value system (beliefs) of the decision makers but also on the social and historical context as well as on the state of the art, a theatre-based dramatherapy supervision curriculum should be open to revision depending on the general developments in the profession as well as on the results of art-based supervision research. It is necessary that such research should be carried out in order for the art of theatre-based supervision to be further developed. As

Grainger (Chapter 8 in this volume) correctly points out, dramatherapy needs as much research as it can get. The same holds true for dramatherapy supervision.

Examples from theatre-based supervision training

In this section we would like to present three examples of the work and learning processes within theatre-based supervision training. The first example from the Greek supervision training course will show the application of the Mandala for the development of a theatre-based supervisor identity and awareness. The second example, also from the Greek supervision training course, will show a dramatherapy supervisor trainee's practice with a music therapist and the containing effect of the art form. The third example, from the Israeli theatre-based supervision training course, deals with the learning processes within the theatre-based dramatherapy supervision training group.

Who is supervising, the German or the Greek?

Within a theatre-based supervision training facilitated by Sue Jennings, the Mandala (see Chapter 2 in this volume) was used to explore and develop personal and interpersonal competence in supervision.

The trainee group consisted of several people who had either had multicultural biographical experiences or were working in multicultural settings. The issue of supervising in multicultural settings had been mentioned. Sue Jennings, the trainer, took up this subject and used it to look at the several levels, facets and perspectives of personal and interpersonal competence in theatre-based supervision.

The trainees were presented with the Mandala and asked to use colours and shapes for each of the sections: the internal supervisor (guide), the internal therapist (skilled person), the internal artist (creative person) and the internal vulnerable client (vulnerable person). The next task was to write in each segment the personal characteristics in terms of culture. In a next step the segments were to be identified with a type of music. Finally, the trainees were asked to locate where, in the Mandala, were the following dramatic archetypal roles: their hero, their trickster, their child, their mother and their old wise person.

We will discuss here the results presented by one of the trainees who, though a Greek, was living and doing her supervision practice in Germany with a multiethnic and multicultural team of women (Germans and non-Germans) working with abused migrant women. We will call this trainee Anastasia. Anastasia filled in the Mandala in the following way:

- *INTERNAL SUPERVISOR*
  colour and shape: straight, ordered, green lines
  personal/cultural characteristic: order
  music: Wagner
  role: none

- *INTERNAL THERAPIST*
  colour and shape: light-yellow mellow covering
  personal/cultural characteristic: light, flowing enlightenment
  music: Mozart
  role: old wise person, mother

- *INTERNAL VULNERABLE CLIENT*
  colour and shape: black chaotic, cloudy circles superseded by a silvery
     covering colour
  personal/cultural characteristic: renegade, refugee, migrant, outcast
  music: none
  role: child

- *INTERNAL ARTIST*
  colour and shape: fiery red rays going from the centre of the Mandala
     towards its outer circle
  personal/cultural characteristic: gypsy
  music: tango, rembetiko[1], fado[2]
  role: trickster

1   The rembetiko is a type of music that was brought to Greece by the Greek refugees of Asia Minor. In 1922, the coast of Asia Minor that by then had been populated by Greeks was conquered by the Turks. One million Greek refugees flooded the mainland of Greece. The music they brought with them was characterized by oriental musical elements and expressed their sufferings, longings and mourning for their lost land.
2   The fado is a Portuguese type of music and song whose name is derived from the word 'destiny' (fatum). It also expresses longings and sadness.

The role of 'hero' was circling the whole of the Mandala, hence containing and holding together all of the segments.

In the subsequent discussion, it was revealed that Anastasia had been having serious problems with her supervision group. The group had chosen her because they wanted a non-German, hence what they called a 'migrant' supervisor. What was explicitly said to her was that they wanted to take the migrant team women's points of view more into consideration. Anastasia, looking Mediterranean, yet brought up and trained in Germany, approached the group in what she believed to be a professional attitude and mainly concentrated on her role as supervisor. She was thereby putting to the fore her ordered, Wagnerian, hence German side. Yet, the German as well as the non-German women perceived her as a 'migrant', on the grounds of her appearance, her name and some information she had given them at the interview before she was engaged by them.

The perception German and non-German women had of migrants was obviously not congruent. What they were projecting onto Anastasia was mirroring the processes of splitting that were going on in the team and between the team and their clients. We will not go into these details here. We will rather concentrate on presenting the insights that Anastasia achieved with respect to her personal and interpersonal competence in the supervision process. The learning was arrived at through contact with the artistic activity and through establishing the relationship with her internal artist.

Anastasia realized through the image revealed by the Mandala that being perceived as a migrant touched her vulnerable internal client. The more she received these projections, the more she activated her internal supervisor, the ordered, Wagnerian side, putting emphasis on its characteristics. This confrontation went to the point that she split into the explicitly played 'professional, rational supervisor' on the one side and into the hidden 'renegade, outcast, refugee migrant' on the other side. She thereby took over the splitting mechanisms of the supervisee and client systems. She also ignored and left unused the resources of the internal therapist and the internal artist, thus remaining unguided. Her inner system was led into an imbalance dominated by the fight between the internal supervisor and the internal vulnerable client. Lacking the nourishment from the internal artist and the mothering and wisdom of the internal therapist, the internal supervisor became devoid of substance, an empty shell trying to keep the internal vulnerable client under control. Anastasia was thus exactly reproducing the mechanisms prevalent between the team of supervisees and their clientele: using authoritarian strategies they were trying to preserve their own 'order' by controlling the 'chaos' of their clients. The connection to the art form (through imagining, painting, expressing metaphorically, playing with colours, shapes, music and archetypal theatre roles) reconnected her to all her parts and their resources, namely also to the internal artist and the internal therapist. Her whole system could be nourished, nurtured and guided and her inner balance and strength restored. In this way she was able to regain her ability to mirror to the supervised team their own dynamics and act as a competent supervisor.

Had the intervention only taken place through discourse emphasizing the relational aspects of the situation, the rational, ordered, Wagnerian part of the internal supervisor would have been allowed to grow further, thus reinforcing the imbalance. Through the artistic intervention, Anastasia realized that many of the characteristics and symbols she connected with her inner artist (gypsy, tango, rembetiko, fado, trickster) were elements that would connect her in a creative, artistic and simultaneously structured way to her group of supervisees and indirectly to their clients. Thus, the relationship to supervisees and clients could be established through the freeing power of the art form. Realizing this, Anastasia could model to her supervisees another, creative, emancipatory way of relating to their clients.

The blending of the two

The cast:

Filotheos	supervisor (trainee)
Dido	supervisee
Xenia	client.

INTRODUCTION

This example is concerned with a practical exploration of some of the issues involved in the supervision process between a dramatherapist (supervisor) and a music therapist (supervisee). The main focus will be:

- on the process of creating a common ground between these two therapeutic approaches, showing that, despite the differences, the creative and healing energies have managed to flow unobstructively within the supervision triangle (supervisor–supervisee–process of supervision)

- on showing how the theatre-based supervision helped both supervisee and supervisor in gaining insight both within the supervision triangle as well as the therapeutic one (therapist–client–therapeutic process).

What follows concerns part of a dramatherapy supervisor trainee's supervision practice done in Greece. We will call this trainee Filotheos. Given his interest in interdisciplinarity Filotheos chose to do his placement (practice) with a music therapist who intended to use dramatic methodology with her client along with the music therapeutic one. Trusting the art form as the common factor for both him and his supervisee and acknowledging the possible difficulties, he embarked on the journey.

THE SUPERVISEE

The supervisee whom we shall call Dido is a 33-year-old music teacher and music therapist trained in the USA, working in Greece, partly as a freelance music therapist and partly as a music teacher. She had participated in several art-therapy workshops whilst studying in the States and also in some dramatherapy workshops conducted by Filotheos.

IMPORTANT ROLES AND ISSUES IN THE SUPERVISION PROCESS

In addition to the issues and difficulties involved in supervising a music therapist, Filotheos was also faced with the following:

- Dido's difficulty in the role of the supervisee stemming from what proved to be a feeling of low self-esteem as a therapist
- Dido's switching from her role as music therapist to that of the music teacher as a form of resistance within the dynamics created with her client
- Dido's negative body-image
- Dido's need to project on him the role of the therapist and his own actions in trying to maintain the role of the supervisor.

In the first supervision session Dido felt quite uncomfortable in her role as supervisee. Anxious and threatened by what Filotheos could have assessed as a 'not so capable therapist' she confessed having a problem with the 'student role' (as she had put it) and with 'authorities in general'. In trying to compensate for her insecurity, she resorted to generalized statements regarding her therapeutic work with her client, her thinking being unfocused and inconcrete. Most of that session unfolded in a verbal and cognitive way, just to make her feel safer. During that session they also touched upon the issue – initially brought by her – of her switching from the role of the music therapist to that of the music teacher. In the beginning he *thought* that there was nothing wrong with that; he actually thought of himself switching from the role of the dramatherapist into that of the director when the situation in a dramatherapy group demands it. However, he *felt* that what Dido had been describing was different. It was at that point that he thought of introducing the dramatic dimension by focusing on the body and letting the non-verbal shed some light on what they had already been discussing.

He suggested that Dido should spend a few minutes considering her two roles and exploring them a little. Then he asked her to find a bodily posture which would represent each role, along with the behavioural patterns connected with them. What she experienced was that she felt the music therapist role as 'more responsible, tense, careful and demanding'; qualities that she felt were 'very heavy' to carry around. On the other hand, as a music teacher she felt she could be 'more of herself' and quite 'friendly with her students'. The bodily postures were very revealing and for the first time Dido realized how uncomfortable the role of the therapist had been for her, at least during that period in her life.

THE CLIENT

Interestingly enough, Dido's client, whom we shall call Xenia, a music student, had come to therapy with her because of what she referred to as an 'inability to play the piano in front of an audience'. Xenia, a dramatic and manipulative personality, had put pressure on Dido to 'heal her' in order to successfully face her piano audition which was about to take place in a month's time! Unable to stand Xenia's pressure and therapeutic demands, Dido slipped into the music teacher's role in order not to confront Xenia's manipulative behaviour and destructive fantasies.

Briefly speaking, there had been an unconscious attempt by Dido to transfer in the supervision what had been going on in the therapeutic triangle. The core of this transference was a multilevel form of *avoidance* and *vague boundaries.*

Filotheos suggested to Dido a short ritual for the opening and closing of her sessions with Xenia, a form of 'container-ritual', which Dido translated into a short and easy piano piece for Xenia to play at the beginning and end of each of their sessions. This musical metaphor finally proved to be very effective in making Xenia feel safer and contained.

It was also at this point of the supervision process that he thought of making overt what had been covert using drama and working through issues in both triangles. He suggested that Dido should role-play the therapist while he took the role of her client, exaggerating somehow while trying to do the 'vocal exercise'. (A vocal exercise is an exercise used by music therapists to assess anxiety level and creativity blockages (techniques of Lisa Sokolov and Diane Austin). Prior to this particular exercise given to Xenia by Dido the former had tried to play the 'audition' piece of music on the piano and Dido recorded her; Filotheos frequently listened to cassettes like this one during the supervision process, working them through with Dido, transforming music into shapes, colours, role-play or embodiment of some sort. Then Dido used the 'dramatically chewed' material as a tool or intervention with her client along with her music therapeutic skills.)

Dido was once again frightened by her 'client's' difficulty and it was at this point that she got into the role of the music teacher, making behavioural corrections and remarks to the 'client'. What had been revealed from this role-play, though, had been the emotional distance the client had from her complaints and surroundings. Dido felt very much helped by this insight and connected it with similar reactions that she had had when avoiding important issues. However the particular role-play revealed more than that: Dido clearly saw her need for Filotheos to become her therapist, a sort of 'magician therapist' that would solve the difficulties for her with her comfortably lying in the cocoon of the 'child-client' role, avoiding …

During another session, while listening to one of Xenia's music attempts, Filotheos had the feeling that the piece was not flowing, as if it was performed in small 'modules' with nervous, small intervals. He suggested that Dido should represent the particular piece with a 'moving sculpt' using her body. What had been revealed was a 'soulless', robot like motion! Dido then thought of using GIM (Guided Imagery with Music) with Xenia; a combination of one of Bach's fugues and Red Riding Hood was the result which threw light on Xenia's fantasies towards Dido. Dido realized that Xenia looked at her as the figure of the grandmother, whereas Xenia's destructive fantasies appeared as the wolf.

Dido's initial negative body-image had already begun making a shift towards change. She felt less uncomfortable with her body and safer in applying action methods with her client. As the process went on, she felt safer as a therapist and Filotheos as a supervisor of a music therapist! In closing their 15-session supervision he suggested that Dido could participate in a theatre group, which he thought would help her affiliate more with her body.

Music was being transformed into drama, and drama into music, and as the wheel of art turned creatively, both triangles changed colours and shapes, changing and transforming all parties involved.

One of Filotheos' roles in this supervision had been a combination of two aspects: educative and supportive. The educative aspect worked on both sides since he was also informed on music therapeutic methodology and practice. Although Dido came from the music therapy area and he himself from the dramatherapy one, there was a smooth and complementary blending of the two methodologies. The use of music as therapeutic tool had always fascinated him and he found the use of pieces of music as metaphors really exciting. He used a variety of dramatherapy models and techniques; art and metaphor being the common healing and containing factors of both methodologies.

Theatre-based supervision had once again proved to be an accurate compass, showing in the 'here-and-now' the way a supervisor and a therapist need to look for solutions and answers. In addition to this, it proved to be a solid, yet flexible, container for all those feelings and fantasies that needed working through. Dramatic distancing almost always works like this: 'zooming in' on an issue using a 'zooming out' approach!

Survival in a storm/garden

The following example is from a theatre-based supervision training course offered in Israel. The Israeli training course is similar to the one in Greece as far as the basic philosophy is concerned. It also has similarities in relation to module 1, whereas it is different in modules 2 and 3. These differences are due to the specific needs and situations in the two countries. The example below is from the first stage of the learning process as it took place within the first module of the training.

The first module of this theatre-based supervision training was aimed at enabling trainees to:

- understand contrasting models of practice of dramatherapy supervision in relation to theoretical supervision models
- become aware of the contrasting demands of supervision of individuals, pairs, teams and groups
- practise skills in relation to continuing supervision, brief supervision, crisis supervision, consultation and specialist supervision
- become confident at drawing up appropriate contracts for supervisees, discussing boundaries, advising supervisees concerning client contracts.

The different sessions were based on the following contents:

1. THE SUPERVISORY RELATIONSHIP COMPONENTS

FOCUS   TRUST   CONTAINED

Within an artistic, in other words, theatrical milieu. Supervision should be empowering rather than controlling, and unhelpful words like 'my way', 'if I were you', 'I know' were explored. Trainees gave examples of unhelpful supervisory situations: critical, dependent, pressured, resistant, chaotic, disinterested, controlling. Practical exploration enabled an understanding that these were also dramatherapist–client dynamics (together with manipulation, identification, escape). Supervisory solutions were explored through practical work.

2. THE SUPERVISOR'S KNOWLEDGE BASE

DRAMATHERAPY   THEATRE   SUPERVISION

Within a broad psychotherapeutic and artistic frame. The dramatherapist supervisees, the non-dramatherapists as well as those being supervised by non-dramatherapists enhanced the knowledge base through the relationship to the theatre art form. The supervisor's skills and the dramatherapist's skills were compared: where are the borders in practice?

The application of dramatherapy supervision skills in practice was discussed. Emphasis was put on not de-skilling the supervisee (or client); practice issues such as feeling split when supervising two supervisees at the same time and cautions ('not curing the world') were discussed. Supervisory situations (crisis, chaos, worst fantasy) were role-played. Working on and with the supervisor's Mandala (see the previous example and Chapter 2 in this volume) was also an important part of this first module. Finally, the supervisor's resources were addressed, the personal and professional process, the practical resources (equipment, time, space) as well as the professional status of the supervisor.

3. SUPERVISOR'S PRACTICE

In one of the last sessions of module 1, that is shortly before trainees started module 2 and hence had to embark on their own supervision practice, one trainee brought a situation that she found distressing and disabling. Her client was dying of cancer and kept changing or cancelling her sessions.

The trainee-supervisee told her story and it seemed that a drama existed from the word 'go'. Her client did not allow her to play the role of dramatherapist but wanted her to be an English teacher from the moment she entered the room. Her client said 'I'd like to learn English and I want to sing songs and tell stories'; so this is what they did. She told her stories and wrote them down – gradually telling more and more about herself.

Sue Jennings, the facilitator of the training session, asked her to use other members of the group to sculpt her client's journey, past, present and future, all of which became symbols in a garden – there was the unhatched egg, the strong wind, the tree blown by the wind, and the rose bush with buds, not blooms. The garden became cyclic in the seasons: the feeling of waiting - the slow emergence of the sap – the bursting into bloom – and the harvesting of the fruit. There was a feeling that the client was somewhere between autumn and winter – fruit had been harvested and winter was approaching.

Group members initially felt very heavy, sorrowful and in despair. Gradually their energy shifted as they became part of the story and even though the client was dying, they felt they could transform and reconcile their experiences through the seasonal garden. One of the training-group members said:

After the heaviness I felt more strength, less hopelessness. As the client I became more relaxed in dealing with my illness and could even allow some hope. I also realized that the therapist will now accept me in a different way – something is happening to her.

The trainee who had brought the case was able to work with the idea that changing time symbolized the client's future: 'there will always be next week'.

4. BECOMING A SUPERVISOR

The final session of module one was tinged with high anxiety and dismay that they would now become co-supervisors with an experienced supervisor for the next stage of their training (which is the content of module 2). Issues around never knowing (or being taught) enough were expressed directly and indirectly. Listening to her inner guide Sue Jennings, the trainer, sensed that this was the trainees' deepest fear – to be challenged by their supervisees. In a parallel process they were challenging their learning on the course. Their learning of theatre-based supervision had opened new ways of perception to them. They had discovered a new and different paradigm than the one they were being taught on their analytically oriented MA training (most of the theatre-based supervision trainees were simultaneously on an MA training course). As expanding as this was, it also implied risk-taking and maybe confusion. In this storm, Sue stayed with the image from last week's garden – the tree being blown by the strong wind, but not being uprooted. Led by her inner guide, she felt she needed to role-model survival – and in this sense, it is very important for supervisor-trainees to map the breadth of their supervisees' work and study load and to reflect on potential areas of conflict or confusion.

Acknowledgement

We would like to thank Robert Landy for his feedback to this article. Of course we bear the sole responsibility for the thoughts expressed here.

References

Booth, D. (1992) 'Foreword.' In J. Neeland *Structuring Drama Work*. Cambridge: Cambridge University Press.

Holloway, E. (1995) *Clinical Supervision. A Systems Approach*. London: Sage.

Huxley, M. and Witts, N. (1996) 'Twentieth-century performance: The case for a new approach.' In M. Huxley and N. Witts (eds) *The Twentieth Century Performance Reader*. London: Routledge.

Jennings, S.E. (1998) *Introduction to Dramatherapy Theatre and Healing. Ariadne's Ball of Thread*. London: Jessica Kingsley Publishers.

Landy, R.J. (1996) 'Training the drama therapist: A four-part model.' In R.J. Landy *Essays in Drama Therapy. The Double Life*. London: Jessica Kingsley Publishers.

Schreyögg, A. (1994) *Supervision. Didaktik and Evaluation (Supervision. Didactics and Evaluation)*. Paderborn: Junfermann.

Dramatherapists' Views of Supervision

Madeline Andersen-Warren and Lorraine Fox

Although clinical supervision is stated to be an essential component of safe practice for dramatherapists there seemed to be little or no information about the forms of supervision practitioners were receiving.

Our ultimate aim was to initiate research-based evidence to test the validity of supervision as a mandatory requirement for full membership of The British Association of Dramatherapists.

With the approval of our research supervisor our first step was to design a broad questionnaire to elicit both a range of demographic information and the subjective views of dramatherapists. This was intentionally wide-ranging in order to gain as much information as possible prior to the actual research hypothesis being formulated. It also provided a trial for devising survey forms.

In September 1996 the questionnaires were sent to all the drama-therapists on the Association's register who were resident in Britain, a total of 240. Of these, 176 questionnaires were returned but 36 were invalid for the following reasons:

- 2 respondents were no longer practising
- 4 had not completed the whole questionnaire
- 30 people had received a form which contained a typing error: 'supervision' in one section had been written as 'tuition'. (However, 10 had corrected the error, and we were able to use their material.)

Our results were compiled from 146 completed forms.

The first section requested information on the gender and age of the dramatherapist, followed by questions relating to the length of time they had been qualified and the percentage of work time spent in dramatherapy-related practice.

These led into requests for specific employment details. The responses were as follows:

Own Practice	62
Community Care Settings	51
Hospitals	35
Voluntary Organizations	26
Educational Establishments	22
Colleges	22
Universities	18
Schools	16
Secure Units	9
Social Services	5
Probation Service	4
Child and Adolescent Units	3
Arts Centres	2
Prisons	2
Theatre	1
Residential Home	1
Police	1
Industry	1

These figures reflected the fact that 55 people worked in multiple settings; 86 people worked for both an organization and had also established a freelance practice; 32 people worked only within an organization; while a further 28 people were in freelance/private practice as their sole employment.

Before moving on to the questions directly related to supervision we provided a list of client groupings according to their age. These categories emerged as the age ranges that people worked with:

a)   Children only, 13; children/adolescents/adults 21; children/adults/older adults, 1; children/adolescents, 8; children/adults 3; children/older adults, 1.

b)   Adolescents only, 3; adolescents/adults, 13; adolescents/adults/older adults, 5.

c)   Adults only, 68; adults/older adults, 9.

d)   Older adults only, 1.

Within these groupings respondents indicated that they provided therapy interventions for a wide range of psychological issues and people with learning difficulties or disabilities. We did not ask about physical capabilities although this will be included in follow-up data requests.

The next set of questions related to frequency and forms of supervision. Exactly half, 73 respondents, received fortnightly supervision; of the remaining 73, 50 people were engaged in monthly sessions, and 23 varied the frequency. We did not establish the duration of the sessions. The forms of supervision were : Peer Supervision, 1; Group, 17; Individual, 75; Individual and Peer, 25; Individual and Group, 13; Group and Peer and all three forms, 11.

This factual data was collected to investigate whether any of these factors would establish any differences on the perceived value or experience of supervision. Before looking at opinions about personal engagement in supervision we provided grids marked from 1 to 10 to solicit opinions on whether it is important that dramatherapists are supervised by dramatherapists and whether the supervisor's clinical practice should be similar to that of the supervisee. A ranking of 10 indicated that it was very important and 1 indicated that it was of no importance. The results are shown in Figures A1.1 and A1.2.

Eighty people were actually being supervised by dramatherapists, 66 people by other therapists/professionals including: body psychotherapists, Jungian therapists, Rogerian counsellors, psychodramatists, child psychotherapists, occupational therapists and psychologists.

Of the therapists being supervised by therapists from other disciplines, 21 had indicated that they thought it was very important to be supervised by a dramatherapist.

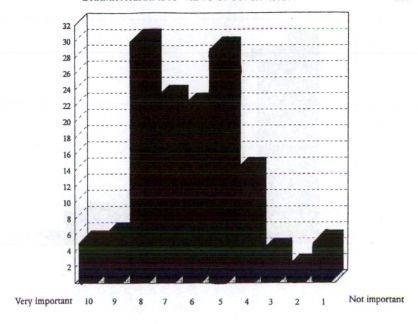

Figure A1.1 Should the supervisor have a similar practice to the supervisee?

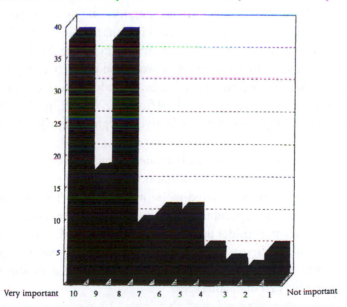

Fig. A1.2 The importance of having a dramatherapist as supervisor

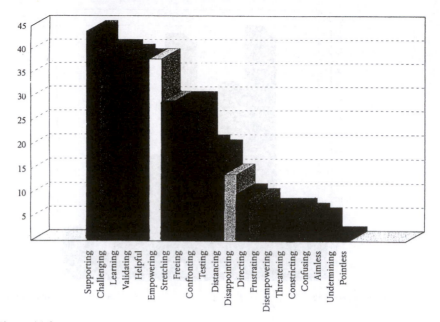

Figure A1.3

Question 19 consisted of words that are provided to describe personal experiences of supervision. Respondents could tick as many as they felt were applicable to their situation. The results are shown in Figure A1.3.

Nobody ticked more than one negative word and no particular patterns evolved in groupings of chosen words. We invited additions to our list and the following words were provided: Affirming, Exciting, Essential, Comforting, Hard going, Enjoyable, Reflective, Enlightening, Questioning, Enabling.

The final part of the survey consisted of nine statements about supervision that we asked people to rank in order of importance. Twelve responses were not completed as ranking was stated to be inappropriate. The remaining respondents ranked: 'The opportunity to clarify dynamics between therapists and client' and 'Time to consider the relationships between therapist, client, organizational/social factors' as the most important components of supervision with 'Time to talk about dramatherapy' placed as the least important aspect by 110 dramatherapists.

Other information obtained was that only 20 per cent of people employed by organizations were funded for supervision and 25 people travelled over 50 miles to their supervisor.

The most problematic area of the survey was the questions about practitioners' theoretical influences. We divided these into theories of theatre and psychological theories but received overlapping answers. For example, 10 people placed Jennings in the section on theatre and 5 people considered her work qualified as psychological theory. The same division of opinion applied to Boal and Moreno. Twelve people objected to the word theory and substituted 'skills' and listed techniques such as sculpting and empty chair work. The most frequently named theorists/theatre practitioners were: Boal, Grotowski, Stanislavski and Brook, with Jung and Rogers as the people who most influenced psychological and theoretical underpinning of practice. Jennings was the only dramatherapist mentioned more than once.

While this survey provided us with a wealth of information about the supervision of dramatherapists we were unable to find any significant differences between experiences of supervision. We found that age, the length of practice, employment basis, client groups and theoretical bias had no influence on the expectations, experience or value of supervision.

However, the information gleaned from this initial questionnaire provided a rich source of material for potential research. We were particularly interested in the imbalance between the named theories of psychology versus the sparse references to those of theatre/drama.

Our next stage will be to refine the questionnaire and carry out structured interviews to provide more robust data which we hope will generate testable hypotheses in this interesting and important field.

Dramatherapy Supervision Training Courses

At the time of printing there existed the following dramatherapy supervision training courses.

United Kingdom

Supervisors' Training Course

Course director: Marina Jenkyns, MA (Cantab), PGCE (London), RDTh (St Albans); Advanced Course in Consulting to Individuals, Groups and Organizations (now MA Consultation and the Organization: Psychoanalytic Approaches), Tavistock Clinic

Teaching staff: Ditty Dokter, MA, RDTh (St Albans), SRDMT. Group Analytic Psychotherapist Visiting Lecturer specialists

Course structure: 12 weekends over two years, totalling 144 hours

Validation: Privately run course approved by The British Association of Dramatherapists

Address for Enquiries: 21a Southcote Rd, London N19 5BJ.
Tel. +44-(0)171-609 1728

Greece

Training Course for Dramatherapy and Playtherapy Supervision

Course director: Katerina Couroucli-Robertson, MA (Dramatherapy), RDTh

Teaching staff: Prof. Sue E. Jennings (Institute of Dramatherapy at Roehampton),Prof. Mooli Lahad (Institute of Dramatherapy at Tel Hai College, Israel), Prof. Robert J. Landy (New York University)

Course structure: 3 modules of experiential teaching on theory, methodology and supervisory self-awareness (90 hours), 2 practice modules of 6 supervision sessions with an individual and 15 supervision sessions with a group or an individual respectively, 12 hours of supervision of practice, written reports of practice and final 3000 word essay

Validation: Privately run course validated by The British Association of Dramatherapists

Address for enquiries: The 'Herma' Dramatherapy & Playtherapy Training in Greece, 5 F.Litsa, Halandri, GR-Athens 15234.
Tel./Fax +30-1-681 6029. e-mail <herma@otenet.gr>

Israel

Further Education in Arts Therapies

Course convenor: Mrs Bilha Givoni DTh

Course Director: Prof. Mooli Lahad

Course lecturer: Prof. Sue E. Jennings

Duration: 3 academic years, total 120 hours. Course meets every other week for 2 hours + intensive workshops

Content: General approaches to SV, SV using dramatherapy and bibliotherapy models and methods, Group SV on cases by participants, Articles discussion, Written essay. Participants receive a reading book on supervision

Participants should have at least 5 years of work experience and should be full members of the Israeli Association of the Expressive Arts Therapies (YAHAT)

Course Recognition Status: As it is the first and only course run so far we are in the process of recognition

Address for enquiries: Institute of Dramatherapy, Tel Hai College, Upper Galilee, Israel.
Tel. +972-6-690 0970, Fax +972-6-695 0697

The Supervision Subcommittee of the British Association of Dramatherapists

The Supervision Subcommittee of the British Association of Dramatherapists is responsible for all issues to do with the provision and practice of dramatherapy supervision. This comprises four main tasks:

a) monitoring the 40 mandatory sessions of supervision required of qualified dramatherapists in order for them to achieve registration

b) producing and revising triennially a register of BADTh approved supervisors

c) advising the Executive Committee of BADTh on the approval of dramatherapy supervisors' training courses

d) maintaining and developing standards of professional practice in supervision, as well as keeping in touch with the needs of the membership and liaising with the executive committee.

To contact the Convenor of the Supervision Subcommittee:

c/o The Administrator, The British Association of Dramatherapists, 41 Broomhouse Lane, London SW6 3DP. Tel +44-0171-731 0160.

List of Contributors

Madeline Andersen-Warren is currently employed by Huddersfield NHS Trust as a Dramatherapist and Health Through Arts Co-ordinator. She is the author of several publications on dramatherapy and a partner in the Northern Trust for Dramatherapy, a training organization which runs post-basic training in dramatherapy. She undertook Marina Jenkyns' training in supervision.

Ann Cattanach, PhD, CSTD, RDTh, is supervisor and course director of Play Therapy at the Roehampton Institute, London. She helped to develop the Dramatherapy course at the Akademie de Kopse, Nijmegen, Netherlands, and supervises the Playtherapy course run by 'Herma' in Athens, Greece. Ann Cattanach is currently a therapist for Harrow Community Health Services.

Anna Chesner, MA, RDTh, UKCP registered psychotherapist, works in London, Germany and Austria as an organizational consultant, psychotherapist, trainer and supervisor. Her background is in dramatherapy, psychodrama and group analysis. Her current research includes the use of action methods and playback theatre in intercultural group work.

Katerina Couroucli-Robertson, MA (Dramatherapy), is a supervisor, dramatherapist and teacher in special education. She is director of the Training Course for Dramatherapy and Playtherapy Supervision in Athens, Greece, a co-founder of the Hellenic Dramatherapy and Playtherapy Professional Association and co-ordinator of the 'Herma' Dramatherapy and Playtherapy training course in Greece. As a dramatherapist she works in private practice. She has been practising with both groups and individuals since 1986. She also co-ordinates a theatrical and music group of people with different handicaps for Very Special Arts Hellas.

Lorraine Fox is a social worker and dramatherapist who works in Forensic Services. She has published several chapters on dramatherapy practice and trained as a supervisor on Sue Jennings' course.

Roger Grainger is a professional actor, dramatherapist and counselling psychologist, who has written extensively in the areas of his own research —

dramatherapy, theatre and implicit religion. His recent books include *Imagination, Identification and Catharsis in Theatre and Therapy* (with Mary Duggan) and *The Glass of Heaven*, both published by Jessica Kingsley. He is a former Convenor of the Dramatherapy Research Subcommittee.

Marina Jenkyns is a dramatherapist, supervisor, director, trainer and organizational consultant. She also runs a Supervisors Training Course. Her writings on dramatherapy include *The Play's the Thing, Exploring Text in Drama and Therapy* (Routledge 1996). She was Chairperson of the British Association of Dramatherapists from 1989 to 1993 and is currently a member of the Training Subcommittee.

Sue E. Jennings' career in professional theatre and dramatherapy spans over 40 years. She has written and edited over a dozen books, including *Introduction to Dramatherapy* and *Playtherapy with Children: A Practitioner's Guide,* and, most recently, *Introduction to Developmental Playtherapy.* Currently, she holds Visiting Professorships at the University of Ulster, Tel Hai College, Israel and New York University, and is Senior Research Fellow at the University of Surrey Roehampton.

Demys Kyriacou is psychiatrist, supervisor, dramatherapist (RDTh, UK), homoeopath and writer. He is the founder and training director of dramatherapy courses in Northern Greece and Cyprus; he runs regular dramatherapy and supervision groups. He is currently preparing the first dramatherapy book to be published in Greek. He has also created many points of contact for dramatherapy on the Internet. He is a trainer homoeopath, member of the Hellenic Homoeopathic Society and the Liga Medicorrum Homoeopathica Internationalis. He lives and works as a freelance drama-therapist and homoeopath in Thessaloniki, Greece.

Mooli Lahad, PhD, Psychologist and Dramatherapist, Founder and Director of the Institute of Dramatherapy, Tel Hai College, Israel. He is the author of 16 books on crisis intervention and the use of creative methods, and a winner of the Highest Israeli Award on prevention and intervention work with communities under crisis and disasters. He is the Director of the community stress prevention training centre in Israel, a Consultant to Unicef and many other international bodies on crisis management prevention and intervention, and an External examiner on the Roehampton PhD in Dramatherapy, the Greek DTh course, the Cyprus DTh course, and in Norway and Sweden.

Robert J. Landy, PhD, RDT/BC, is the Founder and Director of the Drama Therapy Program at New York University. He recently served as the

Editor-in-Chief of *The Arts in Psychotherapy* and Vice-President of the National Association for Drama Therapy. He is a prolific writer in the fields of dramatherapy and drama education and has extensive experience as a theatre artist and composer. His current research concerns ways of seeing and conceptualizing God.

Reinhard Tötschinger is supervisor, trainer, organizational consultant and psychotherapist for integrative gestalt therapy and drama therapy. He studied dramatic arts with Jacques Lecoq and Etienne Decroux in Paris and Vienna. He has worked as lecturer and visiting professor at the University for Music and Performing Arts in Graz (Department of Drama). He is presently lecturer for integrative dramatherapy at the Fritz Perls Institute, Beversee/Düsseldorf (Germany), and works as supervisor and coach in organizational development in Austria and Germany as well as a freelance gestalt- and dramatherapist in Vienna, Austria.

Elektra Tselikas-Portmann, DrPhil, RDTh, works as a freelance supervisor, dramatherpist and trainer throughout Europe and teaches at the universities of Graz and Vienna. She is engaged in the application of dramatherapy in different settings and with different professionals. Apart from supervision, her particular interests include drama in language therapy, language teaching and teacher training, multi-lingual and multi-cultural education, personnel and management development, and soft skills training. She has written three books and several articles on these subjects.

Subject Index

acquaintance, ritual of 140
action methods 21, 24–5, 81
adaptive attachment 145
administrative supervision 15, 16
administrators 16
aesthetic distancing 27
age, in team supervision 58
agencies, working with children 85–7
aims, supervisory training 206
art
  in dramatherapy 23–5
  understanding through art 174
art critics, supervisors as 174
art form, in dramatherapy supervision 95–6, 204
art-based research 168–81
Art-Based Research 174
artistic creation 28
artistic supervision 27
Arts Therapies Research Committee 180–1
Arts Therapies Research Conferences 181
as if, one-to-one supervision 47–8
attachment figures 145
authoritarian stance 190
authoritative stance 189–90

authority 188–90
autonomy, clients' 87

basic assumption theory 196–7
BASIC Ph Model 148–9
  example of 149–51, 152
Bausch, Pina 24
behavioural therapy supervision 19
bereavement, dealing with 75
black hole of trauma 146–7
boundary management 193
boundary setting, lack of, disaster interventions 139–41
Britain, dramatherapy supervision 40, 41–3
broadcasting, disasters 139
burnout, mental health professionals 137
business, supervision of teams in 155–67
button sculpt *see* spectogram

chaos 146, 147, 152
childhood
  playtherapists' exploration of personal 88
  theories and models of 82–5
children, dramatherapy with 80–91
Child's Play 88
CISD procedure 148

client-centred supervision 19–20
client–therapist relationships
  role-counterrole guide 125–8
  supervisory triangle 96
clients
  autonomy, playtherapy 87
  focus on, team supervision 57
  role-counterrole guide 122–5
clinical supervision 43
Clinical Supervision Conference 43
CNN model, electronic media 139
co-operative inquiry 96
coaching, of teams in business 155–67
cognitive discontinuity 144
combat fatigue 143
communication 24–5
compassion fatigue
  concept of 136–7
  development of 142–3
  likely victims 137–8
  urge to help 143–6
competition, in supervision 190–1
complexity, capacity to cope with 28
compromise, dramatherapy research 172
confidentiality, playtherapy 86–7
conflict moderation, in business 158–9
constructivist approach

dramatherapy 23, 28
supervision 20–1
consultants 16
consultation, art-based
research 169–72
consultation supervision
71–2
containment, supervisory
training 192
content, supervisory
training 194–8
context
associated behaviour
111
focus on, team
supervision 56–7
supervisory training
191–2
contracts
in coaching 161–2
dramatherapy
supervision 28–9
control
lack of, in disasters 138
in supervision 15,
16–17
counsellors, group
supervision of 53–4
counterrole see
role-counterrole-guide
countertransference
disaster interventions
141–3
in dramatherapy 22
dramatherapy
supervision 44, 132
creation research 171
creative dramatists 65
creative expressive play
80–1
creative methods 21,
24–5

creativity, art-based
research 171
crisis intervention teams,
supervision 136–52
crisis supervision, medical
team 72–4

death imprint 141–3, 145
dependency,
client–therapist
relationships 126–7,
128
developmental models, of
childhood 82
diagnosis, in coaching
162–4
disasters
urge to help 143–6
vulnerability of helpers
138–43
discourses, about
childhood 83–5
distance, one-to-one
supervision
gaining 48–9
reducing 49–51
distancing
aesthetic 27
by clients 107–8
concept of 22
lack of, disaster
interventions 139,
141
supervision of helpers
150
theatre-based
supervision 63
through stories 99
Dizengoff Shopping
Center disaster 141
drama, in business 155–6,
157–8, 159
dramatherapists

role-counterrole guide
118–22
supervision of 40
views of supervision
220–5
dramatherapy
characteristics and
methods 21–5
with children 80–91
research 170–2, 175–6
supervision and 25–8
Dramatherapy Research
Subcommittee 180
dramatherapy supervision
contracts 28–9
historical perspective
39–43
necessity of training
203–5
role model 114–33
supervisory settings
43–60
training courses 226–7
dramatic imagery, and
group process 45–6
dramatic reality 22

educational supervision
16
educational workshops 41
embodiment 23, 67
emotional intensity,
supervisory
relationships 178–9
empathy
compassion fatigue
137–8
one-to-one supervision
49–51
empty space, in drama
164
enquiring into inquiry
173

envy, in supervision
190–1
EPR paradigm 23, 25,
67–8
sample record sheet 77f
ethics, working with
children 86
ethnographic differences,
supervision 15–17
evaluation
effectiveness of therapy
112
learning, theatre-based
curriculum 208
experiencing ego 198
exposure
compassion fatigue
137–8
disaster interventions
139
external supervisors 17

fairy tales, therapeutic
aspect 102
family metaphor, team
supervision 58, 59
Fay, illustration of role
model 115–31, 133
*Fieldbook of The Fifth
Discipline* 166
Fifth Discipline, The
159–60
first names, using 102
foci, team supervision
55–60
form structure, supervisory
training 207–8
formative aspect, of
supervision 43
functions, of supervision
26

game playing, social
identity 88
Genesis, experience of
chaos 146, 147, 152
geographic proximity,
disaster interventions
141
German speaking
countries, development
of supervision 16–17
gestalt approach 20
in coaching 162–4
goals, theatre-based
curriculum 206
good enough, concept of
126, 186
Greece
dramatherapy
supervision 40
supervision training
course 209–16
group process, and
dramatic imagery,
vignette 45–6
group supervision
for ongoing practice
74–5
supervisory setting
51–4
group-led group sculpt 52
guide *see* role-counterrole
guide

Hansel and Gretel theme
71–2
helicopter ability 27, 98
illustration of 99–112
help, in supervision
16–17
helpers
black hole of trauma
146–7

multidimensional
supervision 149–52
supervising 148–9
urge to help 143–6
vulnerability of, in
disasters 138–43
see also mental health
professionals
historical discontinuity
144
historical perspective
39–43
Humpty Dumpty, urge to
help 143–6

identification, disaster
interventions 141–3
impotence, vs
omnipotence, disaster
interventions 145,
146, 147, 152
imprint of death 141–3,
145
individual supervision, for
ongoing practice 75–6
innocence, childhood 83
intake, ritual 140
integrative
gestalt-oriented
supervision 20
interactions
supervisees and clients
18–19
therapist-researchers and
supervisors 177–8
interdependence,
client–therapist
relationship 128
internal client 97
internal states 64f, 65
internal supervisor 65, 97
internal therapist 97

interpersonal competence,
   acquiring 207
interventions
   by supervisor
      dramatherapists 26
   see also crisis intervention
      teams
irritators 20
Israel
   dramatherapy
      supervision 40
   supervision training
      course 216–19

Kiss that Got Lost, The 145

learning
   theatre-based curriculum
      206–7, 208
   transfer of, coaching
      165–6
light, creation of 147
listening
   developing trainees'
      powers 195
   to supervisees 97
Little Prince story
   99–112

macro role reversal 47
Makendaya, journey of
   73–4
Mandala
   concept 63–7
   in Greek training course
      210–12
media 21, 25
medical team, crisis
   supervision 72–4
mental health
   professionals
      burnout 137
   see also helpers

metaphors
   in dramatherapy 22
   helper–victim interplay
      146–7
   in team supervision
      57–60
Midsummer Night's Dream, A
   69–71
mind, dramatic structure
   of 63–5
mini role reversal 47
MIT Centre for
   Organizational
   Learning 160
multidimensional
   supervision, helpers
   149–52

narratives
   construction of new
      20–1, 28
   deconstruction of, in
      supervision 88
   social construction 75–6
non-artistic supervision
   27
non-dramatherapists,
   techniques in team
   supervision 55–60
normative aspect, of
   supervision 43

object relations theory,
   authority 189–90
observing ego 198
omnipotence, disaster
   interventions 145,
   146, 147, 152
one-to-one supervision
   46–51
ongoing practice
   group supervision 74–5

individual supervision
   75–6
openness, theatre-based
   curriculum 208–9
order, urge to restore,
   disaster interventions
   147
organizations
   supervision in 17
   see also business
overview, one-to-one
   supervision 48–9

parallel processes
   disaster interventions
      142, 145
   therapy supervision 96
peer supervision 60
peer–pair substructure,
   supervisory training
   193
perception, expansion of
   28
performance
   creative process 202–3
   disaster interventions
      140
   supervisory relationship
      176–7
personal competence,
   acquiring 207
perturbation, of the
   system 23, 28
perturbators 20
*Philosophy of Childhood,
   The* 82
physical symptoms, of
   helpers, disaster
   interventions 142
place, ritual of 140
play
   with children 81–2
   value of 87–8

play phase, in coaching
    164–5
playback theatre 53
playtherapists
    exploration of personal
        childhood 88
    responsibility 87, 89
    role conflict 85–6
playtherapy
    illustration of
        supervisory triangle
        99–112
    sample record sheet 78f
    supervision in 80–91
poiesis 27
post-traumatic stress
    disorder (PTSD)
    136–7, 139, 147
potential space, supervisor
    training 191–8
power relationships,
    children and adults
    83–5
powerless, play for 87–8
practitioner research 169,
    171, 176
process, of coaching
    161–6
process-oriented
    approach, drama 156
professional competence
    dramatherapy
        supervision 206–7
    improvement of 17–18,
        25–6
professionalization, of
    dramatherapy 40–3
projection 23, 67
proximity, immediacy and
    expectancy model
    (PIE) 139
psychoanalytic supervision
    19

psychodrama 20
psychodynamic approach,
    training 185–200
psychosocial proximity
    141
psychotherapeutic process,
    supervision of 176
Puer Aeternus 100

qualifications, for
    supervisors 40
qualitative research 171,
    172
qualities, supervisor
    dramatherapists 26
quantitative research 171,
    172
questionnaires,
    dramatherapists' views
    of supervision 220–5

reactions, to disaster
    144–5
realities, construction of
    23
record sheets 76, 77f, 78f
recovery 112
referrals, for therapy 86
register, of supervisor
    dramatherapists 41
relationships
    art-based research
        176–9
    dramatherapy
        supervision 114
    role-counterrole guide
        125–8, 128–31
    in supervision 24
    see also client–therapist
        relationships; power
        relationships;
        supervisor–supervisee
        relationships

rescuers, in playtherapy
    89
research see art-based
    research
responsibility,
    playtherapists 87, 89
restorative aspect, of
    supervision 43
rituals, lack of, disaster
    interventions 139–41
rivalry, in supervision
    190–1
Rogerian client-centred
    supervision 19–20
role, concept of 22, 23
role discontinuity 144
role feedback 52–3
role play 22, 67
role reversal 47, 52–3
role-counterrole-guide
    115–17
    client–therapist
        relationship 125–8
    client–therapist–supervis
        or relationship
        128–31
    within the client 122–5
    within therapist 118–22
roles
    conflict of,
        playtherapists 85–6
    dramatherapy
        supervision 114–15
    internal 97
    playing someone else's
        156–7

scientific approach,
    art–based research
    175
secondary traumatic stress
    disorder 136
seminars, research 181

seniority, team supervision 58

settings *see* supervisory settings

Snow White in the Forest 89–91

social constructions
of childhood 83
narratives 75–6

social discontinuity 144

social identity, game playing 88

sociology, of childhood, new paradigm 84–5

spectograms, one-to-one supervision 48, 49, 50

stories
illustration of supervisory triangle 99–112
in supervisory process 97–8

story telling, in business 160

strategies, dramatherapy research 170–2

structure
supervisory training 193–4
theatre-based curriculum 205–6, 207–8
theatre-based supervision 62

supervisee-led group sculpt 52

supervision
aim of 17–19
approaches to 19–21
art-based research 172–80
authority 188–90
crisis intervention teams 136–52

and dramatherapy 25–8
dramatic element in 198–9
envy, rivalry and competition 190–1
ethnographic differences 15–17
necessity of training 203
in playtherapy 80–91
as potential space 191–8
as support 187
tasks of 20, 25–6, 188
see also coaching; dramatherapy supervision; theatre-based supervision

Supervision Subcommittee of the British Association of Dramatherapists 228

supervisor dramatherapists
qualities required 26
register of 41
resources 30, 112
training
psychodynamic approach 185–200
theatre-based approach 202–19

supervisor–supervisee relationships
co-operative inquiry 96
one-to-one settings 46

supervisors
as art critics 174
as broker of views 20
characteristics 13
debate over professional profile 17
external 17

supervisory relationships, art-based research 176–9

supervisory settings 43–60
group 51–4
one-to-one 46–51
peer 60
team 54–60

supervisory triangles 95–112

supportive supervision 16, 187

symbolic material 76

symbolization
group supervision 53
one-to-one supervision 48
team supervision 56

systems approach
in drama 156
to supervision 20

tasks, of supervision 20, 25–6, 188

team supervision 54–60
in business 155–67

techniques
group supervision 52–3
one-to-one supervision 47–8
in team supervision 55–60

telecommunications, disaster interventions 138–9

text, supervision through 68–71

theatre-based supervision 62–78
dramatherapy principles 63–71

examples of supervision
practice 71–6
training
curriculum 205–9
examples of 209–19
necessity of 204–5
theatrical methods, in
coaching 160
themes
finding, in coaching
162–4
of supervision 18–19
therapists *see*
dramatherapists;
playtherapists;
supervisor
dramatherapists
therapy
evaluation of
effectiveness 112
parallel processing in
supervision 96
see also dramatherapy;
playtherapy
time
in group supervision 51
ritual of setting 140
supervisory training
207–8
timetables, supervisory
training 193
trainees, supervision 43–5
dramatic imagery and
group process 45–6
one-to-one setting
48–51
training courses 41,
226–7
psychodynamic
approach 185–200
theatre-based approach
202–19

transfer of learning, in
coaching 165–6
transference
disaster interventions
142
in dramatherapy 22
dramatherapy
supervision 44, 132
trial identification 198,
199

United States
administrative
supervision 16
dramatherapy
supervision 40

value, of supervision,
auditing 43
victims, black hole of
trauma 146–7
vulnerability, helpers,
disaster interventions
138–43

wickedness, childhood 83
workplaces, in training
191
workspace, one-to-one
supervision 47

Author Index

American Psychiatric
    Association 147
Artaud, A. 23
Ayalon, A. and Lahad, M.
    148
Ayalon, A. and Shacham,
    Y. 149

Bausch, P. 24
Beaton, D.R. and Murphy,
    S.A. 138
Belardi, N. 16, 17
Bettelheim, B. 102
Binyamini, K. 149
Bion, W. 196
Bishop, V. and
    Butterworth, T. 43
Booth, D. 202
Breznitz, S. 149
Brook, P. 164
Buber, M. 174
Buer, F. 20
Burnett, F.H. 75

Canetti, E. 157
Carroll, M. 185
Casement, P. 198
Cassirer, E. 96
Casson, J., Feasey, D.,
    Mitchell, S. and Smith,
    H. 42
Cattanach, A. 23
Cherney, M. 149
Chesner, A. 53

Davis, D.R. 21, 111
Doehram, M.J.G. 96

Dramatherapy North West
    41, 42
Dunning, C. 148
Dyregrov, A. and Mitchell,
    J. 148

Elraz, J. and Ozami, R.
    148
Emunah, R. 21
Evaldsson, A. and
    Corsaro, W. 88

Fatzer, G. 156
Figley, C. 136, 137, 149
Frankel, V. 148
Freudenbeyer, H.J. 137

Gergen, K.J. 23
Gersie, A. 21
Gersie, A. and King, N.
    26
Geus, A. de 158
Goldman, L. 88
Grainger, R. 171, 172

Harris, C.J. 137, 148
Hawkins, P. and Shohet,
    R. 16, 18, 27, 98,
    186, 187, 188, 194
Hendrick, H. 83
Hodgkinson, P. and
    Shepherd, M. 148
Hodgkinson, P. and
    Stewart, M. 137, 139,
    148
Holloway, E. 16, 20, 25,
    26, 203
Huxley, M. and Witts, N.
    23, 24, 202

Jenks, C. 82
Jenkyns, M. 186, 191

Jennings, S. 23, 62, 65,
    67, 73, 74
Jennings, S.E. 22, 23, 26,
    204, 205
Joinson, C. 137
Jones, P. 23
Jones, R. 176
Kadushin, A. 16, 188
Keats, J. 200
Kersting, H.J. 17, 20, 28
Kfir, N. 140, 149
King, G., Keohane, R.O.
    and Verba, S. 170
Kleiner, A. and Roth, G.
    160
Klingman, A. 148

Lahad, M. 25, 26, 99,
    148
Lahad, M. and Ayalon, A.
    148, 149
Lahad, M. and Cohen, A.
    148
Laing, R.D. 103
Landy, R. 115, 198
Landy, R.J. 21, 22, 26,
    107, 108, 109, 112,
    120, 131, 205
Langs, R. 185, 192
Levine, S.K. 27
Lloyd-Owen, D. 191

McCammon, S.L. and
    Allison, E.J. 148
McCann, L. 136
McNiff, S. 23, 168, 172,
    173, 174
Martindale, B., Hörner,
    M., Rodríguez, M. and
    Vidit, J.P. 185
Maslach, C. 137
Maslach, C. and Jackson,
    S.E. 137

Matthews, G. 82
Mattison, J. 185
Maturana, H.R. and
    Varela, F. 20
Mitchell, J. 148
Mitchell, J. and Bary, G.
    148, 149
Mitchell, S. 26
Moran, C. and Collers, E.
    149
Morgan, G. 156, 158,
    166

Obholzer, A. 189
Omer, H. and Inbar, H.
    144

Payne, H. 181
Perlman, L. and Saakvinte,
    K. 148
Pines, A.M. 137
Pines, A.M. and Aronson,
    E. 137
Pritchard, J. 185
Prout, A. and James, A. 84

Rappe-Giesecke, C. 18,
    28
Reason, P. 96
Reason, P. and Hawkins,
    P. 97
Rioch, M. 196
Robertson, K. 99, 102
Robson, C. 169, 170,
    176
Rowan 26
Rutter, M. 145

Saint-Exupéry, A. de 98,
    103
Salas, J. 53
Salmon, T.W. 139
Schaverien, J. 96

Schreyögg, A. 17, 18, 19,
    20, 21, 205
Searles, H. 178
Senge, P.M. 159, 167
Shainberg, D. 178, 180
Shakespeare, W. 69, 70
Shohet, R. and Hawkins,
    P. 179
Solomon, Z. 139
Stokes, J. 196
Stoltenberg, C.D. and
    Delworth, U. 16
Storch, M. and Rösner, D.
    156
Storr, A. 102, 112

Valent, P. 145
Van Der Kolk, B.A. 146
Von Franz, M.L. 100

Walker, A. 200
Webster's Encyclopedic
    Unabridged Dictionary
    of the English Language
    137
White, M. 148
Williams, A. 20, 48
Willke, H. 166
Winnicott, D.W. 126,
    144, 191
Witstom, A. 140